REVIEW 13

REVIEW

Volume 13   1991

Edited by

James O. Hoge
*Virginia Polytechnic Institute
and State University*

James L. W. West III
The Pennsylvania State University

University Press of Virginia

Charlottesville

THE UNIVERSITY PRESS OF VIRGINIA
Copyright © 1991 by the Rector and Visitors
of the University of Virginia

First published 1991

ISSN 1090-3233
ISBN 0-8139-1371-3

Printed in the United States of America

The editorial assistants for volume 13 of REVIEW are
LaVerne Kennevan Maginnis and Tracy S. Bitonti,
both of The Pennsylvania State University.

PENNSTATE

Funding for *Review* is provided by the generous gifts of Mr. and Mrs. Charles O. Gordon, Jr., and Mr. and Mrs. Adger S. Johnson to the Virginia Tech Foundation, and by a grant from the College of the Liberal Arts, The Pennsylvania State University.

Contents

Renaissance Death   1
  by Donald W. Foster
    Review of Michael Cameron Andrews, *This Action of Our Death: The Performance of Death in English Renaissance Drama;* James L. Calderwood, *Shakespeare and the Denial of Death;* Kirby Farrell, *Play, Death, and Heroism in Shakespeare;* Robert F. Willson, Jr., *Shakespeare's Reflexive Endings*

Standing Up to the Wise Guys   31
  by John Goode
    Review of Daniel R. Schwarz, *The Transformation of the English Novel, 1890–1930*

Contextualizing Contemporary Lyric:
Some Aporias of Recent Criticism   43
  by Marjorie Perloff
    Review of Thomas Gardner, *Discovering Ourselves in Whitman: The Contemporary American Long Poem;* Walter Kalaidjian, *Languages of Liberation: The Social Text in Contemporary American Poetry;* Jeffrey Walker, *Bardic Ethos and the American Epic Poem: Whitman, Pound, Crane, Williams, Olson*

Nabokov for the Nineties   59
  by J. E. Rivers
    Review of Gennadi Barabtarlo, *Phantom of Fact: A Guide to Nabokov's* Pnin; Geoffrey Green, *Freud and Nabokov;* Priscilla Meyer, *Find What the Sailor Has Hidden: Vladi-*

mir Nabokov's Pale Fire; Vladimir Nabokov, *Selected Letters, 1940–1977,* eds. Dmitri Nabokov and Matthew J. Bruccoli; Stephen Jan Parker, *Understanding Vladimir Nabokov;* Leona Toker, *Nabokov: The Mystery of Literary Structures*

The Queen's Disraeli 83
 by Stanley Weintraub
  Review of *Disraeli Letters,* 4 vols.

Tennysonian Pastoral 97
 by John Pfordresher
  Review of Owen Schur, *Victorian Pastoral: Tennyson, Hardy, and the Subversion of Forms*

The Return of the Native: Ezra Pound as an American 111
 by Robert Casillo
  Review of Wendy Stallard Flory, *The American Ezra Pound*

Poetic Theorizing in Chaucer's Dream Visions 131
 by Michael D. Cherniss
  Review of Robert R. Edwards, *The Dream of Chaucer: Representation and Reflection in the Early Narratives*

Periodical Verse of the American Revolution 149
 by J. A. Leo Lemay
  Review of Martin Kallich, *British Poetry and the American Revolution: A Bibliographical Survey of Books and Pamphlets, Journals and Magazines, Newspapers, and Prints 1755–1800,* 2 vols.

Historical Fictions 163
 by Alexander Welsh
  Review of James Kerr, *Fiction against History: Scott as Story-Teller;* Stephen Bann, *The Inventions of History: Essays on the Representation of the Past;* Lionel Gossman, *Between History and Literature*

Contents ix

Barbershop Bravery 173
  by Nina Baym
    Review of Mark Spilka, *Hemingway's Quarrel with Androgyny*

Self-consuming Discourse: Spenserian Poetics
and the "New" New Criticism 185
  by Richard A. McCabe
    Review of Harry Berger, Jr., *Revisionary Play: Studies in the Spenserian Dynamics*

Canon or Sixshooters? 201
  by Keen Butterworth
    Review of A. Carl Bredahl, Jr., *New Ground: Western American Narrative and the Literary Canon*

Chronicling the Chronicler 211
  by Juliet McMaster
    Review of R. H. Super, *The Chronicler of Barsetshire: A Life of Anthony Trollope*

Roethke and Medium 219
  by Thomas Gardner
    Review of Peter Balakian, *Theodore Roethke's Far Fields: The Evolution of His Poetry*

Stephen Crane and Poststructuralism:
Fragmentation as a Critical Mode 229
  by James Nagel
    Review of David Halliburton, *The Color of the Sky: A Study of Stephen Crane*

Dear Dialogic Dublin: Three Joyceans
and Mikhail Bakhtin 237
  by Thomas L. Burkdall
    Review of Zack Bowen, Ulysses *as a Comic Novel;* R. B. Kershner, *Joyce, Bakhtin, and Popular Literature: Chroni*

cles of Disorder; Michael Patrick Gillespie, *Reading the Book of Himself: Narrative Strategies in the Works of James Joyce*

Thoreau as Reviser/Revising Thoreau   249
   by Steven Fink
      Review of Stephen Adams and Donald Ross, Jr., *Revising Mythologies: The Composition of Thoreau's Major Works*

Marxism and Its Uses as Criticism   261
   by Frederick C. Stern
      Review of Edward J. Ahearn, *Marxism and Modern Fiction*

Samuel Beckett, Revisionist Translator   273
   by Rubin Rabinovitz
      Review of Brian Fitch, *Beckett and Babel: An Investigation into the Status of the Bilingual Work*

Unspeakable Plots and Unamazing Puzzles   283
   by Virginia A. Smith
      Review of Marianne Hirsch, *The Mother/Daughter Plot: Narrative, Psychoanalysis, Feminism;* Mickey Pearlman, ed., *Mother Puzzles: Daughters and Mothers in Contemporary American Literature*

Correspondence   299

Contributors   301

Editorial Board

Felicia Bonaparte
City College, CUNY

Anthony J. Colaianne
Virginia Polytechnic Institute and State University

Paul Connolly
Bard College Center

Geoffrey Day
Winchester College

A. S. G. Edwards
University of Victoria

James R. Kincaid
University of Southern California

Cecil Y. Lang
University of Virginia

James B. Meriwether
University of South Carolina

Pierre Michel
Université de Liège

George Stade
Columbia University

Peter L. Shillingsburg
Mississippi State University

G. Thomas Tanselle
John Simon Guggenheim Memorial Foundation

Stanley Weintraub
The Pennsylvania State University

Renaissance Death

Donald W. Foster

Michael Cameron Andrews. *This Action of Our Death: The Performance of Death in English Renaissance Drama.* Newark: University of Delaware Press, 1989. 214 pp.

James L. Calderwood. *Shakespeare and the Denial of Death.* Amherst: University of Massachusetts Press, 1987. 232 pp.

Kirby Farrell. *Play, Death, and Heroism in Shakespeare.* Chapel Hill: University of North Carolina Press, 1990. x, 235 pp.

Robert F. Willson, Jr. *Shakespeare's Reflexive Endings.* Lewiston, New York: The Edwin Mellen Press, 1990. xiii, 127 pp.

Shakespeare studies are not what they used to be. At professional conferences, in journals of literary criticism, and even in the theater, bardolatry has given way to apostasy, if not to outright bardemnation. From a traditionalist's viewpoint, "poststructuralist," "feminist," "new historicist," and "postmodernist" approaches may seem to have no common goal other than a shared impulse to degrade both Shakespeare and the "old" Shakespeare industry as twin stacks of oppressive smoke-belching ideology. It has even been suggested, by a radical few, that Shakespeare has held the stage for much too long; that the old man should roll over (not in his grave, but in the academy) in order to make room for Renaissance authors like Elizabeth Tanfield Cary (a woman) and Gerrard Winstanley (a seventeenth-century radical).

Unfortunately, or fortunately, depending on one's viewpoint, those scholars who contribute regularly to academic journals and professional conferences represent only a small (and, some would say, a largely irrelevant) minority of those men and women who think of themselves as professional "Shakespeareans." It is therefore instructive, from time to time, to pause long enough to consider what's happening in the trenches of the typical undergraduate course, where names like Lacan and Derrida and Bakhtin do not signify and where one may yet encounter student-essays on the admirably patterned imagery, in *Hamlet,* of an unweeded garden. Many, perhaps thousands, of English teachers today are bewildered by what they perceive as an inexplicable assault on our greatest poet—an attack seemingly conducted by elitists who profess to be anti-elitist, and who seem to substitute self-promotion for an old-fashioned love of literature. *Shakespeare Quarterly* provides a recent example of that anxiety in an article by Robert F. Willson that asks, rhetorically, "Why Teach Shakespeare?"[1] Reacting to what he perceives as an anti-cultural threat from "neo-Marxist British Shakespeareans, feminist and deconstructionist critics," Willson finds "at least four highly defensible reasons for requiring [*sic*] English literature majors or non-majors to study Shakespeare. One of these is that he is among the few dramatists whose work is studied in any depth in American university English departments" (p. 208). Ergo: let us teach Shakespeare because Shakespeare is so widely taught. What other playwright can take his place? Shakespeare is, in Willson's phrase, "a shining star in the cultural firmament. . . . Banish Shakespeare, and banish the world of poetic truth, felicity, and debate" (p. 206).

Felicitous debate is itself a second reason for preserving Shakespeare from the onslaught of postmodern canon-bashers, in that carefully selected Shakespeare criticism may serve as a model for undergraduate writers who have not yet mastered the discourse. Since a play like *Hamlet* is "widely written about by scholars, critical study of the play can almost certainly assure student interest in both Shakespeare and literary criticism" (p. 209). Ergo: let us teach Shakespeare because it helps to perpetuate Shakespeare studies.

A third argument is that "Shakespeare's plays and sonnets offer rich material for the study of prosody. . . . Shakespeareans have at their disposal such powerful examples of alliteration as 'deep damnation' and 'brutish beasts,' of metaphor as 'salad days.'" On account of his formal mastery of such rhetorical devices as *litotes*, Shakespeare has an "essential place in the teaching of poetry" (p. 206). Ergo: let us teach Shakespeare because he illustrates those qualities that we have privileged, in the modern era, as the very essence of literary achievement. And let us protect our students from an interest in any recent criticism that might problematize Shakespeare's poetic mastery: "Questions of cultural or sexual politics, while of considerable importance to professors actively engaged in such research, seem particularly remote in a classroom peopled largely by learners who share a fear of Shakespeare because they have been told that he is boring and that he wrote in 'old English'" (pp. 207–8).

Willson does not query whether the exclusion of cultural politics from our classroom discussion, the effective silencing of feminist, deconstructionist, or Marxist viewpoints, may not itself have something to do with the impression, among students, that Shakespeare's English is old and boring. Rather, it seems that "today's visually oriented students" are simply thick-headed, and "eager to see on screen what their imaginations can only vaguely conjure." And therein lies a fourth reason for keeping Shakespeare in the curriculum: "his centrality to film studies." Modern filmmakers, unlike poststructuralist and postmodern literary critics, have helped to perpetuate Shakespeare as an icon of Anglo-American culture. The tradition yet lives—on film. "If nothing else, students discover that Shakespeare has inspired other great entertainers whose work can be replayed and studied for years to come" (p. 209).

As a final rejoinder to those Renaissance scholars who are now "opening the door to radical Puritan writers like Abiezer Coppe and Gerrard Winstanley," Willson remarks that Shakespeare alone can give us the best of both worlds: texts like *Hamlet* and *Macbeth* are wonderfully *quotable*, yet *morally uplifting*.

There are obviously many other good reasons for keeping Shakespeare in the curriculum. . . . After all, Shakespeare's work has long been recognized as the source of more quotable quotes than any other 'book' in the English language. Shouldn't moral rearmament begin with *Hamlet* or *Macbeth*? . . . Evil first flowered in the Garden, as Shakespeare so often demonstrates, and this may be a lesson that bears repeating to youthful inhabitants of the American paradise. [p. 210]

This, from *Shakespeare Quarterly*. And the lesson is indeed repeated, for post-Edenic Shakespeareans, in Willson's recent book on *Shakespeare's Reflexive Endings*. In surveying the death scenes of selected Shakespearean tragedies, Willson finds a pattern (poetically just and justly poetical) which suggests that Shakespeare had an "abiding interest in what might be called character fate. That is, each of the central figures creates the circumstances of his or her own demise" (p. vii). Willson's trope for each of the tragic heroes he discusses is that of blindness (p. xi). Hamlet, Othello, Lear, Macbeth, Antony, and Coriolanus (and indeed almost every Shakespeare character mentioned by Willson) is said, at some point, to be blind, and "all perish fittingly as victims of their own schemes or blind passion."[2] Willson is, however, less interested in blindness as thematic material than in the various strategies (foreshadowing, dramatic irony, blind behavior, etc.) whereby Shakespeare prepares for the death of major dramatic characters, and of the protagonist in particular.

Willson is most successful when comparing death-scenes in various Shakespearean tragedies, or when pointing to the ways in which death-scenes are linked structurally to earlier scenes or speeches in the same Shakespearean text. He identifies a number of recurrent patterns in both imagery and structure, including, for example, a pattern whereby Shakespeare maneuvers his tragic protagonists into something like a trap, or confined space, as death closes in on them. But if Willson successfully identifies formal patterns in the Shakespearean death-scene, he does so while falling into his own formalist trap, never doubting that the meaning of a protagonist's death is determined by the narrative curve, which from Willson's viewpoint always takes us from order and truth, to chaos and falsehood, and back again. The structural climax of each tragedy thus heralds a denouement for evil, a recovery of moral equilibrium. In *Hamlet*, for example, the election of Fortinbras "returns the values of the soldier" to a good kingdom "temporarily overcome" by an evil shadow, thereby signalling, with "Fortinbras's martial music," "a new beginning," "a return to order," a wholesome reestablishment of "martial values" (pp. 11–17). No matter that Fortinbras has been noted within the Shakespearean text as a man of "unimproved mettle," a sharker-up of lawless resolutes who thrives on deception, violates the chivalric pact for which his father died, and kills even for an eggshell. In Willson's view, the extinction of Denmark's royal family and the election of Fortinbras clearly represent the finishing providential touches upon what has been a rough-hewn world.

By privileging the "literal" over the Shakespearean subtext, Willson draws from that strict sergeant, Death, some arresting images: In the bedchamber-scene, "Desdemona literally . . . consummates her marriage with the shape of Death" (p. 27). "The ultimate surprise for Macbeth is that his nemesis [Macduff] has literally become the 'naked newborn babe' he described so movingly in I.vii" (p. 69). We see Hamlet, disjoint and out of frame, "facing a portrait of his youthful exuberance in Laertes, literally wrestling it down before the audience of the court." Claudius's "belief that his position as king gives him god-like power is literally exploded in his face" (hubris as trick cigar). And so on. "But the limited notion of a bomb that explodes in the inventor's face," writes Willson, "does not adequately describe the significance of final things in *Hamlet*" (pp. 4–5). Final things necessarily signify predication and completion, the textual fulfillment of readerly desire. Willson's literalizing impulse thus leads him to privilege as Truth any Shakespearean affirmation of providence, especially if uttered by a noble and good-hearted man with martial values who survives to the end of the play. Willson concludes with Edgar that, in the world of *King Lear*, "the gods finally prove just, not capricious" (p. 53). When Antony dies, "we cannot doubt the sincerity of [Caesar's] sorrow (he apparently weeps throughout the eulogy)" (p. 93). In *Macbeth*, Macduff's assertion "The time is free" is immutable truth because Macduff represents "the qualities of a Christian hero" (p. 70). No matter that Edgar sounds throughout the play like Eleanor Porter's Pollyanna, and Caesar like a shrewd Machiavel. No matter that Macduff is the man who fled to safety while trusting his wife and children to the power of positive thinking. These characters are the designated arbiters of value, meaning, and truth.

Shakespeare (like much of his Jacobean audience) knew from Holinshed's *Chronicles* that Scotland became more debauched under vicious King Malcolm than under King Makbeth; and that, when Malcolm was finally slain (with a spear through his head), Donalbain returned to Scotland, slew Malcolm's sons, and usurped the throne. Shakespeare repeatedly hints that his fictive Scotland will endure a corresponding fate, in an endless cycle of violence and retribution—but Willson will not hear of it.[3] His harshest words are reserved for Roman Polanski, whose film version of the play explicitly recalls the historical reenactment of King Makbeth's career by the historical Donalbain. "However justified by actual history this rendering may be," complains Willson, "it distorts the mood of release and return to natural order that marks Shakespeare's ending. . . . 'Providence' guides the course of human events in Shakespeare, and it is this force that returns Scotland to peace at the close of the play" (pp. 73, 75). In Shakespearean drama, Providence measures out life and death and power with great wisdom, to each as he deserves, and with great metaphysical comfort for all readers who will stay close to the text: "Shakespeare leaves no doubt that Scotland can look forward to a peaceful time in which kingly succession will follow an ordered, uninterrupted path leading inevitably to the glorious reign of James VI" (p. 73). Willson describes as "Marxist-determinist" any reading that would resist such closure and thereby distort the peaceful mood (e.g., pp. 73, 75, 76).

Although Willson deplores the cinematographer's impulse "to recreate the plays according to one's personal vision or philosophy," he seems unwilling to acknowledge *as* ideology the ideology that constitutes his own critical discourse. As is often true of other, more fashionable critics, Willson's rhetorical "we" ambitiously seeks to embrace all persons familiar with Shakespeare's plays—but *we* in this case seem to be represented by those New Critics, Christianizers, and archetypalists whose past achievements are celebrated in the endnotes, and by all other readers who are willing to view Shakespeare's tragedies as an argument for Christian manhood. From Willson's insistently phallocentric viewpoint, women constitute a deadly threat to the Shakespearean ideal of compassionate manliness (p. 69). Not Goneril's sororicide (never mentioned here), but her "contempt for Albany's

Renaissance Death 7

milky nature and for the sacredness of their marriage vows shocks our sensibilities" (p. 50). Because Lady Macbeth "holds a power over her husband unmatched by any man in the play," she is able to block Macbeth's "native impulse toward moral behavior . . . She is, in a sense, the fourth Witch, . . . It was she (and they) whose words implied that any act, no matter how horrible, was justified" (pp. 66–67); as a result, her once noble husband "has, by the end, become Lady Macbeth's 'model' man," "a caricatured man" (pp. 65, 70). Similarly, the "blindness-through-rage" of Coriolanus "leads him to put himself in service to his enemy and his mother, proving him mortal and flawed in the end" (p. 101). "In his mother he discovers not the sustainer of his spirit but the instrument of his death" (p. xi). Willson's noble Antony "has been conquered by an Egyptian in Cleopatra, and she has led him to act in ways that undercut the valiant Roman image" (p. 81). Having "Roman responsibilities," Antony "intends to toe the mark. But he cannot break his Egyptian fetters" (pp. 84, 89). Roman values (admirably and responsibly masculine) represent a stable point of reference whereby to condemn Egyptian pleasures (seductively and fatally feminine).

Antony at least dies like a man. Willson finds that Shakespeare's women—evil when manly and always a menace—can neither live well nor die well without strong masculine guidance. Cleopatra is a case point. After having preyed upon Antony's manhood, Cleopatra's death-scene "signals the elevation of her character from gypsy strumpet to majestic queen. There can be little doubt that this royal performance was inspired by Antony, whose noble soul seems to have entered Cleopatra's body" (p. ix; cf. p. 82).

Not just gender, but race, seems to affect the meaning of death in Willson's reading of Shakespeare. Othello's murder of the white Desdemona thus "acquires a quality of horror and perversion that is not to be found in *Hamlet*," or even in Macbeth's murder of Duncan (p. 23). Consider Othello's final scene with Desdemona: "External and internal darkness come together here to create a mood of Gothic dread that is reinforced by the play of the candle's light on Othello's black face" (p. 28). The candle "is surely representative of Desdemona's soul, held in the powerful hands of her dark husband and flickering near the edge of extinction" (p. 29). "In this tomb-like setting, then, Othello's three kisses take on a necrophilic taint.... Othello has turned vampiric, a figure of Gothic horror for whom the crypt is an appropriate home" (pp. 30–31). "As he murders, Othello's state of mind is animalistic, bestial; he sacrifices his wife as if she were a lamb being devoured by the wolf" (p. 24). White Christian society could well do without the likes of an Othello: "By extinguishing the light of Desdemona's life, Othello has threatened civilization with a return to the darkness of the cave, where the law of survival of the fittest prevails." If Othello has a redeemable trait, it is that he finally commits suicide. Othello thereby "manages to destroy the pagan in himself, acting on behalf of the Christian society that has been threatened" (pp. 34–35). Apart from this welcome act of final self-destruction, however, *Othello* is a play in which "the hero appears to serve the aims of Satanic cruelty" (p. 26).

In an endnote, Willson mentions as "convincing" J. L. Styan's view that "through Iago Shakespeare rouses 'the primitive feelings of a white community against a Negro who steals one of their women.'"[4] It may be that Shakespeare's play continues to rouse those same primitive feelings—but surely such a response does not inhere in the text itself. If "we" view Othello, even in his most fateful and misguided act, as a Satanic, bestial, necrophilic, and monstrous vampire, it may only be that we have allied ourselves, somewhat too strongly, with the limited viewpoint of Brabantio.

Is there an important critical insight to be gleaned from all this? Perhaps. If nothing else, Willson demonstrates that it is indeed appropriate to discuss the cultural politics of literary production, and of literary criticism, both inside and outside the classroom (including, one might add, a free discussion of Willson's own conservative agenda).

Following the enormous success of Stephen Greenblatt's *Renaissance Self-Fashioning* (1980), new historicists have come by the busload to map out strategies whereby the ruling elite in early modern England tolerated, yet contained, potential subversion by competing systems of power and value. It may also be instructive, from time to time, to try the shoe on our own foot, since our own dominant discourse is frequently viewed, by silenced minorities, as oppressive. Renaissance studies are perhaps a special case. Despite a tremendous proliferation of critical approaches in recent years, a decidedly patriarchal elite has looked down from above, dismissing psychoanalytic or metadramatic or feminist readings with a single word—"ahistorical!"—as if truth were not ascendant until the advent of the new historicism, and not to be approached from a competing, "unhistoricized," critical platform. "There is subversion, no end of subversion," says Stephen Greenblatt—"only not for us."[5]

The co-optive or coercive power of the new historicism's discursive practice is evident in *This Action of Our Death*. Michael Andrews begins with the *de rigueur* anecdote from the annals of English history (an opening used with success in literally hundreds of new historicist studies during the past decade); and he duly links these historical events to contemporaneous literary production. After recounting the deaths of Sir Walter Ralegh and Mary Queen of Scots on the executioner's stage, Andrews notes that Ralegh and Mary rehearsed for their respective deaths and performed their final roles with the dignity and eloquence of tragic heroes. These introductory observations derive principally from Stephen Greenblatt, to whom Andrews pays deferential acknowledgment. The new historicist introduction is, however, only a gambit, a concession to a domineering discourse. After the Greenblattian opening, Andrews's new-historicist packaging material is promptly discarded, in that his real interest lies elsewhere. Andrews links public execution with theatrical death, not as the key whereby to recover the meaning of a past culture (a familiar new historicist ambition), but only to suggest that the English concern with good form goes *way* back. "The deaths of Mary and Ralegh may serve to illustrate how one's death might be performed 'to a just height'" (p. 15). The question that Andrews asks is this: If Mary and Ralegh could die so well, why didn't it happen that way in Renaissance drama, except in the tragedies of Shakespeare and a few successful imitators?

Andrews is concerned with many of the same Shakespearean death-scenes discussed by Willson. But where Willson looks for the *meaning* of theatrical death, Andrews looks for verisimilitude and emotive power. Andrews is also willing to look for it in more places than Willson. In his search for effective stage-deaths, he turns to dozens of Renaissance plays, written by more than thirty different playwrights—none of whom, as it turns out, can compare with William Shakespeare. If Willson in "Why Teach Shakespeare?" seems to view non-canonical authors as upstart competitors, unworthy of the Bard, some reassurance may be had from *This Action of Our Death*. Andrews surveys a multitude of non-canonical texts but finds that all roads lead us back to "Shakespeare, and his most potent art," as the center of value (p. 128). Marlowe, Chapman, Middleton, and Ford receive honorable mention. Most of the others are also-rans. Women playwrights (Herbert, Cary, Wroth) are not mentioned.

This Action would be more compelling had Andrews paused to contextualize his sense of the theatrical audience, as we have learned to do from the new historicism. Instead, he tends to posit, for us and for everyone, a fixed response that is not contingent even upon such wildly variable conditions as the manner of theatrical performance. For example, the dying words of Marlowe's Faustus "draw us toward him, *forcing us* to experience infinite terror" (p. 29, my emphasis). By way of contrast, the conventional rhetoric of Cosroe's death-speech means that "we are brought no nearer to experiencing the reality of Cosroe's death" (p. 25); Cosroe "says he is in his mortal death throes, but speaks with such imperturbable copiousness that we cannot believe him. Nor should we" (p. 24). With unperturbed copiousness, Andrews thus legislates our response to dozens of dramatic texts, without ever acknowledging, even briefly, that the same death-speech might be received differently by an Elizabethan noblewoman, or by a Jacobean apprentice, or by a ticket-holder at an *RSC* production, or by an undergraduate reader of the Penguin edition.

Fixed standards are applied also to the dramatic texts that produce these fixed responses. Although he never actually lists his criteria for value, it becomes clear, through frequent repetition, that Andrews has seven aesthetic principles that the playwright cannot violate without an attendant loss of literary excellence and dramatic force:

1. Theatrical death should be mimetically "enacted," and not just announced.
2. The death-speech should have unity of style and affect.
3. The death-speech should not be didactic.
4. The death-speech should not be loquacious.
5. Both the action and words should be convincing.
6. To be convincing, the death-scene must be preceded by consistent and convincing characterization.
7. The words should be memorable.

These rules are in keeping with a critical tradition stretching from the neo-classical period to the present. It is a tradition that Andrews knows well, and uses for his argument. That a realistic and tear-jerking enactment of death was often admired by Elizabethans receives support from works as varied as Thomas Nashe's *Pierce Pennilesse* and Montaigne's *Essays*. Andrews mentions these texts, but without ever seeming to doubt that Renaissance playwrights *always* strove for eloquence and pathos. The model adopted by Andrews is one of slow historical progress, from the Medieval to the Jacobean period, towards artistic excellence, peaking with Shakespeare. A decline after Shakespeare, with a sharp falling-off from Ford to Shirley, marks the end of a great era for theatrical death.[6]

Andrews begins his book begins with a famous remark (used also by Willson) from Dryden's *Essay of Dramatic Poesy*. Dryden's Lisideius observes that "in all our tragedies, the audience cannot forbear laughing when the actors are to die; it is the most comic part of the whole play. . . . There are many actions which can never be imitated to a just height: dying especially is a thing which none but a Roman gladiator could naturally perform on the stage, when he did not imitate or represent, but do it; and therefore it is better to omit the representation of it."[7] If Elizabethan or Jacobean audiences likewise guffawed at dying heroes, one may see from Andrews's study that the actors were not necessarily to blame. In what is clearly the most important contribution of this book, Andrews identifies a conventional "rhetoric of death," in which dying characters not only announce their death to the audience, but describe death's effect upon their various body parts. "Despite what would seem its obvious limitations," writes Andrews, "the convention by which the dying refer to the state of their own interior organs courses like quicksilver through Renaissance drama" (p. 169). Here follows an altogether typical example from Chettle's *Hoffman:*

> I feele an Aetna burne
> Within my braines, and all my body else
> Is like a hill of Ice, . . .
> My sinewes shrinke like leaves parcht with the sunne
> My blood dissolves, nerves and tendons fayle
> Each part's disjointed, and my breath expires
> Mount soule to heaven, my body burnes in fire.[8]

On account of their "general enthusiasm for the rhetoric of death" (p. 172), most Elizabethan and Jacobean dramatists are said by Andrews to be aesthetic and dramatic failures. Citing play after play, he observes that this once-popular device cannot elicit either tears or terror. He concludes, "The history of this convention—which should be recognized as a kind of linguistic addiction—testifies to the wisdom of those who, like Shakespeare, focused instead on the way the dying see themselves and the world they leave" (p. 175).

This Action of Our Death is an effective mimesis of that linguistic addiction, consisting largely of plot summary interlarded with illustrative quotation. Each quoted death-speech is followed by a commentary that typically consists of one sentence, or two, about the relative aesthetic merit, or dramatic forcefulness, of the scene or speech under consideration: "It is bad enough to speak these lines at all, but to do so while looking *cheerful!*" "[Nabbes's] 'Painted fire,' it turns out, is the only fire Nabbes has at his disposal." "Rawlins (like Nabbes) is content merely to mix the usual ingredients." "Heywood and Dekker, one may say, are old-

Renaissance Death 13

fashioned." "[Davenant's] 'I spit scum' is a vile phrase. Yet the passage is not intended to be comic." "Ford sounds like a host of his contemporaries" (pp. 173–75). Clearly, most Renaissance dramatists fail to meet Andrews's formal requirements for dramatic excellence.

Perhaps this, more than any other feature, distinguishes "modern" from "postmodern" criticism. We once thought it appropriate to discuss only those texts that conformed in certain ways to the Tradition. Postmodernism is a license to begin anywhere we like, and to discover ways in which the selected text justifies our critical interest in it. If modern standards of formal sophistication are the criteria of value, then Andrews is usually right on the money, not only in critiquing individual speeches but in noting the differences between texts, and between authors. His victory, however, is cheaply won. Looking only for eloquence and verisimilitude, Andrews finds himself, as it were, at a loss for words when confronting an entire era of "bad" death-speeches uttered by incredible or one-dimensional characters. His book is therefore a study in missed opportunities. For example: in Fletcher's *Valentinian* Lucina expires from grief after being raped by the title character. Andrews quotes Claudia's account of Lucina's death but notes only that "what might have been dramatized is reported" (p. 84); i.e., the dramatic force of Lucina's rape is not augmented with a good stage-death afterwards. Similarly, in Massinger's *The Unnatural Combat*, "Theocratine's rape and death, horrible though they are, are chiefly significant in terms of their impact on Malefort. What happens to her is part of his punishment" (p. 107). The death-speech of a raped woman should be theatrically effective, concludes Andrews, and not serve tiresome didactic ends as in Massinger's drama (which is perhaps true, but surely theatricality is not the only critical issue worth discussing in such a case).

Many of the death-speeches quoted by Andrews are richly suggestive of the ways in which un-Shakespearean playwrights conceived theatrical representation itself to be a symbolic triumph over death, quite apart from the relative sophistication of their verse. Consider, as a characteristic example, the dying speech of Eleazar in the anonymous play, *Lust's Dominion:*

> Devills com claim your right, and when I am
> Confin'd within your kingdom then shall I
> Out-act you all in perfect villany. [*Dyes.*]⁹

Andrews's only commentary after reprinting this death-speech of Eleazar is that "he dies, in short, every inch a villain" (p. 32); we then move to a summary of *Antonio's Revenge,* by Marston. Yet surely Eleazar's dying boast acquires a kind of poignancy if we hear in it the player's will to insert his own being between the life that he represents on stage and the death that threatens to consume it. ("Confined within a theatrical space, I become a Platonic form, a timeless and immortal representation of human villainy.") Andrews sees only a stock-villain's stock-death. By ignoring the text's metadramatic affirmation of cultural value, he robs the text of critical value.

In Barnabe Barnes's play *The Devil's Charter,* writes Andrews, "Borgias is no more than a negative example, a learn-thou-by-me moralist," a sorry Faustus:

Holla, holla, holla, come, come, come, what, when, where, when, why, deaf, strike, dead, alive, oh alas, oh alas, alwaies burning, always freezing, always living, tormented, never ending, never, never, never mending, out, out, out, out, why, why, whether, whether, thether. . . .
   *Thunder and lightning with fearefull noise the divells thrust him down and goe Triumphing.*¹⁰

Andrews responds tersely, "Sensationalism and grotesquerie dominate." He then turns to other tragedies, warning in advance that "most are eminently forgettable" (p. 40). But surely a skilled actor could make the death-speech of Borgias less forgettable than Andrews suggests; and even if such lines could not be performed at all, Andrews would be wrong to dismiss them as merely grotesque. Here, in Borgias's dying words, is a dramatization of Andrews's own critical perception: dramatic language is inadequate to express the experience of death; at the moment of death, all words become meaningless repetition, the last syllables of privately recorded time, signifying nothing.

Andrews may be right to assume that some Elizabethan verse was just plain "bad"—that is, intended to produce a pathos greater than the verse was able to achieve even for its original audience. Such an hypothesis is of course hard to prove, using texts that were both fictional and theatrical, and performed long ago by actors who wished for their audience to be well entertained. But most critics will agree, even in today's postformalist climate, that a text may fail to validate its own pretensions, or to achieve what Kenneth Burke has called the eloquence of form (much less sheer verbal eloquence). I have in my own files a collection of howlers from Renaissance elegiac verse, many of them taken from laments for Prince Henry (d. 1612). As we know from their historical context, elegies on Prince Henry were neither fictional, nor intended to be funny. But consider, for example, these verses from George Wither's "Obsequies":

> Prince Henry's dead! What voice is that we hear?
> Am I awake or dream I? Tell me whether.
> If this be true, if this be true, my dear,
> Why do I stay behind thee, to do either?
>
> ... Again, when one had forc'd unto my ear,
> *My prince was dead,* although he much protested,
> I could not with belief his sad news hear,
> But would have sworn, and sworn again, he jested.
>
> ... But when I saw the hearse, then I believ'd,
> And taking breath, thus fell to vowelling.
> Beside, to show I had not causeless griev'd,
> I saw a note of his embowelling.[11]

That these verses are indeed "bad" receives some confirmation from Wither himself, who revised them before reissuing the "Obsequies" a decade later among his *Juvenilia* (1622). All of the most bathetic lines in the poem were removed by Wither's more seasoned pen.

But did fictive death-speeches have to be "tragic," and death "imitated to a just height," in order to find success on the Renaissance stage? Probably not. How else, after all, does one account for the very popularity and durability of what Andrews has called the "rhetoric of death"? Assuming such stuff to be failed pathos, Andrews neglects to consider whether there might not be a playful side to many of the death-scenes that he discusses. Without our resorting to an essentialist view of the dramatic text or of the response generated by its enactment (indeed, without even presuming that Shakespeare is "better"), it is possible that Renaissance playwrights were not, after all, competing always to achieve the theatrical effects produced by the death of Hamlet or Desdemona or Macbeth. Very few stage-plays were written in response to a national tragedy like the death of Prince Henry in 1612, and it is doubtful that many playwrights sought to achieve such pathos in the theater. We can be fairly sure, at least, that none of the playwrights whom Andrews critiques in *This Action* was trying to satisfy modern notions of good form and dramatic forcefulness, and it may well be that none was striving after Arnoldian high seriousness, either. Take, for example, John Webster's *The White Devil*. A theatrical review of the initial performance is unavailable to us; but it may be that such lines as these struck Webster's Jacobean audience as funny, even *deliberately* funny:

> O I smell soot,
> Most stinking soot, the chimney is a-fire,—
> My liver's parboil'd like Scotch holy bread;
> There is a plumber, laying pipes in my guts.[12]

Andrews's book is rife with assumptions about authorial and histrionic intention. The Renaissance drama's rhetoric of death, although "ludicrously ineffectual," is "not intended to be comic" (pp. 45, 173). Andrews repeatedly tells us what "we are meant to feel" (p. 81), and how the playwright "wishes us to respond" (p. 118). Fletcher's deaths are "designed to draw tears" while Middleton's are "designed to astonish and impress" (pp. 78, 109). The strategy employed here might find an apt parallel if a twenty-fourth-century scholar were to compare the script for Martin Scorsese's *The Last Temptation of Christ* with the script for Monty Python's *The Life of Brian*, without being privy to the way in which these two scripts were acted or received; and then to deplore the latter as a failed twentieth-century representation of the crucifixion, citing its relative lack of pathos. Irrespective of what "we" (that is, you or I) may think of Scorsese and Monty Python, we might at least wish to counsel future critics to use another guide than fixed formal standards whereby to judge the relative interest of these two motion pictures, either to a film-audience in the twentieth century, or to an academic audience in the twenty-fourth.

By complaining that most Renaissance death-scenes are simply not credible, Michael Andrews aligns himself, in effect, with Tom Stoppard's Guildenstern:

GUIL (*fear, derision*): Actors! The mechanics of cheap melodrama! That isn't *death!* (*More quietly*) You scream and choke and sink to your knees, but it doesn't bring death home to anyone—it doesn't catch them unawares and start the whisper in their skulls that says—"One day you are going to die." (*He straightens up.*) You die so many times; how can you expect them to believe in your death?
PLAYER: On the contrary, it's the only kind they do believe.[13]

In *Shakespeare and the Denial of Death,* James L. Calderwood has it both ways. This study considers both the grimness of death in Shakespeare's society, and its representation in Shakespeare's drama, in order to show that Stoppard's player is no less right than Guildenstern:

Death in tragedy is denied, demeaned, and diverted. It is also dignified beyond its due. To be touched with a poisoned foil like Hamlet or stabbed by one's own dagger like Othello is not the same thing as coughing and retching one's way to the grave like Keats. Most deaths are ugly, pathetic events, and Shakespeare must have seen his share of them in bodies tettered by the pox, made noseless by syphilis, or festering blackly from the plague. Tragic death transcends all this . . . because it lends an aura of vitality and excitement to the drab deaths outside the theater. [pp. 134–35]

If the daily spectacle of men and women retching their way to the grave was transformed, by some of Shakespeare's contemporaries, into grotesque comedy—one thinks, for example, of Marlowe's poisoned nuns in *The Jew of Malta*—then Shakespeare is in league with modern sensibilities by making death grand, and by loading it with tragic significance. Both strategies, however, contain a repressive element, as Calderwood reminds us in *Shakespeare and the Denial of Death*.

Few Shakespeare scholars have been as prolific, or as consistently interesting, as James L. Calderwood. His best-known work includes *Shakespearean Metadrama* (1971), *Metadrama in Shakespeare's Henriad* (1979), *To Be and Not to Be* (1983), and *If It Were Done:* Macbeth *and Tragic Action* (1986). Although Calderwood is often identified with metadramatic and metatextual criticism, his recent work has taken him in other directions, as in his newest book, *The Properties of Othello* (1989), which looks at the ways in which identity and manhood in *Othello* are shaped by notions of "property" (including claims on women as a self-validating masculine possession).

Shakespeare and the Denial of Death, first published in 1987 and now reissued in paperback, is probably Calderwood's least familiar book, having been ignored by most of the journals to which one might turn for a scholarly response. The only exception, I believe, among Renaissance journals, is a *Shakespeare Quarterly* review in which the reviewer, Arthur Kirsch, grumbles with disapproval.[14] Kirsch complains first of Calderwood's "academic facetiousness," which "seems unbecoming and disconcerting" in a discourse that deals with such grave subjects as God, Death, and Shakespeare. He complains also of Calderwood's "fragmented" argument. Less glum readers will find Calderwood's wit to be thoughtful and incisive, a refreshing change from our usual diet of thickly ponderous prose. (In fact, of the four books reviewed here, only Calderwood's can bear to be taken up for the sheer pleasure of reading.) Whether Calderwood's "argument is fragmented," as Kirsch says, or fully cohesive, or no argument at all, depends on our relative commitment to conventional structure. Far from being tightly organized, Calderwood's discussion proceeds in a series of brilliant flashes, each one briefly illuminating

Renaissance Death

a new stretch of territory. Calderwood leaps from mountain peak to mountain peak, skipping about from play to play with an agility that can only be envied, not imitated; when reading this book one may thus say of Calderwood what Nietzsche says of Zarathustra: one must have long legs to follow him. Not all readers will be willing to make the effort. But those who do will be rewarded with fresh ways of thinking about Shakespeare's entire corpus.

Kirsch's fundamental objection to *Shakespeare and the Denial of Death* has less to do with wit or disorder than with an alleged "neglect of Christian thought": "Shakespeare habitually thought in terms of Christian images"; James Calderwood does not. "Christian images" are for Kirsch the very stuff of Shakespearean meaning; and "to neglect their impingement on [Shakespeare's] drama is to impoverish it." Which is not to say that Calderwood is the only person responsible for Shakespeare's recent poverty: "Except as a new historicist target," complains Kirsch, "the subject [of Christian images] is now regarded as outmoded and unimportant. One can only hope this fashion passes." Kirsch misleads his readers, however, by remarking that "though [Calderwood] mentions Christianity from time to time as a 'strategy' to deny death, the subject is essentially absent" (p. 349). Not so. Calderwood's study has nearly as much to say about Christianity as about Shakespeare. Indeed, the two topics are, in Calderwood's treatment, deeply interrelated. One cannot turn to any portion of this book without finding a reference to biblical texts, or to Christian ritual, or to Elizabethan theology. The real basis for Kirsch's objection seems to be that Calderwood shows small reverence for God's authorial intention; instead, Calderwood studies Christian texts and symbols under the light of feminist, psychoanalytic, and anthropological theory, thereby reading Christianity as a patriarchal and phallocentric symbolic structure that serves (among other functions) to sustain male identity. Calderwood finds that Christianity facilitates the denial of death, and mediates fears of death-like self-nullification, all the way to the grave. Infant baptism, for example, "may have been the first effort of patriarchal societies to deny the potential femininity of males. Baptizing babies shortly after birth, that is, implies among other things that the passage through a feminine body is contaminating. The woman must be washed away to guarantee masculine purity" (p. 51). Not everyone will accept such audacious readings of Christian symbolism—perhaps Calderwood *ought* to have neglected Christian images after all—but the connections that are made here between Christian cultural forms and Shakespeare's art are so illuminating that this reader, at least, cannot wish the book to be other than it is.

Calderwood draws on the work of Ernest Becker, Norman O. Brown, Rene Girard, and others in order to demonstrate that the denial of death is a fundamental and perhaps universally human activity. That we mortals insistently belie the inevitability and finality of death is, moreover, one modern scholarly viewpoint that William Shakespeare seems actually to have shared. He repeatedly dramatizes the various cultural norms, spiritual and otherwise, through which men and women may seek to transcend their inevitable doom and the "biological embarrassment" of their own mortal flesh. "Shakespeare was more than usually aware of man's ironic status as the animal that seeks to deny its mortal limitations by fashioning idealized images of itself. Thus throughout the plays he provides abundant opportunities for man's spiritual highness to come to grief on his corporeal lowness" (pp. 3–4). Nowhere do Shakespeare's characters display their short-sighted ingenuity more clearly than in the various means by which they avoid sharing the ironic vision of their death-dealing creator:

The vast majority of Shakespeare's characters deny death in some positive manner. They deify something and identify with it: a hero, a king, a beloved, the nation, money, knowledge, virginity, honor, and so forth. By so doing they tuck themselves into a niche in the social order and become defiladed against death's arrows. If they cannot survive because they are powerful enough to conquer death on the battlefield, then they will do so because they are good, and God loves the good, or because they are patriotic, and God loves England, or because they are men, and God has strong reservations about women. [p. 197]

When all evasive strategies fail, and doomed characters must face the abyss, Shakespeare's fictive men and women often revise their interpretive strategies, but without admitting the finality and relative unimportance of their imminent demise. With remarkable dexterity, the dying simply refigure their death as a translation to immortality of one kind or another—unless, like Hotspur, their illusions and breath are lost too suddenly. It is not often, however, that the dying hero views himself or herself, in his or her last moments, as food for worms.

Shakespeare, it turns out, dramatized the desire for symbolic immortality in more ways than anyone (including Shakespeare) might have guessed. In Part 1 of this study ("The Denial of Death"), Calderwood finds death-avoidance not just in the representation of fighting, fleeing, or hiding, but in such activities as eating, lust, and self-disguise. Language, money, social class, and honor are similarly figured, in Shakespearean drama, as defensive arguments against mortality or self-nullification.

From these private defenses against death (Falstaff's eating, Hotspur's virtú, Isabella's chastity, the impulse of Shylock and Timon to cannibalize their enemies, etc.), Calderwood moves in Part 2 ("Tragedy and Death") to the ways in which various cultural "immortality systems"—the state, hero worship, the patriarchal family—may likewise infuse Shakespeare's characters, or Shakespeare's audience, with an illusion or hope of transcendence. Among those forms is tragic drama itself, which serves as a kind of amulet whereby the audience (no tragic heroes, there) may ward off death. Shakespeare "creates in us an appetite for death the satisfaction of which compensates us for the pity and fear we have been made to suffer. Yet death is not truly death when it is reduced to playing a culminating part in the plot, a part we expect it to play, and, in our aesthetic perversity, want it to play" (p. 134).

A third and final section ("Immortality and Art") illustrates ways in which Shakespeare both exploits and questions literary immortality as a compensation for literal death. The conventional line is of course that literary discourse provides enduring fame for the poet as well as for those whom the poet eulogizes (e.g., Sonnet 18). Yet words are—as Shakespeare so often reminds us—mortal breath, transient and insubstantial exhalations. The poet mitigates this insubstantiality of speech by asserting (e.g., through poetic form) the corporeality or materiality of words. The poet can see that "Enduring speech is memorable speech, and it is memorable because it is in some degree formal, whether as simply formal as 'Sticks and stones may break my bones' or as complexly so as 'The Canonization'" (p. 172). Publication also helps, of course, as any scholar will tell you. For the Elizabethan playwright, however, theatrical production rather than publication was the usual ground for a continued incarnation. Shakespeare's insistent metadramatizing of experience at a theatrical level—to which Calderwood has directed our attention in recent years—is thus akin to the poet's materializing formality of language at a stylistic level: both strategies foreground the signifier at the expense of their signifieds in continuing to represent the absent presence of the author's "I" (p. 177); id est, here lies the poet's denial of death. Yet life, as Shakespeare insistently reminds us, is a play of illusions. When the Shakespearean revels fade, as fade they must, the illusion of reality merely gives way (at least in Calderwood's version of Shakespeare's vision) to a reality that is itself comprised of illusion.

Calderwood concludes, then, that Shakespeare's art "is not really an attempt to deny death, however much it may in a sense do so. He does not seek to create disembodied worlds without end but dips his art in the watercolors of human action and paints time where she stands. Eternity has to stoop to make an entrance on his stage, because the only immortality we are promised is a performance again tomorrow" (p. 194). It is impossible to sum up the richness of this extraordinary book; but every reader who sees it through to the end will be happy, I think, to promise Calderwood another performance tomorrow.

In *Play, Death, and Heroism in Shakespeare*, Kirby Farrell considers the strategies whereby Shakespeare's characters seek to tame death through imaginative or compensatory play. "Play-death," as used here, is a fairly expansive construct that includes self-effacement, faked death, apparent death, and identification with a death-defying or death-dealing hero. Needless to say, Farrell covers some of the same turf as Calderwood; but if Calderwood's 1987 study seems throughout to inform Farrell's book published two years later, it is a debt that goes both ways, as both authors acknowledge in their notes. Despite notably different critical angles in viewing similar material, Farrell and Calderwood are in a sense collaborators, each having contributed to the other's work in a cross-continental dialogue that has apparently been in progress for several years. The fruitful results of that exchange suggest that we may not be whistling in the dark after all, that it really is possible for an ongoing critical dialogue to generate a richer store of meaning than those studies which seek to preserve the harvest of critical approaches no longer in fashion.

Like Calderwood (who credits Farrell with having got there first), Farrell builds upon Ernest Becker's *The Denial of Death,* written when Becker was terminally ill. Farrell shares Becker's view that all cultural activity springs from our impulse "to avoid the fatality of death, to overcome it by denying in some way that it is the final destiny for man."[15] This explanation for cultural production provides the foundation for Farrell's critical study of death-denying play in Shakespearean drama. Beginning with the observation that "an astonishing range of characters in Shakespeare undergo a simulation of death," Farrell explores cultural forms for coping with the dread of death—mechanisms whereby human beings, fictional and otherwise, deny their mortality. Drawing on psychoanalytic and anthropological theory, and on new historicist methodology, Farrell looks beyond the literary text to other forms of cultural activity (painting, courtly manners, child's play) to show "that imaginative responses to death are inherently cultural processes"—in Shakespeare's age as in our own (p. 6). This, of course, is an observation that no thoughtful critic would deny. But Farrell's book is to be valued for the thoughtfulness and thoroughness with which he illuminates heroic or self-effacing "play" as a process—culturally programmed and psychologically motivated—for subduing mortal dread. Farrell ably demonstrates that we have much in common with Shakespeare's contemporaries (as with Shakespeare's fictive men and women), in that heroic posturing, for example, may reduce an all-too-human fear of death while transforming the pressure of death into a source of creative energy.

Farrell reminds us that play-death is a prominent feature not just of Shakespeare's drama but of the culture that produced it.

In the ordered society of early modern England, one operative fantasy—prescribed for women, children, and servants—was the belief that through self-effacement an individual might achieve autonomy, no less in the home or work-place than in the royal court or the kingdom of heaven. An exemplary instance not mentioned by Farrell is that of Katherine Parr, who was valorized as a champion of the Reformation following the publication of her *Prayers* (1545) and *Lamentation* (1547); both works insist that radical self-effacement and absolute submission to God, king, and husband may lead to immortality. (Unfortunately, none of the four scholars reviewed here expresses much interest in texts by Renaissance women.)

Moving from self-negation and avoidance to self-assertion and symbolic conquest over death, Farrell shows that Shakespeare's society generated forms of heroic significance which, through transference, could sustain a feeling of immunity or transcendence: our apotheosized hero has power over death itself; therefore we share in his immortality. Whether through self-effacement or transference, then, a radical loss of identity could be viewed as leading to compensatory aggrandizement, an escape from nullification. Farrell's central concern is to demonstrate how this rhythm of self-loss and apotheosis operates as an imaginative response to death, both inside and outside Shakespeare's theater.

"To my knowledge," writes Farrell, "no contemporary writer was so richly concerned with play-death and apotheosis as Shakespeare." Perhaps the operative phrase here is "richly concerned," but it is nonetheless unfortunate that Farrell and Andrews did not cross paths a little sooner. Even if (as Andrews has shown) the death-scenes of some Renaissance playwrights more closely resemble Shakespeare's "Pyramus and Thisbe" interlude than the death of Desdemona or King Lear, it seems clear from Farrell's illuminating study that some of the same cultural strategies are at work in every staged death. Farrell's analysis suggests that the "rhetoric of death" delineated by Andrews may not represent a failed mimesis, as Andrews has supposed, but a familiar (and therefore comforting) strategy whereby theatrical production mocked and depleted the fear of death.

If the Elizabethan drama provided an important site of resistance to death and self-nullification, the same may be said of Renaissance social structure, gender relations, and religion. In discussing the cultural context for Shakespeare's drama, Farrell builds upon recent historicist and feminist scholarship with admirable dexterity. He recognizes, for example, that "patriarchy" was not a monolithic agent that oppressed every aspect of women's lives, as in some feminist formulations (a hostile version, as it were, of Willson's controlling "Providence"), but rather a network of assumptions and cultural practices within which women, children, servants, and other disempowered classes could seek autonomy, albeit within constricting cultural norms. "The official network in the Renaissance was an interlocking sequence of upward identification following the chain of being from dead matter to the throne of the everlasting father" (p. 60). Farrell shows that patriarchal values were partly sustained, at all levels of society, by a powerful cultural impulse to identify with a figure or system of potent authority. The "ideal" child (or wife) typically "substituted the patriarchal will for his or her own" (p. 25); through such transference, the subject-self could sustain an illusion of autonomy. Farrell does not attempt to illustrate this hypothesis with respect to nonfictional women of the period; but indeed, it does appear that the usual strategy whereby Renaissance women resisted nullification, at least among the aristocracy, was not one of rebellion *against* patriarchal authority, but of identification *with* it. (Consider, for example, Sidney's proud sister, the countess of Pembroke; or Lady Tanfield, Elizabeth Cary's tyrannical mother.) Such transference was, of course, a deeply ambivalent process, as Farrell goes on to demonstrate from Shakespearean drama and from the history of such figures as Ralegh and Essex. The result, for those who played out these self-effacing or heroic games, was often a radically split self—or literal death.

Although there is not much to complain of in this erudite study, it is perhaps worth noting Farrell's habit of quoting critical commentary without identifying the speaker—as if the quoted remarks were not another critic's perspective, but an exact reformulation of his own prior viewpoint (or even a kind of self-substantiating truth, amputated from its human source). As a result, while reading, one cannot tell who is speaking, except of course Farrell himself. (The names of his predecessors may be found, suitably buried, in the notes at the back of the book.) In an otherwise riveting study, the unidentified quotations are a minor distraction at worst—but they may be viewed also as a point of interest, as a shrewd reversal of Farrell's own subject matter. While demonstrating that Shakespeare's contemporaries, like Shakespeare's characters, efface the self and identify with authority as a means whereby to achieve limited autonomy, Farrell simply effaces his authorities, keeping them behind the arras while he occupies center stage.

At the present moment in Renaissance studies, center stage is an okay place for Farrell to be standing. This impressively learned work violates the boundaries that we have drawn between contending forms of critical discourse. To illuminate Shakespearean texts and the culture in which they were produced, Farrell has drawn upon historicist, anthropological, psychoanalytic, and feminist methodologies without seeming to privilege one critical strategy over the other, and without slipping into a fuzzy eclecticism. While moving comfortably from canonical works to noncanonical texts and back again, his account of the Shakespearean drama is multivalent in its critical insights, conscious of its own ideology, and theoretically well informed. With "traditional" deconstruction now in its death-throes and the new historicism in a mid-life crisis, Farrell's book may represent the wave of criticism's immediate future.

Or perhaps we Shakespeareans have no future. Terry Eagleton, in his *Literary Theory*, contemplates with wicked glee the nightmarish vision of a world in which Shakespeare studies dwindle into irrelevance and finally expire altogether:

We may in the future produce a society which is unable to get anything at all out of Shakespeare. His works might simply seem desperately alien, full of styles of thought and feeling which such a society found limited or irrelevant. In such a situation, Shakespeare would be no more valuable than much present-day graffiti. And though many people would consider such a social condition tragically impoverished, it seems to me dogmatic not to entertain the possibility that it might arise rather from a general human enrichment. [pp. 12–13]

"Anything can be literature," remarks Eagleton, "and anything which is regarded as unalterably and unquestionably literature—Shakespeare, for example—can cease to be literature."[16] True. But it is not very likely that the curricular or critical or dramatic production of "Shakespeare" will die out very soon. With unfailing market-instincts, Terry Eagleton has himself capitalized with two books on the Bard.[17] The Shakespeare market has, indeed, become so resilient that it can respond even to the imminent "death of Shakespeare" with a flurry of books about Shakespeare's eminent representation of death. In the words of James Calderwood, "Shakespeare and immortality seem to have been made for one another. The man himself may no longer be among us in the flesh, but bound in calf he seems a good bet, as he himself predicted, to outlive brass and stone and gilded monuments" (p. 169).

One can, however, detect in many recent studies some hint of sheepishness about contributing to the ever-growing mountain of Shakespeare studies at a time when other texts, both literary and nonliterary, clamor for attention. "Shakespeare dominates my argument," confesses Farrell, "because the pattern that I want to unfold appears profoundly and accessibly in his art" (p. 6). This apparent privileging of the cultural pattern over the Shakespearean text that illustrates it is, of course, a ruse. Shakespeare dominates Farrell's argument, and Calderwood's and Andrews's and Willson's and Eagleton's and my own, because Shakespeare is *Shakespeare*. A clever treatise on *Play, Death, and Heroism in the Bulgarian Romance,* or even one about *George Peele's Reflexive Endings,* would not be published by an Anglo-American press, no matter how accessible or profound; or, if published, it would not be read.

Shakespearean texts have shown themselves able to accommodate virtually every critical perspective, and that's lucky for all of us. Not even Shakespeare's art, however, is potent enough to generate wave after wave of critical "insights." Rather, with two centuries of Shakespeare studies behind us already, the potency of the tradition mandates new critical approaches so that we do not run out of things to say. To take part in that tradition is of course to adopt a death-denying strategy of our own academic subculture. By writing books and essays and conference papers about the immortal Shakespeare, we identify ourselves with a significant cultural hero, in hopes that some of his immortality may rub off on our own enterprise. And yet, given the continued vitality of modern literary scholarship, Shakespeare studies are not a bad place to be.

Notes

1. Robert F. Willson, Jr. "Why Teach Shakespeare? A Reconsideration." *Shakespeare Quarterly,* 41 (1990), 206–10. For another recent work that seeks to preserve Shakespeare while preserving undergraduates from the Shakespeare industry, see Leah Scragg, *Discovering Shakespeare's Meaning* (Totowa, N.J.: Barnes and Noble, 1988).

2. Willson, p. 18. The word "all" at this point refers only to Claudius, Gertrude, and Laertes, but similar remarks appear throughout his study. Shakespeare critics likewise are typically blind or unobservant or perversely short-sighted. Willson's study opens with the example of Dr. Johnson, who complained that Shakespeare "seems to write without any moral purpose. . . . Yet Johnson's blinders have to a great extent misled his judgment" (p. 3).

3. For a more problematic view of *Macbeth,* and of its relation to Holinshed, than that of Robert Willson, see Peter Stallybrass, "*Macbeth* and Witchcraft," in John Russell Brown, ed., *Focus on* Macbeth (London and Boston: Routledge and Kegan Paul, 1982), 189–209, and my own "*Macbeth*'s War on Time," *English Literary Renaissance,* 16 (1986), 319–42. Without turning to Holinshed, James L. Calderwood argues persuasively that Malcolm's victory merely renews the cycle of violence. See *If It Were Done:* Macbeth *and Tragic Action* (Amherst: Univ. of Massachusetts Press, 1986). Such readings as these, in Willson's view, would "refute [Shakespeare's] endings as they exist" (p. vi), making "explicit what can only be called implicit in the plot"—to which "there can be no alternative for criticism than to invoke the text" (p. 75).

4. Willson, p. 36n. Quoted from John L. Styan, *Shakespeare's Stagecraft* (Cambridge: Cambridge Univ. Press, 1967), p. 196.

5. Stephen Greenblatt, "Invisible Bullets," *Glyph,* 8 (1981), 57. This line has since become a formula for new historicists seeking to demonstrate that the subversive potential of literary texts is inevitably contained by the social power-structure. I am, of course, putting a somewhat different spin on Greenblatt's

words from what was intended. Greenblatt's point is that modern critics tend to privilege as subversive those Renaissance texts that partly illustrate our own departure from the values or power-systems of early modern England, i.e., that we "locate and pay homage" to the subversive potential of some Renaissance texts only because it is not our power-structure that is being threatened.

6. For example: "For years theatrical representation lagged behind what may be called the art of life" (p. 18); and again, "If one compares the death of Cambyses to those of characters in medieval drama, one finds that there has been little or no progress" (p. 19).

7. Andrews, p. 13. Quoted from William Frost, ed., *Selected Works of John Dryden* (New York: Rinehart, 1955), p. 350.

8. Andrews, p. 170. Quoted from Henry Chettle, *Hoffman, or a Revenge for a Father* (Malone Society Reprints, 1951), ll. 226–34. Wrongly cited in the notes (Andrews, p. 197) as "1914 (1915)."

9. Andrews, p. 32. Quoted from *Lust's Dominion, or the Lascivious Queen* (1600); in Fredson Bowers, ed., *The Dramatic Works of Thomas Dekker*, 4 vols. (Cambridge: Cambridge Univ. Press), vol. 4, ll. 163–66.

10. Andrews, p. 40. Quoted from Barnabe Barnes, *The Divils Charter* (London, 1607), sig. M2^v; rpt., Ann Arbor, Mich.: University Microfilms, 1954.

11. George Wither, *Prince Henries Obsequies or Mournefull Elegies upon His Death* (London, 1612). Normalized text by D. Foster. Wither's revised text appears in *Juvenilia* (London, 1622).

12. Andrews, p. 171. Quoted from John Webster, *The White Devil*, ed. John Russell Brown (London: Methuen, 1964), 5.6.141–44.

13. Tom Stoppard, *Rosencrantz and Guildenstern Are Dead* (New York: Grove Press, 1967), p. 83.

14. *Shakespeare Quarterly*, 40 (1989), 348–49.

15. Farrell, p. ix. Quoted from Ernest Becker, *The Denial of Death* (New York: Free Press, 1973).

16. Terry Eagleton, *Literary Theory: An Introduction* (Minneapolis: University of Minnesota Press, 1983), p. 10.

17. Terry Eagleton, *Shakespeare and Society: Critical Studies in Shakespearean Drama* (London: Chatto and Windus, 1967), and *William Shakespeare* (London: Basil Blackwell, 1986).

Standing Up to the Wise Guys

John Goode

Daniel R. Schwarz, *The Transformation of the English Novel, 1890–1930.* New York: St. Martin's Press, 1989. viii, 336 pp.

Regrettably, the first point to be made about this book is that it is not what it says it is. The title surely leads us to expect a global discussion of the changing nature of fiction within two dates. In fact it only deals with six writers whose work loosely falls within the period—Hardy, Conrad, Joyce, Lawrence, Woolf, and Forster—and only with selected aspects of them. It does not engage seriously with any writer outside this well-established and largely unquestioned canon: a brief dismissal of Galsworthy, Bennett, and Wells as writers of "comparatively pedestrian journalistic prose" (p. 136) indicates how unquestioned it is. It fails to define the novel of this period against its predecessor because it has an entirely makeshift view of a homogenized mythic beast called "The Victorian Novel," further identified, it is true on page 22, as "say *Bleak House, Vanity Fair,* and *Middlemarch.*" This trinitarian manifestation of the Victorian Novel is not analyzed but is said to "have depended on mastery of space and time and the preeminence of the individual perceiver." The model of the modern, on the other hand, is taken to be Rodin's statue of Balzac which manifests art as self-expression. The Victorian Novel is really Classical Realism, a simple-minded old monster ambling about a God-given universe conferring benign light on all it touched. But this book is little concerned with historical transformation, so perhaps a comic-cuts version of nineteeth-century fiction does not matter.

But not only is Schwarz's volume not what its title says, it is also, it has to be said, not exactly a book; rather, it is a collection of essays, some of them going back to 1972, but rearranged to fit a scheme that a properly designed book might have required. At its worst, as in chapter 8, it is merely a knitted-up sequence of old reviews. The more thematic chapters have the mark of their age, and indeed of their chronological separation. Thus there is a good deal of repetition—deconstruction is described, for example, almost verbatim in the same terms on page 215 as on page 149. Odd phrases recur throughout the book. Zeno is wheeled out several times to make the same point. This is natural enough if you are writing for different journals over a number of different years. I am surprised, however, that an editor did not get the obvious patchwork better stitched.

So once we have got over the disappointment of not having a study of the transformation of the English novel, or even of having a new book, what do we have? Well, at the most positive end, in the final three chapters, we have some specific "readings" of important modern texts—*Lord Jim, Ulysses, Mrs. Dalloway,* and *To the Lighthouse.* In addition to these we have some interesting commentary on aspects of *Sons and Lovers,* and *The Rainbow,* the novels of Forster, and some aspects of Hardy's fiction. But I suspect that the real appeal of the book to the publisher is that it "offers an alternative to the way that the deconstructive and Marxist ethos have sought to transform literary studies." It marks, in other words, a return of the repressed, defined by Schwarz himself as "Humanistic Formalism." "It behooves traditional Anglo-American humanistic criticism to resist the onslaught of deconstruction," he writes, "and to defend the ground of its own formalism" (p. 142). But this is halfway through the book. Coded into this is an attack on theory itself insofar as it leads away from the literary work. The "brief history of deconstruction," (p. 153) has two phases, the replacement of the critic as intellectual midwife by the critic as "Genius" followed by a critique of criticism. Deconstruction (and Marxism) are held to have failed because they do not deliver powerful readings of subtle texts. The overt theoretical discussion thus follows an example of practice.

So let us begin, in the empirical spirit of this volume, with the critical practice. The first section, we are told, "shows how historical and contextual material is essential for humanistic formalism," to which the blurb adds "sophisticated close reading" (p. 1).

Standing Up to the Wise Guys

I am not sure that I would use the word "sophisticated" to describe Schwarz's readings—it is, after all, a highly subjective and at best relative term ("sophisticated" in comparison to what?). But I do think he gives warm, generous, and attentive accounts of the reading process. He argues that each novel has a consciousness evident in the "speaking voice" of the narrator which reveals an imagined world as the object of his shaping spirit. Most of the texts he discusses show a variable relationship between narrator and protagonist which governs a variable relationship between narrator and reader. The best of these analyses show that we have in a sense to trust the teller even though we know that the tale is eluding his grasp. In that tension lies the reader's enrichment. Thus, for example, Schwarz argues that the narrator moves very close to Paul Morel in *Sons and Lovers* and that we are left aware of all that the narrator omits by this empathy, notably the possibility of a different evaluation of Paul's love for his mother. In a different way, *Ulysses* creates a tension between the narrator's drive from lyric through epic and dramatic modes, and the distraction of the reader by rich local detail. The reader becomes Odyssean, the book a sacred text which has to be read profanely. Another kind of tension, between male and female values, dominates the dialectic of order and flux in *To The Lighthouse*. I say these readings are generous, because Schwarz brings out in his chosen writers both their sense of a world unpinned by values and the intense need to give it pattern nonetheless. What he invites us to admire and enjoy is the extent to which these writers do not concede victory to either impulse. There are a couple of bad moments when he seems about to produce God or Jung as an answer waiting in the wings, but most of the "reading" is firmly, as he would put it, "profane."

There are two issues on which the formal criticism seems to me to falter. Both come from an anxiety to assert that the distinctive characteristic of modern fiction is its expressivity—an argument that a proper historical consideration would rapidly demolish. This emerges first in the ellision between authorial presence and omniscient narration. Omniscience survives in certain modern texts without the "concept of a shared value system which originally gave rise to the convention" (p. 13). This is a naive assertion, which is exposed further in the essay on Forster who is described as writing subjective novels in the guise of objective ones by continuing to use the "conventional omniscient narrator" (p. 116). This is not a useful distinction. No one would wish to assert that either Fielding or Eliot uses the omniscient narrator because he or she wrote on the basis of shared values—on the contrary, *Tom Jones* expresses a very personal view of the world, and the author of *Middlemarch* has to intervene so much because she knows that the reader is as likely to be as superficial and deluded as the gossips of Middlemarch itself. Forster *is* very much in a line that goes from Fielding to Meredith—the much vaunted omniscience reflects and emphasizes a rehearsed and contested doubt. The common complaint (of James, for example, or even of Eliot against Fielding) is that such authors are too subjective. And that, indeed, is what raises itself as a question about Forster. Why will he not let the reader alone with the story? Is it because he does not believe it?

Related to this is something that may seem much more local. Schwarz seems to be indifferent to the concept of Free Indirect Discourse. This makes him assert authorial presence in passages which are in overt conflict with the "tale" and to suggest that the reader is confronted with an enriched complexity when the text is clearly still holding all the cards in its hands. Again in the Forster essay, he quotes Margaret's sentimental imposition of Arnoldian aspiration to see life steadily and see it whole on "these English forms" as though it were Forster's view (p. 119). Margaret is to learn otherwise. She is later described as Forster's "surrogate" (p. 128), though this is immediately contradicted ("yet Margaret . . . has her limitations"; if this is visible, how can it be unless the narrator has seen them and therefore is not party to them?). This comes out even more in the essay on *Sons and Lovers*, which falsely polarizes the choice in that text between Paul and his actions (see page 82 especially).

These are local points which do not vitiate the generally sane and attentive expositions. However, they do arise from a more general problem, which is that Schwarz, for all his assertion that historical and contextual material is necessary for developing powerful readings, is almost totally uninterested in history except insofar as occasionally he alludes to biography. This applies both to literary history and real history. In the first case, we are constantly referred back to the "conventional Victorian novel," which apparently deployed an omniscient narrator confident about the world which he portrays in a detached manner, and which is peopled by characters "who often function successfully within the community" (p. 23). That "often" acknowledges tacitly the nonsense that it is. If one could hazard a generalization about the major Victorian novelists, it is that they show a concern for precisely those protagonists who cannot function successfully within a community. The nineteenth century is littered with famous examples from Waverley to Daniel Deronda, and as for the detached outsider, it depends what you mean by "detached." Is Dickens detached? Or George Eliot? Later, we are told that Lawrence's prophetic voice displaces the "ironic gentility of the traditional omniscient narrator of Victorian fiction" (p. 98). It is not easy to measure the genteelness of the Brontës or the irony of Mrs. Gaskell. Of course, the Victorian novel is not homogeneous. It is a constantly changing form which grows up precisely because there is no certainty, no unproblematic community, but rather a fluid social and psychological scene. Schwarz's main aim is to assert the expressivity of the modernist novel, but expressivity, as everyone knows from Abrams if not before, is a major concern of romanticism. Schwarz discusses very few actual premodernist novels, and it is significant that when he does feel himself pressed by wishing to account for Forster's originality, he contrasts him with Jane Austen, or rather something generically dubbed "an Austen novel."

Now, to labor the obvious, Forster is hardly original because he moved beyond Austen—there were one or two writers in between them. This may seem cheap irony, but consider Schwarz's four claims for Forster's originality. First "his novels not only dramatize his characters' search for values, but structurally are quests for values" (p. 116). This is very vague, but we might just suggest that he read, to start with, *Caleb Williams*, *Wuthering Heights*, *Great Expectations*, or *The Mill on the Floss*. Second, Forster writes novels that do not merely clarify what precedes and that do not end conclusively. We do not need to make any further comment than that it was Dr. Johnson who entitled the last chapter of his novel "Conclusion, in Which Nothing Is Concluded." Even Jane Austen wrapped some of her novels up with an ironic awareness that there are no endings. However (thirdly), Forster does challenge "the novel of manners"—but no one surely would claim that nineteenth-century fiction is dominated by the novel of manners. I agree that he tested "Victorian Shibboleths about proper and decorous behaviour, about the importance of reason to control the passions" (p. 117)—but so did the Brontës, Wilkie Collins, and Meredith. Finally, we learn, he expanded the novel's range geographically to Italy and India and sociologically (Leonard Bast). Thus, at a stroke, not only are *Little Dorrit* and *Romola* wiped out, but Meredith's Italian novels, Kipling and the whole Anglo-Indian novel traced with such fine scholarship by Benita Parry; and Dickens, Gaskell, Gissing, and a hundred others might as well have stayed in the drawing room. In fact, of course, Forster is self-consciously concessive about Bast. The poor he refuses to deal with. He does not extend the Victorian novel, but deliberately and justifiably, for his purposes, shrivels it up into something much more like a conventional image of a Jane Austen who in any case was also pulling the novel's horns in, as Marilyn Butler has amply argued. Forster is beating a strategic retreat, and if the Marabar caves (a very "Victorian," Darwinian blow, incidentally) are a cosmic extension, it is to the nothing of the later silence.

Along with the descriptive simplification, goes the unquestioned canonicity. Nowhere does Schwarz ask himself whether some of the marginalized writers of the earlier period might have complicated his portrayal of modernism as self-expression. The period 1890–1930 had a much wider and richer field of fiction than he seems to be aware of. Moreover, in the end he becomes aggressively dismissive of the whole historical enterprise. Praising Herzinger's *D. H. Lawrence in His Time, 1908–1915* on page 180 because it sets Lawrence in a contemporary literary context, on page 195 he uses the letters of 1916–1921 to throw doubt on that work (the anachronism seems unimportant to him). Lawrence, the argument goes, must have been less intellectual than was thought because his letters of those years do not mention many writers. Earlier he decides that we have done enough placing of Lawrence "in the English tradition." It "domesticates" him. This does not mean that we ought to pay more attention to a European (or American) context, but that we should not pursue "tertiary influences" such as Carlyle or Ruskin (p. 188). It is difficult to see, however, where else Lawrence would have got his ideas about Norse myth or the Gothic from if it was not from these.

The indifference to literary history is supported, one can only say, by a colossal ignorance of "the social and historical realities" which he despatches as one of Eagleton's "shibboleths" (pp. 164–65). (There are many "shibboleths" in this book—bad guys have shibboleths, good guys "credos.") However, this obsession of Eagleton's could have served Schwarz better than he thinks in some of his readings. *Sons and Lovers* is certainly one of the few novels that presents English working-class life from the inside. This is totally and disablingly ignored by Schwarz's purely psychological analysis. Mrs. Morel is for him simply a discontented and self-serving pervert who asphyxiates Paul. Any awareness of the complex and contradictory drives to integration and separation in working-class life would have saved Schwarz from this one-sided reading, and given him, too, a greater insight into the contradictory drives of *The Rainbow*. Mrs. Morel marries to escape the barren separation of her petty bourgeois family, and she looks to her sons to take her out of the trap the escape inevitably leads to. Paul is also driven by conflicting drives which are indeed, as Lawrence realized, the source of common tragedy. The same lack of awareness marks the essays on Hardy. Tess and Jude are regarded as neurotic because they uproot themselves. But they do not wander about Wessex, they look for work. To use the phrase "upward mobility" with regard to them is actually an insult to the experience of the English rural working class. The poverty of the context in this book is very disturbing. Even Mrs. Thatcher knows that "the stress on private values, on restoring family relationships, and on developing personal relationships" is not a modern concern in contrast with Victorian values (p. 136).

Where does this leave the theoretical polemic? Certainly

Schwarz is in no position to accuse deconstruction, as he does, of ignoring the real world. Nor is one of his other accusations, that it uses obscurantist language, easy to sustain in the face of his own slack, repetitive style. On page 141, he accuses deconstruction of basking in a "consensual glow conferred by a dominant trend." But immediately it is "spreading like fire in dry grass on a windy day" until, later in the paragraph, it reaches high tide, and *then* he announces that he is going to change the metaphor (into another mix, as it happens, with benign critical teleology expressing itself as in a *Big Bang* to *expunge* deconstruction's evil influence). I suppose you could argue that deconstruction is versatile, but it is surely not protean. "Basking in a consensual glow" is a favorite phrase of Schwarz's, however. Later intertextuality basks in a glow (p. 182) and later still Deconstruction (upper-casing itself) constitutes a "consensual glow" in itself. Schwarz tries to give credit where it is due—deconstruction forces us to reassess the stories of our reading and constitutes a radical skepticism which depends on "the quite accurate perception that nothing is perfect and that certainty is impossible" (come back, Popper, all is forgiven). This makes it the intellectual equivalent of "the urban Wise Guy (the modern picaro) who lives on the margin and knows how to exploit every event as a profit" (p. 147). This level of argument is barely improved on throughout a reiterated but incoherent polemic. Insofar as it makes sense at all, it argues that deconstruction ignores reality, privileges misreading, and abandons the literary work. There is, of course, some truth in this, but Schwarz does not put himself in a position to argue for it.

In the first place, he is not interested at all in Derrida, except to make a few jokes about his name, and requote (from Culler) part of a sentence which he says is incomprehensible but which is, as it happens, a fairly lucid remark, even wrenched from the context of Derrida's discussion of Rousseau's conception of writing. Schwarz quotes it as though it were a wayward quotation about life. The target is not, of course, deconstruction as an intellectual position, but a purely academic, professional grouping. It is one of the protagonists in "the dialectical struggle on today's critical mindscape between the two major ideologies of reading"

(p. 215). As we are several times told that deconstruction is at its high noon, I assume that Schwarz sees himself as the Gary Cooper of the old Anglo-American tradition—a humanist has got to do what a humanist has got to do. The critical mindscape, needless to say, is male, white, and middle class.

Derrida is not a literary critic. Only in a very broad sense could you say that deconstruction is an "ideology of reading." Deconstruction cut some ice in English departments not because it brought new methods in, but because it legitimized (or seemed to) some well-established procedures such as connotative interpretation and polysemy. It equally seemed to legitimize these procedures as though they were radical: it enabled textual analysis to have a happy fall. I do not think you can blame much of this on Derrida, who has primarily been concerned to investigate the ideological parameters of the enlightenment tradition and its roots in classical philosophy. Schwarz calls his own position "humanistic formalism" which he, fairly arbitrarily, decides is the chief opponent to deconstruction. Literary criticism is divided between them. Not surprisingly, though somewhat tacitly, by the end of the book he has got them married up, with the only rider that humanistic formalism is the final arbiter.

"Humanistic formalism" is hard to define, from this book at least, although chapter 7 is "the case for it" and chapter 8 "a primer." It insists that the literary work is "an imagined world" and that in the process of reading we respond to an *imitation* of the real creator of the work. It is difficult to disagree with this or with the five points on pages 171–72 that define this criticism, viz: that form expresses a value system, that the work is both a "creative gesture" of the author and the result of historical context, that there is a world preceding the text, that "man's behaviour" is central to most texts, and that inclusiveness is a desirable quality in a literary work. Only the third of these seems to address deconstruction directly since Derrida states that there is no *hors de texte,* but, in its place in the argument about Rousseau (the very paragraph from which Schwarz unwittingly quotes), it is clear that Derrida does not think there is no real world at all, but that there is no real world in Rousseau's depiction of it. There is an important difficulty here about the relationship of language and conceptualization which might arise with the term "imagined world" (what is imagination, what is a world?), but as Schwarz does not engage with any of Derrida's arguments directly, he never has to face this.

What Schwarz is attacking, of course, is only the American assimilation of deconstruction, but the reader will get little illumination even from this. Hillis Miller is invoked but the only arguments are with texts that predate his apparent conversion. Indeed, so ghostly is Hillis Miller's presence, that he is said to "permeate" *The Disappearance of God* and *Poets of Reality* (p. 214). Deconstruction means Jonathan Culler, "middleman who is midwife," to use Schwarz's definition of a good critic (p. 150) if ever there was one. Culler too is berated for his defense of deconstruction on the basis of quotations from his book on structuralism, so there is little sense that Schwarz wishes to engage in serious intellectual debate even with him. In any case, by the last three chapters, humanistic formalism and deconstruction have given up their dialectical struggle and work manfully together to tease out the complexity of modernist texts. This is not as surprising as the earlier polemic might portend, since Schwarz cannot understand what Culler means by the statement that "to deconstruct a discourse undermines the philosophy it asserts . . . by identifying . . . the rhetorical operations that produce the supposed ground of the argument."[1] This cannot be so, says Schwarz, because rhetoric supports the philosophy of a work. But that is what Culler is saying. If we see through the rhetoric, we see through the ideology. If we then argue that there are tensions within this, "are we moving in a direction necessarily different from the old formalism?" (p. 149). Well, no. As long as we keep the tensions within discourse, they can remain purely rhetorical. This is Coney Island deconstruction, thrills but no spills.

Marxism makes a brief appearance in the guise of Terry Eagleton brandishing his shibboleths of social and historical reality, author it appears only of *Literary Theory* and then mainly of its incompetent index. He is told, as though he had not himself said so (in *Against the Grain*, for example), that his hands are too grimy with real life for deconstruction. Feminists too are warned off but are also taken to task for failing to see that a man cannot live by gender alone and that we are all products of multiple intersections. At this point (p. 170), the real "Dan Schwarz" makes his appearance, with a silent kind of tribute to the power of feminism to make one stand up to be counted. He is, as my review will have indicated, a fundamentally Nice Guy, who does not mind admitting to being a caring father, a thoughtful husband and, as is borne out by the style of the book, a committed teacher. I only wish someone had told him not to publish this volume until he had had a harder look at the Wise Guys and time to brush away the froth at the end of his no doubt anxious and angry pen.

Note

1. Jonathan Culler, *On Deconstruction* (Ithaca: Cornell Univ. Press, 1982), p. 86. Quoted, Schwarz, p. 149.

Contextualizing Contemporary Lyric: Some Aporias of Recent Criticism

Marjorie Perloff

Thomas Gardner. *Discovering Ourselves in Whitman: The Contemporary American Long Poem.* Urbana: University of Illinois Press, 1989. x, 208 pp.

Walter Kalaidjian. *Languages of Liberation: The Social Text in Contemporary American Poetry.* New York: Columbia University Press, 1989. xxii, 263 pp.

Jeffrey Walker. *Bardic Ethos and the American Epic Poem: Whitman, Pound, Crane, Williams, Olson.* Baton Rouge and London: Louisiana State University Press: 1989. xvi, 261 pp.

Neither the New Historicism nor its successor, Cultural Studies, has done especially well by modernist and postmodernist poetry. It is often complained that our field is under-theorized, that there are no studies of modernist poetry comparable to, say, Fredric Jameson's *The Political Unconscious* (1981) or T. J. Clark's *The Painting of Modern Life* (1984). Such exceptions as Frank Lentricchia's *Ariel and the Police: Michel Foucault, William James, Wallace Stevens* (1987) or Cary Nelson's *Repression and Recovery: Modern American Poetry and the Politics of Cultural Memory, 1910–1945* (1989) concentrate on particular problematics of modernism, making no attempt to assess the situation on postmodern poetry. Meanwhile the university presses continue to churn out studies of the "long poem" or the "American epic" that seem to do little more than to replicate the generic and thematic models of an earlier period.

The books under review here include one largely traditional study (Thomas Gardner's *Discovering Ourselves in Whitman*) and one brave attempt to read the "social text" of contemporary

American poetry in the light of post-structuralist, especially Foucaultian, theory (Walter Kalaidjian's *Languages of Liberation*). The third book, Jeffrey Walker's *Bardic Ethos and the American Epic Poem,* appears to be just another study of the "long poem" in the Whitman tradition but is actually the most original and challenging of the three, using rhetorical analysis to provide us with new ways of understanding what Walker calls the "splendid failures" of Pound, Crane, Williams, and Olson.

Thomas Gardner's thesis is stated on the opening age of *Discovering Ourselves in Whitman:*

> What I examine in this book is the way that a number of important contemporary poets, engaged like [Robert] Duncan in creating self-portraits, have also discovered in the 'two co-inherent figures' [e.g., solitary singer and created universe] of Whitman's work ways of framing and finding generative the tensions implicit in singing oneself. [p. 1]

Gardner is aware that the claim for Whitman as poetic father of contemporary poets is hardly news, but he argues that whereas Whitman is usually regarded as epic bard (e.g., by James E. Miller, Jr.) or as spokesman for the self's ability to master its world, an ability no longer possible in late twentieth-century culture (see Cary Nelson's *Our Last First Poets*), his own Whitman is "acutely aware of the distance between self and the medium used to make it visible" (p. 9). What contemporary poets have learned from Whitman, therefore, is that "declaring one's self" (Whitman's phrase) is "deliberately acknowledged to be 'problematic'" (p. 8). And in a brief discussion of *Song of Myself,* Gardner points to places in the poem where the "embrace" of the "vital universe" proves all but impossible to maintain.

The difficulty with this thesis (which sounds suspiciously like an updated version of Meyer Abrams's or Robert Langbaum's accounts of the Greater Romantic Lyric or "poem of experience," with its tension between self and world, inner and outer) is that it is unobjectionable enough to be finally less than useful. What twentieth-century poet, after all, has not been faced with the difficulties of relating the personal to the social, self to world, inchoate feeling to the medium of language, and so on? And why does Gardner choose for his exemplary poets John Berryman and Galway Kinnell, Theodore Roethke and Robert Duncan, John Ashbery and James Merrill, rather than, say, Louis Zukofsky or George Oppen, Allen Ginsberg or Edward Dorn, all of whom, after all, produced significant long poems? More important: why doesn't Gardner's "line of Whitman" include a single woman poet?

I suspect the answer is that Gardner chose those poets whom he happened to find especially congenial. There would be nothing wrong with such personal choice, were it not that Gardner sets out to define the genre of "*The* Contemporary American Long Poem." The method, in any case, is to take up pairs of poets and to establish linkages between them:

> The first two writers I discuss, John Berryman and Galway Kinnell, locate the limitation of the embrace in the perceiver, the poet. For them . . . the embrace is frustrated by personal problems, and that tension is best explored by studying what in themselves blocks contact. Accordingly, Berryman's *Dream Songs* are structured as an attempt to tease out and confront the personal difficulties that stand as blinds between him and the world, while Kinnell's *Book of Nightmares* can be seen to be progressively working through his fear of death—a fear that at first holds him away from the world but eventually, when understood, draws him toward it. [p. 21]

I cite this explanation at length because it provides a capsule account of what is put forward in chapters 1 and 2 of *Discovering Ourselves in Whitman*. The second set of writers, Roethke and Duncan, "more usefully understand the limited nature of the embrace as issuing not from a resolvable personal problem, but from the act of using a medium itself" (p. 21). And for the third pair, Ashbery and Merrill, the "cold neutral surface of assumed voices" (Renaissance self-portrait in the case of Ashbery's "Self-Portrait in a Convex Mirror," otherworldly "spirit" voices in the case of Merrill's *The Changing Light at Sandover*) "invite but ultimately refuse a full embrace" (p. 22). Both Ashbery and Merrill "make Whitman's embrace primarily a language issue," language being an external medium that both invites and ultimately discourages union.

From hereon out, it is plain sailing as the book settles down to the business of explicating specific long poems. Many of Gardner's readings are excellent, particularly in the case of Duncan's difficult "Passages," a poem whose body of "shifting particulars" makes it very hard to determine where the participation of the "I" begins and ends. Gardner is also acute in detailing the gradual unfolding of the interaction of fission and artifice in Merrill's *Changing Light at Sandover.* But if the book's individual readings are sensible, informed, and acute, some nagging problems remain. For one thing, Gardner regularly equates the poem's "I" with its author. "Because he can neither embrace nor take warning from the painting," we read in chapter 5, "Ashbery is free to view it in a more detached manner, curious about the artistic problems it raises" (p. 154). But of course Ashbery isn't "free to view" anything, since he is the one who has set up the whole viewing situation, and the "curiosity" Gardner speaks of is qualified by the fact that the "artistic problems," far from being necessarily inherent in Parmiagano's painting, are ones that Ashbery's poem attributes to it.

In reading his long poems as so many experiences of the poets themselves, Gardner takes the works in question almost entirely at face value. In asserting, for example, that the "poet's opening 'howl'" in *The Book of Nightmares* has been "made out of Kinnell's sense of a division within himself" (p. 75), Gardner never questions the rhetoric by means of which this "sense of division" is conveyed, a rhetoric that, so many critics have argued, is bombastic and portentous. Indeed, *The Book of Nightmares* (1971) has not stood the test of time well, which is not to say that a case can't be made for its importance. But Gardner doesn't make that case; he takes as a given that the poem *works* and that its Whitmanian dialectic consequently merits attention.

Discovering Ourselves in Whitman thus opens itself to the charge, made by Walter Kalaidjian in *Languages of Liberation,* that the criticism of contemporary American poetry has "consistently repressed" its "social text" (p. xii). It is true that Gardner is silent on issues of culture and class, race and gender, a situation Kalaidjian sets out to rectify in his own study. Of the three books under review, Kalaidjian's is clearly the most up-to-date and the most theoretically sophisticated, its aim being to "look at how contem-

Contextualizing Contemporary Lyric 47

porary American verse is both swept by and resistant to the commercial, institutional, and social pressures of our historical moment" (p. xii). "Strong poems," he argues, "not only disrupt the world outlooks of reigning ideologies but frequently resist incorporation by ruling narratives of literary criticism." Whereas most criticism is content to read poems for their "expressive lyricism," Kalaidjian's purpose is read them for their "powers of subversion" (p. xiii).

That such a project is long overdue is suggested by the curious silence about social text and ideology in Gardner's and related studies. But my doubts were raised almost immediately by Kalaidjian's choice of "subversive" poets. Adrienne Rich and Gwendolyn Brooks are predictable choices in any discussion of the politics of contemporary poetics. But W. S. Merwin? Robert Bly? James Wright? Are these not exemplars of precisely the "expressive lyricism" Kalaidjian claims to scorn? I will come back to this question, but first I want to have a close look at Kalaidjian's introductory chapter, "Poetry's Institutional Settings," because it raises extremely troubling issues, not just about the poetics of postmodernism but about the state of scholarship today.

The dust jacket of *Languages of Liberation* bears strong words of praise from two distinguished critics, J. Hillis Miller and Catharine R. Stimpson. Miller calls the book "an important contribution to the currently flourishing 'cultural criticism.'" Stimpson calls it "Impeccable and adventurous . . . an indispensable account of contemporary culture." Kalaidjian's "indispensable account" begins with a chapter about "the contexts of postwar history and, in particular, today's conglomerate publishing market" (p. 4). These are important matters, but Kalaidjian's account is riddled with misleading statements, not to mention ordinary inaccuracies that the manuscript's readers should certainly have caught before it went into production.

"During the Great Depression and World War II decades," we read, "literary humanists all along the political spectrum were driven to the fringes of a spreading transnational consumer society" (p. 4). Driven, one wonders, from where? When had literary humanists (one assumes from what follows that Kalaidjian means literary critics) been at the center of society? If he means the university, English professors of the 1910s and 1920s were primarily philologists, and certainly they didn't study contemporary poetry.

"Throughout the postwar years, the New Critics waged a tireless campaign to reverse the decline of English studies" (p. 5). What decline? English studies, as we now know them, didn't even exist before the advent of the New Criticism. Nor was the New Criticism guilty of having "little truck with history," as Kalaidjian asserts, mouthing a tired cliché. Anyone who has ever read W. K. Wimsatt's work on the eighteenth century or Cleanth Brooks's on the seventeenth knows that they were acutely aware of history, which is more than one can say for a "cultural critic" like Kalaidjian. The point, of course, was that the New Critics felt that the *value* of a poem, as opposed to its *meaning* (which could only be determined by historical study as well as by close reading), depended on aesthetic criteria.

But Kalaidjian has a more serious score to settle with the New Critics. It seems they set up "rigid generic boundaries discriminating theoretical rhetoric from poetic discourse. Significantly... Cleanth Brooks popularized the view that verse writing is ontologically prior to criticism" (p. 6). Quite a view to "popularize," given that from Plato and Aristotle, Horace and Longinus, to Sidney, Johnson, Kant and Hegel, to Marx, Lucacs, Adorno and Raymond Williams, poetry was considered "ontologically prior" to the criticism of it. There was, it seems, a life of the mind even before Deconstruction taught Kalaidjian that poetic discourse has no priority over the "theoretical."

In the conservative New Critical climate of the fifties, in any case, poets were evidently characterized by their "disavowal" of history. "Considering the collage of crises America faced throughout the postwar decades, the prevailing tendency to ignore history, common to most contemporary poets and their critics, is striking indeed" (p. 7). Never mind that "collage of crises" is a curious vulgarism, for if "crises" are really "collaged" together, they are no longer perceived as crises. More important: does Kalaidjian think that the "collage of crises America faced throughout the postwar decades" was worse than what occurred in the pre-war (not to mention the war) decades, decades whose horrors and brutalities make the cold-war American fifties look like a pastoral idyll by comparison? Evidently he does, for he now launches into a capsule list of "events" that are designed to make us shudder at the iniquities of our time and our nation. "Tom Hayden's 1962 'Port Huron Statement,' inaugurating Students for a Democratic Society, summed up the apocalyptic angst of the 1950s. 'We may be,' Hayden said, 'the last generation in the experiment with living'" (p. 8).

Surely this is pop cultural history. The familiar items are trotted out—"global tensions," the "Red Scare," "McCarthyism," the "civil rights movement"—like so many ciphers. Along the way, there are simple errors of fact, for example: "The urban 'massification' of American culture was fostered by the growth of print journalism and the spread of television during the 1950s and 1960s" (p. 9). Wrong. As television expanded, print journalism declined, the number of newspapers gradually decreasing so that today cities like Washington have only one newspaper. Or again (pp. 15–16), in a discussion about the state of poetry publishing in the fifties, Kalaidjian argues that Charles Olson "arguably had access to the major publishing houses and influential academic journals. But he deliberately avoided them, choosing instead to publish with alternative outlets such as Jonathan William's [sic] Jargon Press and small independent periodicals like Robert Creeley's *Black Mountain Review*" (p. 15). Here Kalaidjian seems to assume that because Olson had gone to Harvard, he had access to major publishing houses, whereas the opposite is true. Even *Call Me Ishmael*, Olson's critical study of Melville (1947), was rejected for Harcourt Brace first by Eliot and then by F. O. Matthiessen, and Paul Christensen informs us that mainstream little magazines (let alone the major publishing houses) wouldn't print Olson's poems because of their unconventional lay-out on the page.[1] What Kalaidjian refers to as "Olson's refusal to publish with the big publishing houses" (p. 16) is thus simply myth.

The garbling of information continues throughout the chapter. In discussing the academicization of poetry in the fifties and sixties, Kalaidjian observes that "even the more radical so-called anti-academic poets of the 1950s and 1960s became, in some cases, the university's most distinguished academics" (p. 24). True, Olson, as the footnote to this statement tells us, "could not adjust to the state university system of New York" (not quite accurate, since Olson was trying to get teaching appointments again and again and did teach at the University of Connecticut at Storrs in the last years of his life), but "Creeley is now the David Grey Professor of Poetry and Letters at SUNY, Buffalo," A. R. Ammons has a chair at Cornell, Marvin Bell administers the Iowa Writers Workshop, James Dickey teaches at the University of South Carolina, W. D. Snodgrass at Delaware, and so on (see p. 210). The only possible "radical" on this list is Creeley, who had been writing for over three decades by the time he became a professor. Ammons and Bell radicals? James Dickey and W. D. Snodgrass?? And where were the real radical poets of the period: Jack Spicer? George Oppen? Philip Whalen? Were they in the university? The statement on page 24 is thus entirely misleading.

On the next page, Kalaidjian describes the "postwar inflation of practicing poets," the glut produced by "creative writing" programs, and so on. Has he forgotten that he began his chapter by mourning the fact that "literary humanists" had been driven to the "fringes of a spreading transnational consumer society"? How is it that that same society produced such a poetry glut, thus creating what Kalaidjian calls a "legitimation crisis for critics who must define career status and form a canon" (p. 26). This last statement is extremely revealing: Kalaidjian's opening chapter has, in fact, little to tell us about the publishing history of postmodern poetry, its modes of production and reception, Kalaidjian's real aim being to reverse the priority of poetry to theory that he finds so objectionable in the New Criticism or in neo-New Critical poets like Stuart Friebert and David Young who edit *Field* at Oberlin, and who mistakenly take themselves to be poets first, critics second (p. 24).

The confusion between what poetry does and what criticism chooses to see in it runs through *Languages of Liberation*. Kalaidjian never makes clear, for instance, whether the "staging of the private self" is the "bourgeois aesthetic" of the poet himself or herself, or whether it is the wrong sort of criticism that insists on foregrounding that staging (see p. 22). Not surprisingly, then, when Kalaidjian turns to the poetry itself, his methodology runs into a curious impasse. In chapter 2, Kalaidjian compares the "lyric minimalism" of James Wright to that of W. S. Merwin. Wright, he argues convincingly, turned his back on "America's industrial scene," "pursu[ing] a poetics of lyric disclosure" (p. 43). His "pursuit of authentic lyric expression ends in a dubious phenomenology of place," staking his career "on an 'authentic' style of sheer lyric assertion" (p. 45). But what about Merwin? "Unlike Wright's poetry, Merwin's does not depend on registering authentic authorial presence. Instead, he speaks to an absence at the heart of language" (p. 46). His later verses "describe a chiaroscuro of indeterminacy. His mature work resembles an extended web of fragments or a palimpsest" (p. 51). The implication, evidently, is that "indeterminacy" negates the lyric self, but common sense tells us that the opposite is the case. To speak of "an absence at the heart of language" is to posit a "longed-for but unattainable presence"; to write fragments or palimpsests is hardly a manifestation of social critique. Indeed, when Kalaidjian comments on poems like "Sybil," in which "the poet addresses his muse with . . . tragic irony," he seems to be describing the ultimate "staging of the lyric self" that he has dismissed so derisively.

The conclusion that "Merwin's lyric project serves as a powerful foil to the existential and phenomenal aesthetics that shaped Wright's career" (p. 64) is thus puzzling. If Merwin really does "release the lyric into transpersonal expressive registers," he would exemplify Paul de Man's theory of lyric rather than Fredric Jameson's theory of social text. Indeed, a case could be (and has been) made for the extreme escapism of Merwin's poetry, his refusal to grapple with social actualities, his inward turn into a natural world stripped of all human complexities. The maskings of ideology in Merwin's poetry are extremely interesting, but there is no discussion of them in *Languages of Liberation*.

The next chapter, which deals with Charles Olson, is hardly more satisfactory. The *Maximus Poems* are presented as "moving beyond the failure of modernism in Pound and Williams" onto the "horizon of what Olson called 'post-humanism'" (pp. 75–76). The "failure" of modernism as well as its "elitism" are taken for granted, even as Olson's own elitism, which, as we shall see, is subtly analyzed by Jeffrey Walker in *Bardic Ethos*, is safely ignored. *Maximus I* "returns epic to its worldly foundations of nonliterary discourse," and that seems to be sufficient to make it a satisfactory "cultural critique of American consumer society" (p. 86). Never mind what recent feminist criticism has defined as the "phallacy" of Olson's heroic masculinist stride, his self-presentation as arrogant bardic prophet. The prophet's voice rails against American "greed" and "selfishness," and that seems to be enough for Kalaidjian.

In the chapters that follow, something curious begins to happen. In his commentaries on Bly, Rich, and Brooks, Kalaidjian seems to forget his Marxist base and his Foucaultian/Derridean/Bakhtinian superstructure and returns to a mode of explication not different from that of Thomas Gardner, although Gardner is a much better reader. The Rich chapter is largely explicative; subject matter rather than social text is all. At the end of the chapter, for example, Kalaidjian cites as an instance of Rich's "dark vision of history" and "dedication to social justice" the following passage from a lyric in *The Fact of a Doorframe* (1984):

> The almost-full moon rises
> timelessly speaking of change
> out of the Bronx, the Harlem River
> the drowned towns of the Quabbin
> the pilfered burial mounds
> the toxic swamps, the testing-grounds
>
> and I start to speak again [p. 169]

"Rich's feminist agenda," Kalaidjian comments, "leads finally to broader 'testing-grounds' of political change. . . . In the mid-1980s, her writing seeks alignment with other ethnic, racial, and Third World movements of social liberation from patriarchy's 'crumbling form'" (p. 170).

Cleanth Brooks, that benighted New Critic, might have dismissed this "reading" as the "heresy of paraphrase." Kalaidjian simply "translates" what Rich has already said. It should go without saying that this is hardly a Jamesonian analysis of the poem's "political unconscious," hardly a Frankfurt School placement of the poem in its culture. Most important, Kalaidjian seems to have forgotten everything he said about "the staging of the lyric self" and of the need to go beyond the "romantic doctrine of expressive lyricism." For if Rich's stanza cited above is not an example of "expressive lyricism," what is it? Indeed, by the time we reach the final chapter of *Languages of Liberation*, which is about the poetry of Gwendolyn Brooks, we seem once again to be confronted by one of those synoptic surveys of American poetry, surveys that contain chapters on representative and exemplary figures, in this case the African-American woman poet.

If Kalaidjian's book makes claims it cannot satisfy, Jeffrey Walker's *Bardic Ethos* is deceptively modest. Like Thomas Gardner, Walker takes "the fundamental enterprise in which modern [American] poems participate" as being "Whitmanesque" (p. xi), but his sense of what that epithet means is quite different. His subject is that old warhorse, the "modern epic," specifically Pound's *Cantos*, Williams's *Paterson*, Hart Crane's *The Bridge*, and Charles Olson's *Maximus Poems*. All four of these works, he argues, are "splendid failures," their problem being one of "rhetoric—of finding the means of persuasion adequate to their grand, and sometimes grandiose, suasory desires" (pp. xi–xii).

Walker's thesis is that the "discourse of the modern epic bard" arises from the "intersection" of two mythologies: a "Jeffersonian historico-political vision, as revised according to vitalistic premises; and a belletristic theory of bardic utterance, as filtered through an Emersonian and subsequently modernist orphism" (p. xii). The *bardic poem* that results is distinguished from the personal epic (e.g., Robert Lowell's *Notebooks*, Berryman's *Dream Songs*, Ginsberg's *Howl*) by its use of voice, by which Walker means not its orality or even its "oratoricality," but "its broad rhetorical function as an instrument of ethical authority" (p. xiii).

The first four chapters focus primarily "on the motives and the conventions that the moderns have inherited from Whitman and revised" (p. xii). Walker has wisely decided not to ask the perennial question whether it is possible to write an epic poem in the twentieth century, his concern being rather with the varieties of rhetoric poets who, for better or worse, have chosen to write epics, adopt. The bardic poet, as Whitman conceived of him in the 1855 preface to *Leaves of Grass,* is the Shelleyan legislator of the world whose extraordinary power over public consciousness permeates all things. But he is a legislator, not by virtue of representing his culture so much as by opposing it, by seeking to transform society and educate the fallen masses. It is thus "Whitman's fundamental problem," according to Walker, "to find some ground upon which polemical bard and fallen (or simply unawakened) audience can meet" (p. 19).

But how could the bard of *Leaves of Grass* hope to move and persuade those "thirty millions of live and electric men" eulogized in its pages? Analyzing Whitman's Transcendentalist and Romantic audience, Walker concludes that Whitman's dream of merging his voice with the voices of all men and the voice of destiny was bound to be a failure, that "democracy" invoked as a kind of national mythology inadvertently transformed itself into "the virtual dictatorship of a sanctified elect" (p. 31). In the hands of Whitman's twentieth-century successors, Walker argues, the problem has been exacerbated, the difficulty for the would-be bardic poem being the enactment of a sublime historical intelligence that would involve the reader in its process.

Walker's training in Longinian rhetoric stands him in excellent stead, especially in the first four chapters that sketch in the nineteenth-century background and take up the larger issues of readership. Chapter 5 is devoted to Pound: here Walker studies the author-figure in the *Cantos,* suggesting that from the opening Canto with its mix of Homeric tale, medieval Latin archaism, and Anglo-Saxon prosody, its intruded utterance ("Lie quiet, Divus") and learned citation ("In officina Wecheli, 1538, out of Homer"), the poet emerges as a "scholarly knower of obscure texts" who "alerts the reader to the exegetical task" (p. 88). The "master/student relationship" thus established with the reader persists throughout the *Cantos,* as does the "convergence of the authorial and ancestral voices" which produces the poem's "mantic" stance. Incantatory, ritualistic, sacerdotal, the bardic voice invites the reader into the text as a witness or observer of the

Contextualizing Contemporary Lyric

mantic performance, a performance in which America is presented as an unrealized pagan civilization, thwarted by bad economics, bad politics, and the suppression of the light.

At their best, Walker suggests, the *Cantos* have a "double perspective": the "more permanent, authoritative, ancestral perspective of tradition," and the "fluctuating perspective of the personal, fallible 'Ezra Pound,' who is a character within his own text and a factive partisan of particular causes" (p. 104). This is very well put (although one might object that such "double perspective" also characterizes mock-epic and that the *Cantos* have often been placed in the tradition of Byron's *Don Juan*), and Walker further shows that where Pound's bardic poem falters is in the eventual breakdown of this doubleness, the text coming more and more to seem "a massive, obsessive illustration of a relatively small number of fixed ideas" (p. 105).

Pound's admirers, of whom I am one, would want to quarrel with this stricture, would want to point out that at many later points in the poem (and not only in the *Pisan Cantos*, which Walker reads, incorrectly, I think, as the testament of a "chastened survivor"), reader involvement is achieved by presenting us with an accumulation of images that the various voices fail to understand and measure, the pathos being precisely the gap between the two. It is, of course, impossible to account for the rhetoric of the *Cantos* in a short chapter or two, and there are places in Walker's argument that one wants to amend, but his discussion is extremely suggestive in its analysis of the poem's attempt to win over and assimilate its audience.

The chapters on *The Bridge* and *Paterson* are somewhat less impressive, if only because the ground has been covered so frequently. *The Bridge* has been criticized so often for failing to fulfill Crane's epic ambitions that Walker's treatment seems anticlimactic. True, he has a new argument: namely, that far from being "incoherent," as critics from Allen Tate and R. P. Blackmur on down have maintained, *The Bridge* suffers from being too coherent, each section of the poem repeating the binary opposition between ideal possibility (flight, liberty, the open space of the sky of the Proem) and actuality (modernity, urbanity, the "chained bay waters"). Crane's "hopeful sense of a possible redeeming, transfiguring fusion of the two antithetical terms" (p. 129) is asserted rather than enacted; his "mythic ideal is beyond the boundaries of American history and actuality, and indeed requires the erasure of that actuality for its fulfillment" (p. 135). In sum, the "would-be Pindaric bard . . . is at odds with the fundamental assumptions he must work with" (p. 138).

All this is true enough; indeed, it is so true that I'm not sure it bears repeating at such length, especially since any number of earlier critics have made similar points, regardless of whether they begin with the incoherence or the coherence theory. The treatment of *Paterson* is similar. Walker interestingly explains the dialectic between the suppression of a vital American "primary culture" by the spirit of a mercantile, puritanically oppressive "effigy culture" which animates Williams's bardic poem, and he convincingly argues that in Book V, the poet increasingly moves toward versified, direct statement so as to satisfy his rhetorical urge to speak directly to "the people" (p. 199). In the end, Walker suggests, Williams couldn't reconcile the needs of his primary audience (the literary world who read Pound and Eliot) and his fantasy "popular" one, and the Cloisters sequence of Book V marks a retreat into the "aesthetic that defines the artwork as a sacred locus for the communion of a sacerdotal elect" (p. 200).

But even if one shares this view of Book V, as I myself do, one may feel that Walker has slighted the marvelous complications of language in *Paterson,* the varieties of idiom and speech base that, "elitist" as they may be in relation to the poem's projected mass audience, have set a standard for what poetry can do with "ordinary" material. To put it another way: one critic's "splendid *failure*" may be another's "*splendid* failure," the rhetorical anxieties embedded in *Paterson*'s composition also constituting a measure of its strength.

The final chapter, on the other hand, is brilliant. The question of Olson's rhetoric is rarely raised; on the contrary, it is regularly assumed, not only by critics like Kalaidjian but also by those who find Olson's bardic voice tedious, that he was the spokesman for an "advanced" community. But as Walker points out, Olson's voice is an eclectic compound of "the oratorical, the rhapsodic, the primitivistic, and the abysmic, in his self-representation as an American sacerdotal literatus" (p. 215). Claiming to speak for a live humanism of active, independent "yeomen," Olson's "abysmic voice" came more and more to "exclude the very audience that a "cultural revolution must 'meet and win'" (p. 230). A sermonizer and pedagogue, Olson became increasingly distant and elitist, speaking for the few even as he sought a transformation of the many (p. 235). In presenting his more absurd fantasies, as in the account in *Maximus III* of legendary Roman soldiers turned to stone in Gloucester, "he resembles Tom Sawyer more than he does Thoreau" (p. 233).

The ironic fate of the bardic poet in the twentieth century, Walker concludes, is to become the poetic spokesman for the tribal ethos he represents—but only in the eyes of the tribe itself. His failure is "to engage and cultivate the ethical will of the nation." In this sense, Walker argues, a figure like Martin Luther King, Jr., has been a more successful "rhetor" than have the poets.

Exceptionally fine a book as *Bardic Ethos* is, it may, ironically, suffer the same fate as the bardic poems it discusses. For Modernist scholars, especially for Pound, Williams, Crane, or Olson insiders, its treatment of the poetry may be dismissed as too cursory. For a wider audience, on the other hand, individual chapters may seem too detailed, too absorbed in finding yet another instance of Longinian rhetoric in a given Pound or Williams passage. Walker's would have been an even better book, I think, if it had taken a larger view of twentieth-century poetry, reading, say, Olson's sermonizing voice against those of other poets of the fifties so as to come to terms with the larger readership problems of the period.

As I was reading *Bardic Ethos*, I kept wondering why certain poets have wanted to write the bardic poem while others, like Wallace Stevens or Marianne Moore, John Ashbery and Elizabeth Bishop, have not. What are the cultural and social determinants of the "bardic" or "mantic" voice? What is the fate of that voice in the 1990s? These are questions that the new Cultural

Criticism will have to take up. But for the moment, Jeffrey Walker has given us a subtle and acute examination of the rhetoric of modernist poetics.

Note

1. Paul Christensen, *Charles Olson: Call Him Ishmael* (Austin and London: Univ. of Texas Press, 1979), pp. 39, 81–82.

Nabokov for the Nineties

J. E. Rivers

Gennadi Barabtarlo. *Phantom of Fact: A Guide to Nabokov's* Pnin. Ann Arbor: Ardis, 1989. 314 pp.

Geoffrey Green. *Freud and Nabokov.* Lincoln: University of Nebraska Press, 1988. x, 128 pp.

Priscilla Meyer. *Find What the Sailor Has Hidden: Vladimir Nabokov's* Pale Fire. Middletown: Wesleyan University Press, 1988. x, 277 pp.

Vladimir Nabokov. *Selected Letters, 1940–1977,* eds. Dmitri Nabokov and Matthew J. Bruccoli. New York: Harcourt, 1989. xxvi, 582 pp.

Stephen Jan Parker. *Understanding Vladimir Nabokov.* Columbia: University of South Carolina Press, 1987. xii, 160 pp.

Leona Toker. *Nabokov: The Mystery of Literary Structures.* Ithaca: Cornell University Press, 1989. xvi, 243 pp.

Whatever term or trope I use, my purpose is not to be facetiously flashy or grotesquely obscure but to express what I feel and think with the utmost truthfulness and perception.
——Vladimir Nabokov[1]

Vladimir Vladimirovich Nabokov died in 1977. His career had been remarkably prolific: poems, plays, stories, novels, translations, scientific papers, literary criticism, an autobiography, a screenplay, and several kinds of occasional prose. During the last years of his life, in declining health, he had continued to work, wrestling with a new novel called *The Original of Laura*.[2] He did not live to finish this last book. He had, however, published seventeen other novels, including five masterpieces: *The Gift, Lolita, Pnin, Pale Fire,* and *Ada*. Primarily on the basis of these five books, he has often been called one of the century's greatest writers. During the decade that just ended, critics in increasing numbers echoed that judgment. In Nabokovian scholarship, it was a decade of steady productivity, characterized by a dawning realization that Nabokov's work will occupy critics for as long as there are critics, that it is, in a word, inexhaustible.

In the last three years of the decade, those spanned by the books reviewed here, the pace of scholarship, already swift, accelerated, spurred not only by the challenge and charm of Nabokov's own writing but also by a major critical book that had appeared at mid-decade, Brian Boyd's *Nabokov's* Ada: *The Place of Consciousness* (Ann Arbor: Ardis, 1985). This book, a beautifully written, profoundly searching look at Nabokov's epistemology and metaphysics, set a new standard of excellence for Nabokov critics. Moreover, by focusing on *Ada* alone, it implied that Nabokov's entire vision is contained in each of its parts. In this respect, it seems to have started a trend toward books on individual novels.

That trend is with us as we enter the 1990s. Of the books here reviewed, two treat individual novels: Gennadi Barabtarlo's guide to *Pnin* and Priscilla Meyer's study of *Pale Fire*. Both rest on solid scholarship and reveal a good deal about Nabokov not previously known. Barabtarlo's *Phantom of Fact: A Guide to Nabokov's* Pnin, a recasting of his dissertation, is not a sustained interpretation of *Pnin* but a collection of annotations to it. Barabtarlo goes through the novel line by line, explaining whatever difficulties or allusions he finds. In addition, he points out cases where the novel differs from chapters first published in the *New Yorker*. He also includes an introduction and five indices to *Pnin:* persons, dates, places, flora and fauna, and colors. The index to colors is remarkably detailed. It lists them first alphabetically and then in the order of the spectrum. Then, in a table and four graphs, it shows the frequency of the various colors in each chapter and in the novel as a whole (reds predominate, occurring in *Pnin* fifty-three times).

To the non-specialist, such detailed indexing of *Pnin* may seem trivial. To scholars of Nabokov, however, it will be enormously valuable. Of special value is the index to colors. Nabokov possessed *audition colorée*, a form of synaesthesia in which a person sees certain colors when hearing certain sounds.[3] In light of this special trait, it is not surprising that he sometimes referred to himself as a painter in the medium of fiction.[4] For Nabokov, language was, quite literally, color, a fact reflected in obvious and subtle ways throughout his work. Barabtarlo's index to colors—presented, like his other indices, virtually without commentary—could serve as an excellent starting place for an interpretative study of color in *Pnin*. That such a study is needed is shown by the length of the index itself.

What is true of the index to colors is true of the book as a whole. This book presents basic research, new facts and figures. It is a study from which other scholarship, especially that of a more interpretative nature, can be born. Despite the obvious value of such basic research, however, *Phantom of Fact* has a serious and sometimes disabling flaw: its style. The author's difficulties with English are apparent. (I assume that English is not his native tongue.) To be sure, a rough or awkward style can be tolerated, grimly, if it is consistently clear. Barabtarlo's style is not. The most serious problems occur in the introduction, where Barabtarlo argues at some length about themes and structures in *Pnin*. As these arguments become increasingly complex, the style becomes progressively more obscure. Here is an example, a comment on memory in *Pnin:* "Even the strongest memory, that peculiar channel to the past, loses much of its vividness when exposed, as if our light veiled and blurred the preserved images previously viewed only in the darkroom of one's solitary recollection. The moment one's private memory becomes public property, it cuts somehow its natural fragile capillary vasculature connecting it with the prototype through a series of intermediate refueling reminiscences" (pp. 27–28). As far as I can tell, this passage does not mean anything. And it is not uncharacteristic.[5]

The editor of Barabtarlo's book should have intervened in this and similar passages, working them over with the author until they were clear. To aim for anything less than total clarity is to sin against the whole purpose of writing, especially critical writing.

Worse, to write muddy or muddled prose about Nabokov violates the spirit of Nabokov's own work, which strove for absolute precision of expression—"to express," as Nabokov put it, "what I feel and think with the utmost truthfulness and perception."

The sin of obscurity does not mar Priscilla Meyer's book on *Pale Fire*. Lucid, artful, at times even poetic, it marshals a style worthy of its thought. I would call Meyer's *Find What the Sailor Has Hidden* the second best book on Nabokov ever published. (The best, in my view, is Brian Boyd's study of *Ada*.) The virtues of this book are many; chief among them is Meyer's striking originality. According to Meyer, *Pale Fire* is Nabokov's response to a cataclysmic event in his life: the assassination of his father. One evening in 1922, while attending a lecture in Berlin, Nabokov's father (Vladimir Dmitrievich Nabokov) was struck down by an assassin's bullet. Ironically, the killer was after another man, the lecturer. Nabokov describes the event in *Speak, Memory:* "My father shielded the lecturer (his old friend Milyukov) from the bullets of two Russian Fascists and, while vigorously knocking down one of the assassins, was fatally shot by the other."[6] In Meyer's view, this tragic episode, a murder by mistake, inspires— "conspicuously" (p. 4)—the accidental shooting of John Shade in *Pale Fire*. Like Nabokov's father, Shade is shot by an assassin who is gunning for someone else.

Meyer is not the first to associate the shooting of John Shade with the assassination of Nabokov's father.[7] She is, however, the first to claim that the assassination of V. D. Nabokov permeates the whole of *Pale Fire,* not just the scene of Shade's death. For Meyer, *Pale Fire* is Nabokov's "attempt to make sense of his father's assassination," an attempt that sends him on an extraordinary artistic quest—an "exploration of the history, literature, natural evolution, and language of the North over the last thousand years" (pp. 4–5). By "the North," Meyer means, roughly, the northern hemisphere, especially northerly regions such as Scandinavia. By "the North" she also means Ultima Thule, an ancient name for the northernmost point on the earth and one associated in Nabokov's work with the hereafter, with life after death (p. 45, pp. 193–211).

Striking out from these ideas and associations, Meyer presents a remarkable explication of *Pale Fire*, combining, for the task, a detective's shrewdness with the style and vision of an artist. As she develops her analysis, she summons a second thesis, intertwining it with the first. According to Meyer, Nabokov does more in *Pale Fire* than grapple with his father's death: he recapitulates certain trends of literary history and certain patterns of world history and merges them with themes from his own life. In Meyer's view, *Pale Fire* is the story of Nabokov's life, the story of literature, the story of history itself, told as a single story. Meyer supports these ideas with evidence so abundant and so tightly woven that it can't be summarized without quoting the whole study. Like *Pale Fire* itself, Meyer's book resists paraphrase. It grows from an immense fund of slowly accumulating detail, sometimes turning, as Meyer herself puts it, on "one highly specific word" (p. 42).

Although I can't reproduce the full range of Meyer's evidence or summarize all that it implies, let me give an example of her scholarship. In *Pale Fire* there is a painter named Eystein, said to be a "prodigious master of the trompe l'oeil."[8] Eystein tricks the eye by inserting real pieces of wood or cloth into his own painted representations of wood or cloth. When I teach *Pale Fire*, students sometimes notice this character and say: "Aha! A reference to Albert Einstein and therefore to Nabokov's relativism." Not according to Meyer. Avoiding Einstein altogether, Meyer shows that the name Eystein alludes to the *Heimskringla* of Snorri Sturluson (1178–1241), which contains the biographies of three kings named Eystein and presents numerous tales of murder and revenge. Once focused on Snorri, readers confront among the host of revenge tales the most famous one of all, the story of Hamlet, an early version of which appears in another work by Snorri, the *Younger Edda*. Meyer believes the name Eystein is one of several that Nabokov uses in *Pale Fire* to evoke not only the work of Snorri but also the whole tradition of Scandinavian revenge lore (pp. 44, 46, 48–49). By embedding in the novel this and other allusions to works about murder and revenge, Nabokov sweeps into his narrative an ancient and recurring pattern in world history and literature. At the same time, Meyer argues, he poses by means of such allusions a wrenching moral problem in his own life, one that he shares, in fact, with Hamlet: how to avenge the death of his own father. Precisely how Nabokov avenges his father in *Pale Fire* and how that vengeance turns on allusions to Snorri, Shakespeare, and other writers—this is the subject of an ingenious argument (see pp. 41–52, 96, 108). It is an argument that grows directly from (though it does not depend exclusively on) Meyer's explication of the name Eystein and her tracing of that obscure name back to its source in the *Heimskringla.*

In spite of my admiration for Meyer's study, I do find it vexing in one respect: its assertions about Nabokov's religious views. Meyer states, without proving, that Nabokov believed in God (p. 145). She also states, without proving, that he believed in an afterlife and thought he would meet his dead father in a better world after death. Comparing Nabokov to Wordsworth, she says, "Nabokov too believes that the before- and afterlife are the true reality" (p. 147). Later, in the chapter called "Ultima Thule," she says: "Nabokov's exploration of the other world is particularly urgent: that is where he expects to be reunited with his father" (p. 194).

In these and similar statements, Meyer leaps to conclusions supported by the wispiest of evidence. Whether Nabokov believed in God and the afterlife is a complicated question, more complicated than Meyer seems to realize. The evidence is scant and hard to interpret. On balance, it suggests that he was an agnostic, admitting the possibility of a supreme being and of survival after death but never reaching a firm conclusion on these matters and certainly never preaching about them any rigid doctrine. Insofar as his attitude toward the afterlife can be deduced from his fiction, Brian Boyd aptly sums up the recurring strain of agnosticism: "Nabokov asks what happens to human consciousness at death, and suggests two possible answers: it ends; it continues. (He sees *both* as possible throughout his work, from *Smert'* to *Look at the Harlequins!*)."[9]

On the subject of God, Nabokov's position is harder to pin down. In interviews, his comments about God are sibylline, open to varying interpretations. He once told an interviewer: "I can only explain God's popularity by an atheist's panic." On another occasion, asked by an interviewer, "Do you believe in God?," he responded, "I know more than I can express in words, and the little I can express would not have been expressed, had I not known more."[10] Such tentative remarks as these stand behind Meyer's assertion that Nabokov believed in God—that his study of nature, as she puts it, "convinces him of the presence of the Almighty" (p. 145; cf. pp. 184–85). If that study did convince him, he never said so publicly.

Fortunately, Meyer's assertions about Nabokov's religious beliefs have nothing to do with her principal arguments. Her close reading of *Pale Fire* is a distinguished achievement, depending not at all on Nabokov's personal religion or lack thereof. In the bulk of her study, Meyer displays an honest attention to detail and a willingness to let the text speak for itself rather than through filters devised by the critic. These traits are scarcer in criticism than they ought to be and would serve well the critics of the nineties, who could do worse than to follow the stylistic and interpretative model of Priscilla Meyer.

Gennadi Barabtarlo's *Phantom of Fact* and Priscilla Meyer's *Find What the Sailor Has Hidden* show what complexities can be uncovered in a single novel by Nabokov. Three other books under review here discuss not one work but several, attempting thus to establish a synoptic view of Nabokov's art. In *Nabokov: The Mystery of Literary Structures*, Leona Toker discusses ten novels, emphasizing works that have received relatively little attention (for example, *Mary* and *King, Queen, Knave*). In *Freud and Nabokov*, Geoffrey Green rushes in where angels fear to tread, daring to suggest that Nabokov, who detested and denounced Freud, is a Freudian in spite of himself. In *Understanding Vladimir Nabokov*, Stephen Jan Parker, the editor of *The Nabokovian*, introduces the master to the student and general reader. Each book reveals some trends of Nabokovian scholarship in the 1980s and implies some directions and problems for the coming decade.

The longest of these books, Toker's, is the least satisfactory, length being in this case no virtue. The main objection I have to Toker's book is that it's boring. The style is riddled with jargon and fashionable literary clichés (*"mise en abîme"* gets a tedious workout). The passive voice goose-steps through the text. The book takes a long time to read—you can't take much of Toker's style at one go—and, once read, reveals little that is worth knowing.

Toker's subtitle—*The Mystery of Literary Structures*—is a quotation from Nabokov, who called his lectures on literature "a kind of detective investigation of the mystery of literary structures" (p. 3). What Toker herself means by "mystery" and "structures" is hard to fathom. Here is her definition of "mystery":

The word "mystery" here is polysemous. Each great work has a structure of its own, to be investigated by a minute Sherlock-Holmesian attention to detail until its mystery—that is, its specific relation to specific dreams, desires, and limitations of human life—begins to emerge. Yet the mystery of a literary structure can be approximated rather than solved. It lies in the quaint appropriateness of the structure to an attitude; the "aesthetic bliss" produced by this harmony retains mysteriousness even after the approaches to it have been mapped. An attempt to unravel the *enigmas* of Nabokov's structure ultimately confronts one with a *Mystery*. [pp. 3-4]

I take this to mean that mysteries are mysterious. For opaqueness and sheer clumsiness, Toker's style rivals Barabtarlo's. Barabtarlo, however, writes a better book than Toker, because he has fits of lucidity during which he imparts valuable information, facts not previously known. Toker presents flatulent interpretation—abstract, overly cogitated, tautological (as in the example above), and, for the most part, unconvincing. Since it's often impossible to tell what Toker is trying to say, the word "mystery" is wickedly appropriate in her subtitle.

Toker's concept of structure, like her concept of mystery, is mystifying: "The structure of each novel is based on a specific manner of combining the perspective (the 'point of view,' variations of the camera eye's trajectory, the presence or absence of an illusion of spatial depth) with recurrent imagery and self-referential games" (p. 18). Because of such failures of definition, I read the entire study never quite knowing what the subject was. Toker's writing is the kind for which we have the Yale School to thank. Under the sway of that school, many critics of the eighties gave up the attempt to write clearly, assuming, apparently, that cant and obfuscation equal profundity.[11] That trend is a great pity. The more difficult the writer being interpreted—and Nabokov is among the most challenging of modern authors—the more urgent the need for clarity in the criticism.

Though "mystery" and "structures" never come together in Toker to form a comprehensible thesis, she does state a very general purpose for her study. She wants to correct "an imbalance in the critical literature devoted to Nabokov," namely, that some critics talk too much about "subtle techniques" and others too much about "humanistic themes." According to Toker, "only a few" studies, most of them "of limited scope," achieve the golden mean for which Toker herself will strive, a balanced assessment. Toker wants to reveal "the combination of formal refinement and poignant humanism in Nabokov's fiction" (p. ix). A noble goal, to be sure, though Toker never shows how it relates to "mystery" and "structures" (as non-defined above). Toker's revelation of "subtle techniques" usually amounts to a tracing of recurrent imagery—for example, doors in *King, Queen, Knave* (p. 60). This is not an original approach to Nabokov and hardly qualifies as structural analysis. To chart the recurrence of an image is one of the oldest tricks in Nabokovian criticism, especially popular in the late seventies and early eighties. When such an approach works, it reveals that the novels cohere in a New Critical sense. But to call such coherence a "structure" is to use that term, I think, rather loosely. The recurrence of an image tends to generate not a structure but a symbol, as Toker herself observes in analyzing doors in *King, Queen, Knave:* "The shutting of doors (and lids) is endowed [in *King, Queen, Knave*] with unmistakably symbolic significance" (pp. 60-61). I have no special quarrel with Toker's tracings of recurrent imagery: the images that she identifies certainly do exist, and do recur. I just don't see why they amount to, or suggest, or solve, a "mystery" of "literary structures" or reveal the "poignant humanism" which, according to Toker, fuses in Nabokov with "subtle techniques"— techniques like recurring imagery.

Another problem with Toker's book: it lacks, itself, a structure. The reader searches in vain for some sense of direction, for the firm guiding hand that Priscilla Meyer, for example, brings to her book on *Pale Fire*. Lacking a clear thesis, the book wanders more or less randomly from topic to topic, following its own mysterious course. Schopenhauer keeps popping up like a jack-in-the-box, not because he has anything to do with "mystery" or "structures" but because his philosophy, according to Toker, has affinities with Nabokov's (pp. 5-8, and see "Schopenhauer" in Toker's index).

What about the "poignant humanism" that Toker claims to see in Nabokov's work? I find it almost totally missing from her book. True, Toker does pronounce some ritual abhorrences of the Nazi-like characters in Nabokov's fiction. True, she singles out some examples of characters who suffer. And true, she gives extended attention to Lolita's implied anguish under Humbert's ministrations (following a lead given by Gladys M. Clifton in 1982).[12] All this, however, is embedded in such dry, bloodless, technical writing that Toker finally reinforces the very image of Nabokov that she is trying to qualify—"a cold virtuoso aesthetician" (p 2). It is precisely this image that emerges from Toker's convoluted, divagating, jargon-ridden explications. Toker's failure to reconcile Nabokov's "subtle techniques" and "poignant humanism" leaves that problem open for critics of the nineties.[13] Toker has at least identified this polarity in Nabokov (cold aestheticism on the one hand, fervent moralism and humanism on the other) as one in need of explaining. The critic who finally does explain it will have to bring to the task less mystery than Toker, and more structure.

Two other general studies, Green's and Parker's, belong to the tradition of the little book in Nabokovian criticism—the small, slim volume with wide margins. It is a rather distinguished tradition, boasting two widely quoted studies: Julian Moynahan's *Vladimir Nabokov* (47 pages, 8 × 5½) and Donald E. Morton's *Vladimir Nabokov* (164 pages, 8 × 5). Nabokov himself practiced the art of the little book: his critical biography *Nikolai Gogol* is small but powerful (172 pages, 7⅛ × 4¼).[14] The very title of Geoffrey Green's *Freud and Nabokov* (128 pages, 7¾ × 5¼) is provocative. Nabokov, of course, abominated Freud, never missing an opportunity to heap scorn on the father of psychoanalysis, whom he called "the Viennese quack."[15] In a *Playboy* interview, he issued an especially fiery denunciation of "Freudism" (note the spelling): "The ordeal [of psychoanalysis] is much too silly and disgusting to be contemplated even as a joke. Freudism and all it has tainted with its grotesque implications and methods appears to me to be one of the vilest deceits practiced by people on themselves and on others. I reject it utterly, along with a few other medieval items still adored by the ignorant, the conventional, or the very sick."[16] One would think that such a withering blast would discourage critics from trying to ferret out parallels between Nabokov and Freud. To the true Freudolater, however, denial means acceptance. Accordingly, Green does not hesitate to investigate what he takes to be close affinities between the two. Notice that Freud is the first one mentioned in Green's title. That sequence of names gives Green's whole game away. Yes, he's a Freudian critic. To conduct his investigation, he proceeds in the usual Freudian manner. He assumes that when Nabokov says x, he really means, at least some of the time, y. Summarizing what he takes to be Nabokov's view of the novel (a scientific report from which the author's own personality is absent), Green writes: "Think of the novel [Nabokov would say] as old-fashioned case history: I am merely reporting the specific clinical findings, but other than my scientific role, I have nothing to do with this case (p. 22). To which Green replies: "Oh, really?" (p. 22). The air of smug superiority that often characterizes Freudian criticism has rarely been more obvious.

Although Green's know-it-all posture makes his book hard to take, he does write more clearly than Barabtarlo or Toker. Like Toker, however, he has trouble deciding where he wants to go, and how he wants to get there. On the first page of the introduction, he states: "A work devoted to Freud and Nabokov would seem to be the occasion for a psychoanalysis of Nabokov's characters, or a psychoanalytical discussion of Nabokov's aversion to Freud, or else a principled recounting of the multitudinous criticisms that Nabokov wielded against Freud. But I intend to do none of these things" (p. 1). Oh, really? As a matter of fact, Green does every single one of these things.

Here is Green doing the first thing that he promises not to do, offering a psychoanalysis of Nabokov's characters: "Kinbote [in

Pale Fire] substitutes a new world and a new system of associations in order to bolster his reading of the text. In so doing, he is acting out Freud's description of the paranoid Dr. Schreber from his case history, 'Psychoanalytic Notes upon an Autobiographical Account of a Case of Paranoia': 'And the paranoic builds it up again, not more splendid, it is true, but at least so he can once more live in it.'" (p. 105).[17] And here is Green doing the second thing, presenting a psychoanalytic discussion of Nabokov's aversion to Freud: "Nabokov might be said to have borne a 'narcissistic love' for his hated fictional creation 'Freud,' not unlike his ambivalent attitude toward many of his characters—for instance, Humbert and Van Veen" (pp. 79–80). Green also promises to avoid "a principled recounting of the multitudinous criticisms that Nabokov wielded against Freud." Whether he keeps this promise depends on how you define the word "principled." Certainly, he recounts the famous aversions (p. 77). For whatever mysterious reasons, Green simply can't keep his hands off those three big cookie jars that he—no other—has labelled "VERBOTEN." The temptation to play that old Fruh-hoidian rag was, I guess, just too great.

Aside from a schizophrenic pursuit of everything that the author forswears, the overall purpose of Green's book seems to be to vindicate both Freud and Nabokov—"two great men" (p. 116)—by showing that they thought along similar lines and echoed each other's pronouncements. In this respect, Green's study amounts to elementary comparative literature. A quotation from one is set beside a quotation from the other, while the critic steps back and shouts: "Behold the similarity!" Trouble is, the similarity sometimes exists only in the mind of the critic. Take the following comparison:

Freud's achievement in the "Rat Man" case, according to [Steven] Marcus, was to avoid "seeking therapeutic alleviation in some grand, novelistic design." Instead, "Freud intuitively and brilliantly concentrated on small, often non-narrative units of thought and memory. He repeatedly prompted [the 'Rat Man'] to speak directly about small matters and come to the point on minor segments of experience rather than trying to construct large story-like structures of thought." To

Nabokov for the Nineties 71

"speak directly about small matters" and avoid "large, story-like structures of thought": the idea recalls Nabokov's belief that there is a "delicate meeting place between imagination and knowledge, a point, arrived at by diminishing large things and enlarging small ones, that is intrinsically artistic." [pp. 101–02]

No. The Freudian concept, as expressed by Marcus, does not recall Nabokov at all, as a second glance at Green's discussion will show. The two concepts—Freud's and Nabokov's—are, in fact, quite different. Freud urges the Rat Man to speak about small matters. Nabokov views art as a process of "diminishing large things and enlarging small ones." Where's the similarity in that? In the Freudian procedure, nothing is diminished, nothing enlarged. Freud's approach is one of focus: large "structures of thought" are avoided in order to focus on discrete units of experience. Nabokov's procedure is one of change, distortion, transformation: small things are enlarged, large ones diminished. Freud follows one course; Nabokov follows two. The only similarity between the techniques is the concept of largeness and smallness, which occurs in both, or, rather, which occurs in Steven Marcus's description of one and Nabokov's description of the other. This seeming similarity is nothing but a chance echo. In each case, what is done with largeness and smallness is quite different.

But Green's argument goes farther awry than that. The passage quoted above compares Nabokov not to Freud but to Freud as understood by Steven Marcus. Not only does the comparison fail to reveal any similarity: it strays from the book's topic, which is Freud and Nabokov, not Steven Marcus and Nabokov. A few pages later Green does it again, in a passage that compares Nabokov not to Freud but to another Freudian, Peter Brooks (p. 107). Green's discussion of largeness and smallness is an unintentional parody of comparative literature.[18] The antidote to such "passionate comparison" (Nabokov's phrase) is a comment made by John Shade in *Pale Fire:* "Resemblances are the shadows of differences."[19]

Green's book is, at bottom, at attempt to build on one of the most daring and influential essays on Nabokov to be published in the 1980s, Phyllis A. Roth's "Toward the Man behind the Mystification." Green praises Roth's "richly suggestive" essay (p. 39), as well he might. It is still the most compelling view of Nabokov from a psychoanalytic perspective. The reason is that, for Roth, Nabokov's actual practice takes precedence over Freudian theory. Like Priscilla Meyer, Roth allows Nabokov's texts to speak for themselves. She shows that Nabokov was well aware of the demons lurking in his life, totally lucid on the need to imprison them in art, where they could be understood, mastered, manipulated, and conquered. In Roth we do not get the insinuating elbow in the ribs, the condescending smirk, the suggestive wink of Green. Instead, we hear Nabokov speaking in his own voice about his complex, mysterious, disappointing, richly rewarding life and the need to deal with that life through the medium of art.

Nothing in Green equals Phyllis Roth's conclusion, stated in various ways throughout her essay—"[Nabokov's] fiction, then, is a way of controlling the uncontrollable, of creating not only a world generated by memory in which, as a result, nothing is ever lost, no one ever dies, but also a world of which Nabokov is the engineer, able to assert and perpetuate his distance from the grotesque. As he put it so plainly, 'the writing of a novel relieved me of . . . fertile emotion.'"[20] In Green's *Freud and Nabokov* psychoanalytic criticism never gets beyond tags and catch phrases like "paranoic" and "narcissistic love.'"[21] To make further progress, it needs to find its way back to Phyllis Roth, to the primacy of Nabokov's own text, and to the realization that Nabokov is his own best analyst and critic.

Stephen Jan Parker's *Understanding Vladimir Nabokov* is a step in that direction. In no way psychoanalytic, Parker's book nonetheless charts a course from which Freudian critics such as Green could learn. Parker assumes that a reader can best understand Nabokov by listening to Nabokov himself. Accordingly, throughout his book, Parker gives the word to Nabokov, quoting liberally from his public statements about life and literature. Green does this too, but there is a difference. In place of Green's "Oh, really?," Parker gives us "Yea, verily."

Parker's study belongs to the series "Understanding Contemporary American Literature," published by the University of

South Carolina Press under the editorship of Matthew J. Bruccoli. In an editor's preface, Bruccoli states the goal of this series: to provide introductions to contemporary American literature "for students as well as good nonacademic readers." Because of this intended audience, Bruccoli goes on to say, the series is "aimed at a level of general accessibility" (p. ix). Such an aim has its advantages. For one thing, we will probably not encounter any pneumatic disquisitions on "catachretic gaps" (Toker), or *"epoche"* (Barabtarlo), or the "subjective presence-ing of a meaning" (Green),[22] such concepts being beyond the patience of the general public, who might, in this respect, know a thing or two. Also according to Bruccoli, the books in this series "are meant to be applied in conjunction with the works they cover. Thus they do not provide a substitute for the works and authors they introduce, but rather prepare the reader for more profitable literary experiences" (p. ix). To write an intelligent introduction to a difficult writer—not an outline or a crib or a trot—is a demanding task, requiring total mastery of the material. Stephen Jan Parker acquits himself admirably. Always plain, straightforward, and direct in his criticism, free of the deadly tendency to overinterpret, uninfected by critical fashion, he is the perfect critic of Nabokov for this particular series.

At one point Parker quotes a beautiful passage from *The Gift* and comments, simply, that such beauty of style "needs no purpose other than its own being" (p. 23).[23] The comment is startling after a reading of Toker and Green, critics who, like Mark Twain's Jim, must always "start in and 'terpret it."[24] Parker refrains from marring the fragile beauty with a critical interpretation. Instead of 'terpreting it, he sits back and enjoys it. Such an introductory maneuver is shrewd, saying to the student that the work of Nabokov, whatever larger implications it may have, is principally a source of pleasure. Isn't that, after all, the best reason to read him?

Like Phyllis Roth, Parker instills respect for Nabokov's literal meanings, his unambiguous effects. As Parker clearly shows, it is on the surface of Nabokov's writing, not just full fathom five within its undulating depths, that some of the most stunning beauty is to be found. Not that Parker renounces interpretation.

As he surveys Nabokov's life and work, he presents astute commentary and explication. In fact, he solves one of the oldest mysteries surrounding *Pale Fire* (a mystery that Priscilla Meyer also solves):[25] the hiding place of the Zemblan crown jewels. As it turns out, the crown jewels, like Poe's purloined letter, have been in plain sight all along. They repose in the text of the novel itself. They *are* the text of the novel itself. Parker: "Kinbote never divulges, in commentary or index, the location of the stolen crown jewels of fantasy-Zembla. But the reader is meant to find jewels where Nabokov's poet, John Shade, has secreted them— in the 'diamonds of frost' (line 19), 'jade leaves' (line 50), 'opal cloudlet' (line 119), 'emerald egg case' (line 238), and 'topaz of dawn' (line 881) of 'Terra the Fair, an orbicle of jasp' (line 558)" (p. 104).

In remarkably short space (160 pages), Parker surveys Nabokov's life and aesthetic views, discusses five Russian novels *(Mary, The Defense, Despair, Invitation to a Beheading, The Gift)* and four American ones *(Lolita, Pnin, Pale Fire, Ada),* then glances at several other novels, the short stories, the translations, and the lectures on literature. By ranging over so broad a field, he dramatizes the variety of Nabokov's achievement. At the same time, by keeping his book short (others in the series are longer), he allows a new reader of Nabokov to see very clearly the underlying unity of Nabokov's vision, to hear the echoes chiming between one work and another. Parker's book concludes with a valuable bibliography of works by and about Nabokov. Carefully and sensitively annotated, it displays the thoroughness, accuracy, and keenness of judgment that one would expect from the editor of *The Nabokovian.* All told, Parker's *Understanding Vladimir Nabokov*—plain of speech, elegant of style and interpretation—is a fine addition to the tradition of the Nabokovian little book (7¼ × 5¼).

Stephen Jan Parker is one of the correspondents in Nabokov's *Selected Letters,* the last of the six books reviewed here. Parker's presence in *Selected Letters* is appropriate. His introduction to Nabokov will help to train some of the up-and-coming critics of the nineties, those who are now undergraduates, and the training they get from Parker will be of the same sort that they get from Nabokov in *Selected Letters*. Both books—Parker's and Nabokov's—say, implicitly, that to understand Nabokov, you should listen, first of all, to Nabokov.

The publication of *Selected Letters* is an event long awaited by scholars and general readers alike. Until now, only two volumes of letters have been available, one in English *(The Nabokov-Wilson Letters)* and one in Russian *(Correspondence with My Sister)*.[26] By collecting previously unpublished correspondence, *Selected Letters* throws open to scholars of the nineties a vast new field of evidence for understanding Nabokov. The book is co-edited by Dmitri Nabokov and Matthew J. Bruccoli, who provide helpful annotations to each letter. In addition to serving as co-editor, Dmitri Nabokov (in collaboration with his mother, Véra Nabokov) translates into English those letters originally written in Russian or French. The translations are quite distinguished, maintaining throughout the book smoothness of tone and precision of diction.

This is the first collection of Nabokov's letters to show him writing to many different correspondents. As such, it contains a few surprises, modifying, if not destroying altogether, some long-held impressions of Nabokov. One impression that crumbles is that of Nabokov the literary dictator. Nabokov himself carefully cultivated this image, of course, with his sneers and snarls at critics and reviewers, not to mention Freud, and his domineering pronouncements on how his works ought to be, or ought not to be, interpreted. Despite Nabokov's famous strong opinions, he was not always so stubborn or dictatorial as he pretended to be. In *Selected Letters* we encounter not the choleric literary dictator who stalks through *Strong Opinions* but a rather more complicated person—firm of opinion, to be sure, and staunch of principle, but also, when the occasion demands, reasonable, flexible, and open to advice and suggestion, even on matters concerning his own art.

For example, when Maurice Girodias, the publisher of the first edition of *Lolita*, decided that the manuscript contained too much French, he asked Nabokov to eliminate some of it. Seeing that Girodias had a point, Nabokov sent to him "a new set of corrections where I have taken into account what you say about the over-abundance of French phrases in the MS. Of your list of sixty I have cancelled or translated one third, but this is as far as I can go" (pp. 166–67). Without this objection by Girodias and Nabokov's accession to it, *Lolita* would have a slightly different tone—more Gallic, less indigenously American. To the strongly American flavor of *Lolita* Maurice Girodias made a small contribution.[27] It's hard to write those last two sentences without a shudder, so conditioned have critics become to the image of Nabokov standing, as creator, cheek by jowl with the Almighty, perfect in the beginning and perfect also in the end.

In a similar vein, Nabokov accepted from Katharine A. White, an editor at the *New Yorker,* some thirty suggestions about a chapter of *Pnin.* Perusing these suggestions, he commented, in one case: "Bed head is good English. You will find it in the Oxford dictionary. But 'bed headboard' is better, I admit" (p. 157). Responding to another of White's suggestions, he said, "I have made this a little clearer." In another case, he said simply, "O. K. Good suggestion" (p. 159).

These were minor changes, to be sure, as were the changes to *Lolita* initiated by Girodias. Moreover, in such cases Nabokov makes it plain that on matters concerning his own art he is the ultimate judge, suggestions or no suggestions. Still, when working on the screenplay for *Lolita,* he was flexible enough to write to the film's director, Stanley Kubrick: "I hope I have won you over to my vision of the last act, but if not, I am ready to discuss alternate renderings" (p. 317). That Nabokov did sometimes accept artistic criticism and advice contradicts rather strongly his long-standing image as a writer who holds his own views and decisions to be non-debatable. In light of *Selected Letters*, critics who have drawn conclusions from that particular pose will have to rethink their positions.[28]

Perhaps the greatest value of *Selected Letters* is that it contains extended interpretation by Nabokov of his own work. Though it is now hard to imagine, there was a time when he was not famous, when he had to seek publishers for his books. During that time, he wrote letters to publishers describing his novels in some detail, voicing his own conception of what makes them worthwhile, and unique. These letters, too, hold some surprises.

In fact, they are quite astonishing, considering the widespread view of Nabokov as a remote aesthetician—solipsistic, heedless of the human condition, constructing ever more ornate dwellings for his own habitation—and considering Nabokov's own reminders, in novels and interviews, that his characters are nothing but fictions, "galley slaves," unreal figments of his own imagination.[29]

In these letters, Nabokov repeatedly stresses the living, breathing, true-to-life people that he creates in his novels—their struggles, accomplishments, failings, humanity. In only two letters does he call attention to a hidden puzzle in his fiction, and that is the acrostic that appears in the last paragraph of "The Vane Sisters" (pp. 115–18, 285–86). These two letters, with their emphasis on puzzle and game, are uncharacteristic. Elsewhere, Nabokov stresses not the games or puzzles or elaborate structures of his novels, or even their shimmering style. He stresses the reality of their characters. It is as if he knows, instinctively, that novelists ultimately stand or fall on their ability to create real people, with no quotation marks around the word real. Unsophisticated as that idea may sound, paradoxical as it may seem, it was of central importance to Nabokov. After all, in a letter to his mother, as yet unpublished, he said about the characters in his first novel, *Mary*, that they are "real people, not characters invented by me. I know the odour of each of them, how he walks, eats."[30]

The importance of realistic character: that is the hallmark of Nabokov's letters of self-interpretation. And little wonder. One of the best-known stories about Nabokov, one that he told about himself, describes how, when he was writing *Lolita*, he "travelled in school buses to listen to the talk of schoolgirls."[31] That is the writer for whom character is paramount, and that is the writer we encounter once again in *Selected Letters*. Speaking of *The Gift*, Nabokov says: "*The Gift* is thoroughly realistic, as it tells the story of a definite person, showing his physical existence and the development of his inner self. As he is an author, I naturally show his literary progress. Moreover, the whole story is threaded on my hero's love-romance" (p. 27). Of *Despair:* "[it is] a purely psychological novel . . . essentially concerned with subtle dissections of a mind anything but 'average' or 'ordinary': nature had endowed my hero with literary genius, but at the same time there was a criminal taint in his blood . . . . It is *not* a 'detective novel' " (p. 17). And of *Pnin*, he says, "When I began writing *Pnin*, I had before me a definite artistic purpose: to create a character, comic, physically inattractive—grotesque, if you like—but then have him emerge, in juxtaposition to so-called 'normal' individuals, as by far the more human, the more important, and, on a moral plane, the more attractive one. Whatever Pnin is, he certainly is least of all a clown. What I am offering you is a character entirely new to literature—a character important and intensely pathetic—and new characters in literature are not born every day . . . . It is [a] combination of the grotesque and the gentle that makes him so pleasingly bizarre. And this is also what apparently endeared him so much to the readers of the New Yorker. I have never had so much fan mail from readers with my other stories as I had with the four Pnin chapters" (pp. 178, 182). In these letters, and others like them, Nabokov suggests a new direction for critics of the nineties—if, that is, they want to respond to what was for the author himself so obviously the main point of his fiction. *Selected Letters* makes it very clear: character is what gives fiction its power. A novel works when a reader hates or loves or believes in or wants to be or shudders at the thought of being the people that the novelist creates. It's an ancient idea, beneath the high-flying theory of the eighties—too old-fashioned, too simple, not mysterious enough.

But I wonder if this old idea, which entered criticism when Aristotle first pondered Oedipus, and which has not yet had its day among Nabokov's critics, doesn't contain mysteries yet unplumbed. The creation of realistic character can't be as simple as taking notes on other people's conversations. If that were all there is to it, everybody who aspires to write novels could, with only minor effort, be as skillful with character as Nabokov. When we read a novel by Nabokov, why, exactly do we weep at the plight or cheer at the victories of people we know are not real? What magic does he unleash to create this response in us? How, precisely, does it work? Is it somehow psychological? In some sense social? Partly sexual? Or is it mainly aesthetic? If the last (as I suspect), what images, structures, tricks of style give these characters their robust, ineradicable life? We know what makes them fictional. What, exactly, makes them real?

The answers to these questions, if they exist, would explain much about Nabokov. They could also open some new perspectives on literature in general, given that critics have neglected now for so long the mysteries of characterization. They are the mysteries that Nabokov himself, in *Selected Letters*, lays before the critics of the nineties.

Notes

1. Vladimir Nabokov, *Strong Opinions* (New York: McGraw-Hill, 1973), p. 179. I want to say in this first note that I am deeply grateful to Earl D. Sampson for help with things Russian while I was writing this essay. I am also grateful to Elissa Guralnick, Paul Levitt, Rolf Norgaard, and William Walker for criticism of a late draft. Any errors or shortcomings that remain are, of course, mine, not theirs.

2. On *The Original of Laura*, see Dmitri Nabokov, "On Revisiting Father's Room," in *Vladimir Nabokov: A Tribute*, ed. Peter Quennell (New York: Morrow, 1980), p. 129. See also Vladimir Nabokov, *Selected Letters*, pp. 560, 562.

3. Vladimir Nabokov, *Speak, Memory: An Autobiography Revisited* (New York: Putnam's, 1966) pp. 34–36. See also Nabokov, *Strong Opinions*, p. 17; and Nabokov, *Selected Letters*, p. 59.

4. Nabokov, *Strong Opinions*, p. 17; Alfred Appel, Jr., "*Ada* Described," in *Nabokov: Criticism, Reminiscences, Translations, and Tributes*, ed. Alfred Appel, Jr., and Charles Newman (Evanston: Northwestern Univ. Press, 1970), p. 161; Nabokov, *Selected Letters*, p. 411.

5. For prose even more debilitating and obscure, see Barabtarlo's attempt (pp. 35–38) to explain Pnin's denial of certain things said about him by the narrator.

6. Nabokov, *Speak, Memory*, p. 193.

7. See also, for example, Andrew Field, *VN: The Life and Art of Vladimir Nabokov* (New York: Crown, 1986), pp. 339, 346.

8. Vladimir Nabokov, *Pale Fire* (New York: Putnam's, 1962), p. 130.

9. Brian Boyd, *Nabokov's* Ada: *The Place of Consciousness* (Ann Arbor: Ardis, 1985), p. 214; cf. p. 70.

10. Nabokov, *Strong Opinions*, pp. 147, 45.

11. For a searing critique of the Yale School and recent literary theory in general, see Frederick Crews, *Skeptical Engagements* (New York: Oxford Univ. Press, 1986), pp. 115–78.

12. Gladys M. Clifton, "Humbert Humbert and the Limits of Artistic License," In J. E. Rivers and Charles Nicol, eds., *Nabokov's Fifth Arc: Nabokov and Others on His Life's Work* (Austin: Univ. of Texas Press, 1982), pp. 153–70. Clifton's essay is mentioned on p. 206 of Toker's book. A good deal of what Toker says about Lolita echoes Clifton's points.

13. The most successful treatment so far of Nabokov's humanism is Ellen Pifer's *Nabokov and the Novel* (Cambridge: Harvard Univ. Press, 1980). See especially her chapter "On the Dark Side of Aesthetic Bliss: Nabokov's Humanism," pp. 158–71.

14. Julian Moynahan, *Vladimir Nabokov,* Univ. of Minnesota Pamphlets on American Writers, 96 (Minneapolis: Univ. of Minnesota Press, 1971); Donald E. Morton, *Vladimir Nabokov,* Modern Literature Monographs (New York: Ungar, 1974); Vladimir Nabokov, *Nikolai Gogol* (New York: New Directions, 1944).

15. Nabokov, *Strong Opinions,* p. 47.

16. Nabokov, *Strong Opinions,* pp. 23–24.

17. Green psychoanalyzes not only Kinbote but also Humbert Humbert (p. 102), John Shade (pp. 109–10), and the protagonist of "'That in Aleppo Once . . .'" (pp. 65–70).

18. See also p. 42, first paragraph, of Green's book. Here Green quotes a statement by Freud and one by Nabokov and asserts that the two are similar when they are, in fact, quite different.

19. Nabokov, *Pale Fire,* p. 265. Nabokov uses the phrase "passionate comparison" in the foreword to *Invitation to a Beheading* (New York: Putnam's, 1959), p. 6.

20. Phyllis A. Roth, "Toward the Man behind the Mystification," in Rivers and Nicol, eds., *Nabokov's Fifth Arc,* p. 51.

21. I should also mention an error of fact in Green's book. Green says (p. 58) that at the end of *Bend Sinister* Nabokov transforms Krug "into a moth." Actually, it is Krug's wife Olga, not Krug, that Nabokov transforms into a moth, as Nabokov states in the introduction to *Bend Sinister* (see Vladimir Nabokov, *Bend Sinister* [New York: McGraw-Hill, 1973], p. xiii).

22. Toker, *Nabokov,* pp. 130–34, 182; Barabtarlo, *Phantom of Fact,* p. 35; Green, *Freud and Nabokov,* p. 86.

23. Parker quotes from Vladimir Nabokov, *The Gift,* trans. Michael Scammell and Vladimir Nabokov (New York: Putnam's, 1963), p. 91, beginning with "Trimmed with ferns outside" and ending with "tortuous and unweeded neighbors."

24. Samuel Langhorne Clemens, *Adventures of Huckleberry Finn,* ed. Sculley Bradley, Richmond Croom Bailey, and E. Hudson Long (New York: Norton, 1961), ch. 15, p. 71.

25. Meyer, *Find What the Sailor Has Hidden,* pp. 51, 75, 105.

26. Vladimir Nabokov and Edmund Wilson, *The Nabokov-Wilson Letters: Correspondence Between Vladimir Nabokov and Edmund Wilson, 1940–1971,* ed.

Simon Karlinsky (New York: Harper, 1979); Vladimir Nabokov, *Perepiska s sestroi [Correspondence With My Sister]* (Ann Arbor: Ardis, 1984).

27. Subsequently, Nabokov had a mighty row with Girodias over publication rights to *Lolita* and other matters. See Maurice Girodias, "A Sad, Ungraceful History of *Lolita*," in *The Olympia Reader*, ed, Maurice Girodias (New York: Ballantine, 1965), pp. 520–32, and Vladimir Nabokov, "*Lolita* and Mr. Girodias," in Nabokov, *Strong Opinions*, pp. 268–79. See also Nabokov's other letters to Girodias in *Selected Letters*.

28. For a very recent interpretation of Nabokov based on his image as literary tyrant, see the section called "Who's in Charge Here?" in Green, *Freud and Nabokov*, pp. 29–34. For other examples of Nabokov's receptivity to editorial suggestion, see *Selected Letters*, pp. 77, 215, 347–48, 514.

29. When Nabokov calls his characters "galley slaves" (*Strong Opinions*, p. 95), he is, of course, punning on the printer's term "galley." On the fictionality and ultimate unreality of Nabokov's characters, see Vladimir Nabokov, *The Annotated Lolita*, ed. Alfred Appel, Jr. (New York: McGraw-Hill, 1970), pp. xxxi–xxxii.

30. Quoted in Andrew Field, *Nabokov: His Life in Part* (New York: Viking, 1977), p. 182.

31. Nabokov, *The Annotated Lolita*, p. xl.

The Queen's Disraeli

Stanley Weintraub

Disraeli Letters: 1815–1834, ed. J. A. W. Gunn, John Matthews, Donald M. Schurman, and M. G. Wiebe. Toronto: University of Toronto Press, 1982. lxxi, 482 pp.

Disraeli Letters: 1835–1837, ed. J. A. W. Gunn, John Matthews, Donald M. Schurman, M. G. Wiebe. Toronto: University of Toronto Press, 1982. xliii, 458 pp.

Disraeli Letters: 1838–1841, ed. M. G. Wiebe, J. B. Conacher, John Matthews, and Mary S. Millar. Toronto: University of Toronto Press, 1987. lxx, 458 pp.

Disraeli Letters: 1842–1847, ed. M. G. Wiebe, J. B. Conacher, John Matthews, and Mary S. Millar. Toronto: University of Toronto Press, 1989. xciv, 449 pp.

When Benjamin Disraeli gave up his post as prime minister in 1880, the year before his death, telephones were just beginning to be installed in London. He lived, then, in the spacious age of letter-writing, which antedated the experience of Winston Churchill, his only rival to eminence in both literature and politics in England. Aside from those in biographies, Churchill's letters have yet to be published. The pace and the technology of the world into which he reached maturity suggest that his correspondence will not have the verve, the sweep, and above all the intimacy of Disraeli's letters, which, in multi-volume, definitive form, are still in the process of publication. The research effort is almost certainly the major scholarly undertaking in the humanities and social sciences (Disraeli fits into both camps) in Canada.

With the fifth volume to be issued by the Disraeli Project at Queen's University (in Kingston, Ontario) in press, covering the years 1848–51, and over sixteen hundred letters and associated documents in print in the first four volumes, it is already possible to assess the scope and the possibilities of the eventual complete edition. Several questions come immediately to mind. What changes have the volumes published so far made in our picture of the only major English political figure who was also a substantial novelist? What is our revised view of Disraeli as a writer in the great tradition of English epistolary literature? And how do the letters as edited and published in this edition differ from earlier texts of the letters as published?

The questions are best answered in reverse order, and some answers to all three are already apparent, although in each case our assessments must be tentative and incomplete until all the volumes are published.

Disraeli's "home letters," largely to his sister, Sarah, were "edited" and published by his brother Ralph in 1885 and 1886; his gossipy letters to Lady Bradford and Lady Chesterfield, the sisters with whom he was infatuated as an elderly widower, were edited by the Marquis of Zetland in two volumes in 1929; and his letters to a patroness, the Marchioness of Londonderry, written between 1837 and 1861, were edited by a descendant in 1938. Further, hundreds of letters have been published or extracted from in the many biographies of Disraeli, especially the six-volume official *Life* by William Monypenny and George Buckle (1910–20).

Every such letter is suspect. Aside from minor misreadings of handwriting, misunderstandings of dates and typographical errors, letters have been censored, rewritten, altered on grounds of taste or privacy or possible libel. Sometimes several letters have been conflated into one text, with an invented date. Even judicious recent biographers often have had to resort to such published letters in lieu of the real thing. Headnotes in the ongoing Queen's edition make apparent the hazards involved. A typical one, into which are tucked, efficiently, publication history and editorial comment, rescuing the reader from flurries of *sic*, identifies a letter (2 April 1832) to Sarah Disraeli, as published by Ralph Disraeli in 1886 in *Lord Beaconsfield's Correspondence with His Sister*. That version, "[mis]dated 28 April 1832, omits the first and second paragraphs, the last three sentences of the fifth and all of the sixth and seventh." Some letters addressed to Isaac were also attributed to Sarah—as if one writes to a sister in the manner and with the same information that one writes to a father.

To find such originals and other surviving letters is a matter of sleuthing that has been underway since the initiation of the Disraeli Project in 1972. Letters thought to have been destroyed have surfaced, even those to Queen Victoria. Letters to politicians, patrons, confidants, lawyers, literary colleagues, society hostesses, relatives, and random acquaintances have turned up. In a postscript (8 December 1829) to a friend, Benjamin Austen, from whom he often borrowed money, Disraeli had advised, at twenty-five when he was still a nobody, "By the bye, I advise you to take care of my letters, for if I become half as famous as I intend to be, you may sell them for ten guineas a piece...."

Austen and others did save them. A letter dated in 1832 sold in 1989 for $1500.00—not a Lord Byron level, but good enough to validate the young man's cockiness. Yet most correspondents who kept his letters did so either because it was a businesslike thing to save one's correspondence, or because Disraeli's letters were a thing of personal rather than pecuniary value. Even so, the first recorded sale of a Disraeli letter dates from 1866, before his first tenure as prime minister although well after his first fame as a novelist.

Many seemingly intimate letters to female correspondents survive. "Disraeli's letters to women," the editors observe, "managed to achieve a tone of instant and almost conspiratorial intimacy. We have encountered cases where Disraeli had written to female correspondents who, in each instance, had cherished the letters and preserved them carefully. Following their deaths, the members of their families had found the letters and, disturbed by the implications of the familiarity of tone, had destroyed them. In none of these cases had Disraeli and his correspondent even met!" But these letters are gone.

One must remember, in drawing biographical inferences from Victorian letters, that excess was part of the epistolary convention. Letters that suggest to us a heterosexual intimacy or a homosexual tendency may merely be employing contemporary diction. Yet that effusion can sometimes be moving, as when Disraeli writes to his father as "My dearest father and friend," or when—at age thirty-eight—he signs a letter to his mother as "Your affectionate child. . . ." Some of Disraeli's letters to his sister are prefaced "My Darling" or "My dearest Angel," as if to a mistress. We sense psychological needs—perhaps on both sides of the correspondence—when Disraeli's mistress, Lady Henrietta Sykes, and his future wife, Mary Anne Wyndham Lewis, both offer him quasi-maternal affection, and he responds accordingly. "Tell me that you love your child," he would write to Mary Anne. Disraeli's letters, especially to his wife, are filled with gushy affection and fulsomely bad poetry, as he celebrated birthdays and anniversaries and mere nights away from the nuptial bed with hasty verses for each occasion never intended for the public gaze. And to Lady Seymour he offers an elaborate invitation to see, from his windows overlooking Hyde Park, a military review at which Victoria will officiate: "The Queen of England will be before our windows, & if the Queen of Beauty be beneath our roof, it will almost recal[l] the field of the Cloth of Gold."*

Sometimes the differences between earlier texts of letters and the definitive ones are subtle, matters of punctuation and spelling which nevertheless alter meaning, or the correct dating or interpretation of a letter. One re-dating (chronologically only the third letter extant) is remarkable for what it implies about young Ben's status among his elders, who already received him, at fifteen and a public school drop-out, as an intelligence far beyond his few years. A letter to the second John Murray reporting on a play manuscript offered to the influential publisher is assigned by the editors to August 1820. In it D'Israeli (he did not drop the apostrophe until he was nearly eighteen) wrote confidently, "I ran my eye over 3 acts of Wallace, and as far as I can form an opinion I could not conceive these acts to be as effective on the stage as you seemed to expect." And Ben went on to offer a critique of Charles Edward Walker's *Wallace,* which would be presented on the Covent Garden stage in November 1820, with

---

*The scene of a famous meeting in Picardy, in 1520, between Henry VIII and the French King Francis I, reportedly a gorgeous chivalric display.

William Charles Macready in the title role. Since it was published before the year was out—but by Oxbery, rather than Murray, it is clear, the editors observe, that the August 1822 dating proposed by Murray's biographer must be in error. Yet he noted on the strength of the misdating that Murray's assessment of Ben's abilities was "so firm that he consulted him as to the merits of a MS when D had scarcely reached his eighteenth year." As he predicted, the drama, despite the young tragedian's brilliance, was not a success. Ben was fifteen. In another hand at the head of the first page of the letter appear the words, "MSS rec / B. D'Israeli / in packet for / Aug. 1820." It was an implication that Murray's biographer could not accept.

The 28 April 1832 letter to Sarah on first meeting the "pretty little woman, a flirt and a rattle" who would become his wife turns out, as already noted, to be a letter of 2 April 1832. And a letter of 5 August 1834 to Lady Blessington reads reasonably of the "pangs of parting" from London, and Disraeli's feeling that "it is a great shame, when people are happy together, that they sho[u]ld be ever separated; but it seems the great object of all human legislation that people never sh[oul]d be happy tog[ethe]r." So it is left in Monypenny and Buckle, but the Queen's edition notes that the lines were not extravagant graciousness toward a favorite hostess. Instead they were an allusion, which both understood, to Lady Sykes, from whom he parted to return to his family at High Wycombe. Comprehending, Lady Blessington would respond knowingly and diplomatically that she had seen, at the Opera, "'The Lady of Your Love' looking as handsome as usual, and *much less* gay, this is all as it should be." For one hundred thirty years after the affair ended it was not mentioned in biographies of Disraeli, or identified in his letters.

Even in volume 5, in press, we find the relentless unscrambling of conflated letters, a puzzling necessity since Monypenny and Buckle had access to the originals yet utilized the corrupt published texts. A letter in Ralph Disraeli's *Lord Beaconsfield's Correspondence* dated 29 December, 1848 uses the first paragraph from a letter of that date and part of the third paragraph of a letter ascribed by the project editors to 13 December. At least both are to the same recipient, Sarah. Even if the letters had been undateable, their sequence should have been clear. In the earlier manuscript, Disraeli talks of his imminent visit to Sir John Hobhouse's palatial estate, Erlestoke; in the later letter he complains of "Erlestoke indigestion" from the succulent table provided by the "firstrate cook" who was part of the "magnificence."

The editors also caution us about the necessary dishonesty of certain Disraeli letters, not only the frequent excuses as to why he has not paid up his loans, or his many promises that the check will be in the mail shortly, but also his post-marriage adroitnesses in handling the power games of his wife, who intended to supplant his family and run his life. "I want a confidential man of business," Disraeli writes to a young solicitor, Philip Rose, on 28 April 1846, "in whose talents, zeal & fidelity, I can repose a complete trust. The pressure of public life has become so extreme of late on me, that I can no longer attend to my private affairs, wh: require great consideration. . . . But I fear, that the engrossment of your parliamentary business may perhaps render it difficult, or even impossible, for you to undertake the transaction of my affairs. If however I be mistaken on this head, oblige me by sending me a line, directed to me at the *Carlton Club*. . . ." Rose would be Disraeli's confidant and friend the rest of his life, and executor and trustee (with Lord Rothschild) after that. And the Carlton was already a necessary alternative address.

His uxorious letters to Mary Anne proving insufficiently persuasive—Mary Anne saw the D'Israeli family at Bradenham as continuing rivals for his affections, especially Sarah—Disraeli was forced to send surreptitious messages to his sister. She then would write to him at the Conservative bastion of the Carlton, open to no prying females. And to deflect suspicion, Sarah carefully sent harmless letters to Disraeli at home for Mary Anne to read. Even then, to keep peace at home, Disraeli had to write abjectly to his wife, then away tending her dying mother, "My correspondence, almost my cordial intercourse, with them has ceased; & as for Bradenham, I can truly say, that after all that has occurred there, I never go there but with disgust & apprehension." It is a shamefully low point in Disraeli's life, and indeed, since there are a few letters to "Sa" on either side of this fabrication of 27 February 1842, one can imagine the actual destruction of any incriminating evidence.

Only a week earlier, Mary Anne had written to her "Dis" that "Sa & I are great friends." But the letters make clear that the marriage with Mary Anne was not always the unalloyed sentimental romance of the earlier biographies. There was much affection between them after a marriage made coldly on both sides. The ageing widow sought companionship and saw her Dis as a rising young star; Disraeli needed to be saved from overwhelming debts and the social stigma of being wifeless. But there was some fiction as well as some friction in the bliss and rapture, and few marriages were contracted with less spurious sentimentality.

In the most truthful letter he ever wrote to Mary Anne, at a time when his social embarrassments at the postponements of their nuptials were only exceeded by the desperateness of his debts, he penned a proposal which earned him credit for candor and a restoration of his fortunes with Mary Anne. It was not only that he was insolvent, he observed (7 February 1839). "The continuance of the present state of affairs, could only render you *disreputable;* me it wo[ul]d render *infamous.* There is only one construction which Society, and justly, puts upon a connection between a woman, who is supposed to be rich, and a man whom she avowedly loves, and does not marry. In England especially there is no stigma more damning; it is one which no subsequent conduct or position ever permits to become forgotten."

While her head spun from that implication he added bluntly, "I avow [that] when I first made my advances to you, I was influenced by no romantic feelings." He now found her "tender" and her income "much less than I, or the world, imagined." Yet that was now helpful. He could love her for herself. "If society justly stigmatises with infamy the hired lover, I shrink with equal disgust from being the paid husband."

They were married on 28 August 1839. The letter has been published only in extracts, in Lord Blake's 1966 biography, and, the editors note, even there "with errors and omissions."

On more than one occasion thereafter, Mary Anne nevertheless viewed her "Dis" as a stock company of great growth potential in which she owned the controlling shares. As a result his many letters to Mary Anne are his most dishonest and least witty, however informative and dramatic about his affairs and necessarily often self-congratulatory for her satisfaction—as with his quoting (9 March 1842) Sir Richard Vyvyan's praise after a long speech, "I observed that you never consulted a single note—a very great demonstration."

The letters to "Sa" do diminish with the years and Disraeli's increasingly busy and complex political life, but they never cease, and they regularly fill his family in about his life, and show Sarah still performing business for him. Further, she was his preferred audience, and still lived vicariously in the penumbra of his achievement, as he knew when he wrote (5 March 1847) about Baron Meyer Amschel de Rothschild's determination to fulfill his office as High Sheriff of Bucks with the utmost liberality by hosting a dinner for citizens of some significance at John Kersey Fowler's White Hart Hotel. "I go to Aylesbury for the Assizes, & to dine with De Rothschild who has sent a legion of French cooks & wines to the astonished Fowler at the White Hart." Wit was never lost on Sarah.

Disraeli and his sister—two years his elder—had always been close, especially so when his friend William Meredith had become affianced to her. The couple were to marry after he completed a "Grand Tour" of the Mediterranean countries in the traditional fashion, much of it in tandem with Disraeli. In Cairo in July 1831 Meredith fell ill with smallpox. On the 19th he died. It was left to Disraeli to inform the family. The next day he wrote to his father, to Sarah, and to Georgiana Meredith, William's sister (for her parents, as he felt unable to tell them directly).

"If you were not a great philosopher, as well as a good man," he began his letter to Isaac D'Israeli, "I do not think, that I could summon courage to communicate to you the terrible intelligence which is now to be imparted by this trembling pen; but I have such confidence in your wisdom, as well as in your virtue, that it is your assistance to which I look in the saddest office that has ever yet devolved upon me. . . ."

With that letter, published heretofore omitting all the graphic medical details, was included the most heartfelt page that Disraeli ever penned. A letter to Sarah. More than anything else Disraeli wrote, it also shows his deep reading in the Bible, as it becomes almost a Song of Songs to a sister. "Ere you open this page," he began to "My own Sa!" "Our beloved father will have imparted to you with all the tenderness of parental love the terrible intelligence which I have scarcely found courage enough to communicate to him." And he told her what he knew would mean—as she was nearly twenty-nine—a life thereafter of lonely near-widowhood.

"Oh! my sister," he went on, "in this hour of overwhelming affliction my thoughts are only for you. Alas! my beloved! if you are lost to me, where, where, am I to fly for refuge! I have no wife, I have no betrothed, nor since I have been better acquainted with my own mind and temper, and situation, have I sought them. Live then my heart's treasure for one, who has ever loved you with a surpassing love, and who would cheerfully have yielded his own existence to have saved you the bitterness of reading this. Yes! my beloved! be my genius, my solace, my companion, my joy! We will never part, and if I cannot be to you all of our lost friend, at least we feel that Life can never be a blank while illumined by the pure and perfect love of a Sister and a Brother!"

While Benjamin could never live up to all his earnest promises, he meant them all at the time, and remained a deeply affectionate brother all her life. For years she was his chief confidante, and to keep her feeling useful he even collaborated with her upon a novel which research in the letters by the Disraeli Project identified as *A Year at Hartlebury,* published in March 1834 as by "Cherry and Fair Star." A poor try at a political narrative—Sarah was no great shakes at fiction—it was nevertheless Benjamin's first experiment at a political novel. And the preface by the pseudonymous pair suggested that a young husband-and-wife team were the authors, possibly Sarah's post-Meredith fantasy of herself as surrogate wife to her rising brother. "Our honeymoon being over," her preface went, "we have amused ourselves during the autumn by writing a novel. All we hope is that the Public will deem our literary union as felicitous as we find our personal one." Benjamin, the novel affirmed, was making good as a brother-and-more.

The Disraeli letters are crucial for novels more significant to his career than that mediocre and long-buried one. A long letter home from his travels in Europe turns up almost word-for-word in his fiction, and the editors call attention to the re-use. The letter to his mother dated 1 August 1830 from Granada is inserted almost unchanged in the fifth part of *Contarini Fleming* (1832), and a reader of Disraeli's novels will find anticipations of other characters and events in his correspondence. It was apparent to the knowledgeable that the Marquis of Monmouth, a selfish voluptuary who is the eponymous hero's grandfather in *Coningsby* (1844), was drawn from the third Marquis of Hertford (copied in Thackeray's Marquis of Steyne in *Vanity Fair*, 1846–48), but there need be no doubt whatever to readers of Disraeli's letter to Mary Anne, 11 March 1832, on the death of Lord Hertford as he heard it. "He went to Richmond to give a dinner to three French Women. . . . They got so tipsy with champagne that they were sick coming home & wd. have all the windows open, & the Marquis caught a cold & died." And Disraeli reports from his source, whom he quotes, *"Do you know—they say he saw the Devil before he died. He jumped up, I understand, & gave a hell of a stare in[to] the corner of the room."*

The letters are more than a mine of London scandal and gossip—many of the scandals Disraeli's own doing. His competitive instincts are acute from the start, as are his assessments of people and politics. To Lord John Manners, an ally, he writes (17 December 1845) of Sir Robert Peel, the prime minister he never forgave for refusing him office, "He is so vain, that he wants to figure in history as the settler of all the great questions, but a parliamentary constitution is not favourable to such ambitions; things must be done by parties, not by persons using parties as tools; especially men with[out] imagination or any inspiring qualities, or who rather offer you duplicity instead of inspiration." A connoisseur of political oratory, and in time one of the masters of the art, Disraeli quickly disparaged those who played the game badly. One M.P. with a "bad delivery . . . and the most ungainly action conceivable," he told Sarah on 23 January

1838, in his own first months as an M.P., was nevertheless impressive. "Lord Francis Egerton spoke with all the effect which a man of considerable talent and highly cultivated mind, backed by the highest rank and 60000 pr ann: wd naturally command." And here the editors add some informative wit of their own—that "For once D[israeli] was underestimating an income. Under the will of his uncle, the 8th Earl of Bridgewater, Lord Francis Egerton inherited property estimated at £90,000 a year."

Between the paragraphs of parliamentary business, financial problems, literary and social activities, and epistles evidencing his need to keep wooing his wife, Disraeli could be an entertaining correspondent. Before his marriage, affecting the cautious bachelor, he writes (2 April 1832) to Sarah that he had remained at a soiree (the one at which he had first met Mary Anne) for hours after most guests had gone home, quietly smoking, when Colonel Henry Webster observed to him, "Take care my good fellow. I lost the most beautiful woman in the world by smoking. It has prevented more liaisons than the dread of a duel or [of divorce proceedings at] Doctors commons."

"You have proved then," Disraeli claimed to have rejoined, "that it is a very moral habit."

Romance, once his own flings were over and he had settled into domesticity, left him—except in his novels—cynical. He had never thought that romantic passion was a good reason to marry. "Horace Pitt," he informed Sarah on 5 September 1845, "from pure ennui has gone and married Nelly Holmes, his chere amie for many years." Politics, he claimed to Mary Anne (22 April 1838) while still courting her, was difficult to re-enter after a pause of "domestic bliss" at home. "I experience a reluctance in once more entering the scene of strife and struggle, but after all, like the shower bath, it needs only a plunge."

Politics of all varieties fascinated him. Reporting to Sarah (16 January 1843) on a conversation at dinner in Paris with the Turkish ambassador, who had just been recalled to Constantinople, Disraeli wrote, "He did not know whether he was to be disgraced, or to be made Prime Minister." There was much controversy in London a few years later about erecting an oversized, forty-ton equestrian statue of the Duke of Wellington on the Marble Arch. "By the time you return," Disraeli wrote to Lady Londonderry on 1 September 1846, "you will see the Duke's statue on the Hyde Park arch. In future he is to be call'd the Arch Duke." The best place for it, suggested Lord Strangford, the Harry Coningsby of Disraeli's novel, was the bed of the Serpentine. The commotion about the Wellington sculpture was an embarrassment to the old campaigner, but the colossal bronze would remain atop the Arch for more than thirty years, until road reconstruction at Hyde Park Corner required moving the Arch to an oblique position. The Archduke came down and was trundled, with difficulty, to Aldershot.

One of the least liked of Englishmen in Disraeli's early years in politics had been the Duke of Cumberland, a Royal Prince and brother of George IV and William IV. A scarred face from a war wound did not improve his personality, and there had been many until 1837 who thought that he sought the throne, which would be his if the late Duke of Kent's daughter, Victoria, were out of the picture. Since a female, according to Salic law, could not inherit the German holdings of the family, Prince Ernest became King of Hanover. His return visits to England were dreaded by Victoria and Albert, but he was a profligate spender, Disraeli wrote to Sarah (19 June 1843). "London, that a little while ago seemed so dull, that the shopkeepers were in despair, is suddenly favoured by the most animated season, for wh: the cockneys are indebted to the King of Hanover, now the most popular man in town—for the first time in his life."

A steadfast Imperialist, Disraeli was opposed to giving up lands in western Canada claimed by the United States as part of the Oregon Territory. The U.S., he felt, made extravagant demands although its control of vast areas in the West under its flag was minimal. Writing to Baron Lionel de Rothschild on 3 December 1845, he scoffed, "The American government . . . governs nothing, except the customs-houses. It has no more influence upon the Western States, than over Devonshire or Dorset." Later, however, he would support the Union against the Confederacy. His rival, W. E. Gladstone, did not.

Politics obsessed him. In one letter to Lady Londonderry (8 May 1839), about the Duke of Wellington's turning down the

The Queen's Disraeli 95

Queen, who preferred him to Sir Robert Peel as prime minister, Disraeli referred to the chances of Lord Glenelg, Tory leader in the Lords, who was known more for falling asleep during debates in the House than for his acuity as a Cabinet minister. "The joke is, the Queen sent for Glenelg and offered him the Premiership, and he said he would sleep upon it." But that office was no joke to Disraeli, who called it the top of the greasy pole. When it was available to him, at long last, at sixty-three, he did not need to sleep on his decision.

Reaching the top was an achievement all the more remarkable for its unlikelihood. His past was public with scandalous womanizing, with debts so enormous that once after he thought his marriage had saved him he still had to flee to France with Mary Anne to escape his creditors, and with political imbroglios from discreditable job-seeking to betrayals of party colleagues. He was also, whatever the paper evidence of his baptismal certificate, of the tribe of Shylock and Fagin. But his letters show how he had become easy with at least that element of his notoriety, once writing to Sarah (9 December 1839) of a dinner party that he and his wife had "dined en famille with Mrs. Montefiore to meet Antony [de] Rothschild who is to marry one of the Montefiores, Charlotte.* There were Rothschilds, Montefiores, Alberts, and Disraelis—not a Xtian name, but Mary Anne bearing it like a philosopher."

The marriage, given his wife's age, was childless, but, Disraeli wrote to Lady Londonderry on 15 March 1847, "There is an accession to my family; & as you have always been very gracious to my offspring, I hope you will receive 'Tancred' kindly." He was sending her his new novel.

A melange of Christianity and Judaism, *Tancred* was in that quality typical of his fiction and representative of his thought, which attempted to reconcile the faith of his fathers with the religion into which he had been baptized, at twelve, to open up career possibilities limited otherwise by law as well as by prejudice. Despite the fact that it was impolitic for him to call attention

---

*The editors note that Disraeli identified the wrong daughter. The bride would be the younger daughter, Louisa.

to that by responding to attacks on Jews and Judaism, he did so regularly—after one cowardly moment when as a new M.P. he was too timid to vote in favor of the removal of legal disabilities against Jews. Although he knew he could not escape his origins, he did not so hide again. In one of his letters, rather than suggest in sly fun, as he did about the Montefiore dinner, that he was comfortable with himself, he rose to the combat, a stance by then more typical of him. Henri Avigdor, a French scholar, had responded to an attack on the Jews of France with a book of his own, which he dedicated to Disraeli. "You have greatly honored me," Disraeli wrote on 28 December 1845, "by the dedication to my name of your reply to the attack of M. Hallez upon our ancient race. I have not seen his book, but I dare say, that the children of Israel, who baffled the Pharoahs, the Assyrian Kings & the Roman Caesars, to say nothing of the Crusades & the Inquisition, will not be overwhelmed by M. Hallez, of whom I never heard."

Although the Disraeli letters are not "literary" in the sense of Lord Byron's, maniacally single-minded as D. H. Lawrence's, or bitchily gossipy as Virginia Woolf's—Disraeli had too much political and associated business for that—the Nineteenth Century in England comes alive in his letters, abetted by the encyclopaedic skills of his editors. The volumes still to be released, with their letters to Queen Victoria, to political cronies, to dowagers and patronesses, and to leading figures on the Continent, will further enrich our portrait of the exotic Londoner whom his detractors called "the Asian mystery."

Tennysonian Pastoral

John Pfordresher

Owen Schur. *Victorian Pastoral: Tennyson, Hardy, and the Subversion of Forms.* Columbus: Ohio State University Press, 1989. ix, 238 pp.

We were sitting (1857 or so) late at night in the Farringford attic-room . . . and Tennyson read over to me the little Theocritean Idyll "Hylas"; eminent for beauty in a treasure-house where all are beautiful. He dwelt particularly on the tender loveliness of the lines which describe how the fair youth, carried to the depths of a fountain by the enamoured Nymphs, faintly answered the call of his companion Herakles . . . *thrice he called on Hylas, and thrice too the boy heard, and faint came the voice from the water, and near as he was, he seemed afar off.* Tennyson . . . ended with that involuntary half-sigh of delight which breaks forth when a sympathetic spirit closes, or turns from, some masterpiece of perfect art, in words or colours. "I should be content to die," said the author of "Locksley Hall" and "Maud" and "In Memoriam," "if I had written anything equal to this."[1]

In this anecdote, recalled almost half a century later by F. T. Palgrave, we find condensed Tennyson's admiration for a very particular, and peculiar, kind of poetry, the pastoral art of Theocritus. The scene is itself an example of how the traditions of Theocritean pastoral came to be translated into forms which Victorians found deeply moving. The poetic art of living song recreated and celebrated—Tennyson reads Theocritus' lament aloud—shared with a fellow spirit in a removed, virtually secret setting, the attic room of a country house late at night. Theocritus' idealized pastoral landscapes and their melodious shepherds have been transformed into nineteenth-century terms, but their root characteristics remain. The poem which the friends share works within strictly defined traditions; it is "little," focuses on a specific moment of loss, and is, within its own limits, aesthetically perfect. The fact that Theocritus' work celebrates homoerotic love doesn't seem to trouble Tennyson or his listener. They may well have unconsciously understood it in terms of an ideal of Victorian male friendship, which this very scene exemplifies.

Finishing the reading, Tennyson, speaking as a modern poet, utters the wish that just one of his works might equal the quality of his Greek predecessor. Palgrave, the loyal friend, indicates with his list of Tennysonian masterpieces that the modern writer has indeed succeeded in this aim already. Together, the wish and the list represent a traditional rhetorical gesture: the expression of a baffled artistic aspiration—which the writer has, paradoxically, already achieved.

Palgrave's list itself constitutes a suggestive bit of critical commentary. The Tennyson masterworks he mentions picture a contemporary, mid-Victorian world. They use isolated locations from the English country landscape expressively, and each employs a speaker who finds himself alienated from the power structure and the received wisdom of his day. None of these works is "pastoral" in any strictly traditional sense of the term. Even *In Memoriam,* which at times elaborately echoes the elements of the pastoral elegy, does so only as it reaches beyond them.[2] And yet all three can be read as complex responses to, and transformations of, the pastoral tradition. Palgrave cites three works which dramatically illustrate Tennyson's implicit understanding that he cannot simply repeat Theocritus' achievement by a literal revival of pastoral tradition.

Some of Tennyson's readers agreed. The *Times* review of *In Memoriam* celebrated the fact that Tennyson's book-length elegy did not simply echo Moschus, Bion, and Milton.

We regard it as a most happy judgment of Mr. Tennyson that he resolved to forget *Lycidas,* and to place the charm of his own longer elegy in its biographical passages and domestic interiors. We hear nothing of Damon, and are thankful for the silence. The age, whether for better or worse, has left the pastoral behind it. Corydon is forever out of the question with people who have anything to do; the close of the 18th century witnessed his burial. That rather insipid shepherd-swain, whom Pope patronized, will never lead his flock along the banks of the Thames since the South-Western crossed it at Twickenham. Not even Theocritus could have outlived a viaduct.[3]

This neatly presents the problem Tennyson faced. On the one hand, he wished to write something "equal" to a couple of lines by Theocritus. On the other hand, he recognized that he could not achieve this end through simple repetition. It was only through a refashioning of elements from Theocritus' achievement into distinctly nineteenth-century modes, only through a modern transformation of pastoral, that he could hope to achieve his wish.

A series of recent, important works on Tennyson's art have thrown fresh light on some of the ways the Victorian laureate strove to equal his beloved "Hylas." Robert Pattison's *Tennyson and Tradition* (1979), Donald S. Hair's *Domestic and Heroic in Tennyson's Poetry* (1981), and Angela G. O'Donnell's "Tennyson's 'English Idyls': Studies in Poetic Decorum" (1988) all examine Tennyson's complex use of literary antecedent and tradition. Now they are joined by Owen Schur's *Victorian Pastoral. Tennyson, Hardy, and the Subversion of Forms*. What does this new book add to our understanding of Tennyson's pastoral art, and his dream of writing "anything equal"?

Angela O'Donnell suggests that when Tennyson was a boy he read Theocritus in Greek, and, thanks to the discoveries of nineteenth-century philology with which he was familiar, that Tennyson understood the specific and characteristic nature of Theocritus' art with a clarity unavailable to earlier writers. Citing an important essay by Walter Savage Landor (published in 1842), O'Donnell concludes that Tennyson would have been able to grasp the distinction between the "idyl" as a generic term and "pastoral" as a term signifying a tradition that dictates a particular setting, specific kinds of characters, and a limited range of themes.[4] The Introduction to Owen Schur's *Victorian Pastoral* draws upon some of the most important recent work on pastoral, and his discussion of the tradition is rich with suggestive possibilities for literary critics. Considering the irreducible core of pastoral, its use of rural landscape and of speakers who at least pretend to be shepherds and goatherds, Schur notes a series of inherent, constructive oppositions: "the tension," for example, "between the sophisticated . . . speaker and the 'naive' subjects whom he describes" (p. 2); the "bucolic world" in which these poems are set, and its necessary "urban counterpart" (p. 3); the isolation, even the alienation, of the pastoral singer from a larger society.

Pastoral art is essentially playful. Hence its fondness for depicting song contests. Governing the tradition are a series of expectations which each writer then tests. "Part of the play of pastoral stems from departures from the expected pattern" (p. 4). Transgression thus becomes part of the tradition. A dialectic emerges in which various oppositions work against one another to produce fresh variations and innovations. Schur, however, ignores other, important aspects of the pastoral tradition. Theocritus wrote in literary Doric, a dialect which struck his readers at once as distinct and quaint. Or, as "E. K." suggestively puts it in his introduction to Spenser's *Shepheardes Calender,* the language of traditional pastoral is "straunge"—"of many things which in him be straunge, I know will seeme the straungest, the words them selues being so auncient . . . ." The consequent distancing of the diction in pastoral poetry from the daily idiom spoken by its author and reader remains an issue for writers of pastoral, whether they comply with or ignore the precedent. In listing themes found in Spenser's pastorals, "E. K." includes what he calls "Moral" issues, "which for the most part be mixed with some Satyrical bitternesse." And indeed either through explicit satire, or through the implicit contrast which pastoral establishes between an idealized rural landscape and the faults of ordinary, daily life, pastoral functions, as Anthony Holden argues, as "a yardstick for other kinds of society . . . . It can be used as a spur, a means of cleansing or redemption, never as a retreat."[5]

Schur's book began as his doctoral thesis, under the title "Developments and Transformations of Pastoral Melancholy in Some Poems of Keats, Tennyson, and Hardy." That title indicates a peculiar stress in Schur's argument which may perhaps have made him uninterested in the linguistic experimentation and social satire which are a part of the larger pastoral tradition. In what he calls "the second half of our subject" (p. 11), Schur focuses on the history of a literary emotion—melancholy—something difficult to define and even more difficult to trace. He is interested in a tradition which links together Milton's "L'Allegro" and "Il Penseroso," eighteenth-century poems of melancholy such as those of the Whartons and Gray, Keats's "Ode on Melancholy" and "To Autumn," Tennyson's works, and the poems of Hardy. Many of these works employ elements from Greek pastoral poetry. Milton recalls "Corydon and Thyrsis," and there is a "hoary-headed swain" in Gray. Keats's autumnal landscape, though devoid of people, suggests their recent activity. But in all these instances writers work allusively rather than directly with pastoral.

It is that allusive tradition which most interests Schur and which leads to both the strengths and weaknesses of his book. When there are traces of a specific pastoral melancholy within a text, Schur frequently reads it with revealing ingenuity. When the tradition is not markedly present, Schur is tempted to blur his terms in order to draw other works into the range of his study. But, as Anthony Holden observes, "The distinction between pastoral as form, as convention, and pastoral as subject, as content, is a vital one . . . . The seductive conclusion of overlooking these distinctions is to subvert to pastoral ends any work which treats of nature or the natural life, of the humble and remote, of the simple as opposed to the lofty or the complex, of states of innocence, of the processes of corruption."[6] Such blurring of terms and distinctions can weaken the point of sustained critical inquiry.

Schur's title is misleading, for he is not interested in Victorian England generally. His book contains scarcely any reference to the social, cultural, or political history of the era. Schur makes no effort to survey the myriad forms which pastoral took in the painting, theater sets, gardening design and theory, and decorative arts of the era. While he promises to discuss Hardy, that writer receives a scant 62 of the book's 239 pages. Schur passes over all the Hardy fiction as well as *The Dynasts* to concentrate on a strictly limited number of brief lyric poems. One soon recognizes that this is a book primarily about pastoral tradition in Tennyson's art, but even here Schur disappoints the reader eager for a comprehensive survey. For unexplained reasons he avoids what one might presume to be the central text for such an investigation, *In Memoriam,* as well as any examination of the pastoral elements one might find in *The Idylls of the King* and in *The Princess* as a whole. Schur's book concentrates on a careful examination of eight Tennyson poems, all of relatively brief length: "Mariana," "Oenone," "The Lotos Eaters," "Ulysses," "Tithonus," "Demeter and Persephone," and two lyrics from *The Princess,* "Tears, idle tears" and "Come down, O Maid."

At first the reader may be surprised at this list since, on the face of it, at least, we have here no shepherds, no rural singing matches, not even a traditional elegy. While there are many descriptions of nature in these poems, one must wonder whether Schur is being tempted to blur the line between traditional, pastoral landscape and any old scene out-of-doors. It is at this point that one must remember Tennyson's involvement in a modern transformation of elements from the past into his own creative work. That is what Schur is pursuing, and it can be, as Robert Pattison suggests, "possibly the most interesting aspect of Tennyson studies."[7] To test that possibility, I would like to examine, for a moment, two of Schur's readings, one quite successful, the other slightly more problematic, and then, to round things off, I would like to consider a kind of poem which Schur conspicuously ignores in his book, but which represents a significant further dimension of Tennyson's Victorian pastoral.

In discussing "The Lotos Eaters" Schur considers some of the ways Tennyson alters the idealized landscape of pastoral tradition into something far more ominous, a world of "deceptiveness, falsity" and "stagnation" (p. 49). Whereas a trip to the countryside helps lead the shepherds of Theocritus and Virgil "back into the social community where humanity is realized" (p. 54), the natural world of "The Lotos Eaters" does the opposite, becoming a narcotic trap they have no desire to leave. The poem becomes a perverse "celebration of [human] placelessness, of nature as the place of exile" (p. 56). It is equally suggestive to compare, as Schur does, the Choric Song to the shepherds' songs in classical pastoral. Such a comparison underscores the fact that Tennyson's Choric Song is uttered not by the commander, whose orders begin the poem, but by sailors, the working-class men he once dominated. Pastoral tradition leads the reader to consider how this poem stresses social and economic difference, and how Tennyson's mariners define their difficult lives: "Trouble on trouble, pain on pain, / Long labour unto aged breath, / Sore task to hearts worn out by many wars / And eyes grown dim with gazing on the pilot-stars" (ll. 129–32). These are not, indeed, the happy shepherds of Sicily, but rather the brothers of early Victorian workers.

Schur's Introduction has already alerted the reader to "the tension between the sophisticated . . . speaker and the 'naive' subjects whom he describes within the pastoral world" (p. 2). In the Choric Song Tennyson's persistent undercutting of the mariners' words establishes the disparity between their desire to degenerate into a purely organic life, to resemble the "full-juiced apple" which "waxing over-mellow, / Drops in a silent autumn night" (ll. 78–79), and the "correct" attitude, an attitude which they explicitly reject, the resolution to strive with life by "ever climbing up the climbing wave" (l. 95). In seeking a permanent alienation from their families and from responsibility the mariners try to prolong the pastoral interlude into a life-long vocation. They transform pastoral into amoral escape. Pastoral's traditional play with language becomes compromised, rhetorical skill serving tainted ends. While at first glance Tennyson's "The Lotos Eaters" might not seem to participate in the pastoral tradition at all, Schur's ingenious comparisons connect the ancient, idealized tradition and Tennyson's isolated, superficially desirable, but ultimately malign, tropical island.

As he progresses, however, Schur strains his topic to its limits. He wants to include the dramatic monologue "Ulysses" in his discussion. Here the reader draws up short. Where, one wonders, are the fundamental elements of the tradition? Schur suggests that Ithaca, with its "still hearth" and "barren craigs" (l. 2), is "an emblem for the pastoral retreat that has failed and from which Ulysses feels psychologically banished" (p. 73). Which is to say that the poem fits into the tradition only in an inverse fashion, as an antipastoral, but not even in the tradition of Gay's "Shepherd's Week" or his *Beggar's Opera* and its "Newgate pastoral." The only connection with the tradition is that of absence. Ulysses faces two equally unwelcome choices, the "barren craigs" of his home island, and the "sounding furrows" (l. 59) of the ocean and the certain death it brings. It is the absence of any pastoral retreat which defines the world of this poem. The same argument, based upon a kind of implicit comparison, must serve as the basis for a discussion of its speaker. Though Schur never tangles with the issue, it is clear that Ulysses in no goatherd. There is, instead, a negative image of the pastoral tradition in Ulysses' description of a goat-like, "rugged" (l. 37) people, and in his sense that the luckless Telemachus must bear the burden of subduing them. As with the landscape, we see through inversion the disheartening distance between the dream world of pastoral tradition and the ethically complex dilemmas which confront Tennyson's "modern" protagonist. Schur's book is a study of pastoral melancholy, and he includes "Ulysses" because he detects that feeling in the poem. Following Robert Langbaum, in particular, Schur argues that the final verse paragraph depicts "Ulysses's knowledge that the only mythical act of heroism left is one of actively seeking his own end" (p. 77). Consequently, Schur hears in Tennyson's celebrated last lines, in Ulysses' assertion that he and his mariners are "strong in will / To strive, to seek, to find, and not to yield" (ll. 69–70), not a tone of ringing affirmation, but rather the "language of an elegiac self-consciousness, a language of melancholy . . ." (p. 77). Certainly this is a conclusion some readers may question.

It is unfortunate that Schur largely passes over the less well-known Tennyson lyrics, since among them one finds a number of poems in which the poet's experiments with pastoral take quite a different form. These are "idyls" set in Tennyson's own day, which ingeniously reinvent elements from Theocritus and Virgil in a contemporary key. Pattison discusses some of them in a chapter on "The English Idyls and Other Poems," and Donald S. Hair, in a book which Schur inexplicably ignores, offers a lengthy discussion of others. In "The Golden Year," for example, an unnamed speaker recalls a memorable moment during a walking tour of the Lake District the previous summer. On that day he, his friend Old James, and the poet Leonard climb "half way up" (l. 6) Mt. Snowdon and then stop to rest amidst the rocks. In this transformed, English pastoral retreat these "shabby-genteel swains"[8]—Tennyson's reworked version of Theocritus' shepherds—listen to Leonard recite a poem he has written. Its subject is progress, and hope in the "golden year" to come. Old James, a choleric character, is infuriated by what he takes to be the folly of Leonard's millennial expectations, and in response he invents a parody of the poem which uses the same stanza form. In terms of narrative content "The Golden Year" replicates the favorite subject of pastoral poetry, a singing contest. And in so doing it uses a favorite Theocritean formal element, inserted song texts. But whereas Theocritus' shepherds sometimes argue in verse over the relative merits of their goats and rams, Tennyson's Victorian intellectuals debate theories of history. This too, however, enjoys important classical precedent. In Virgil's Eclogue IX, which shares a number of characteristics with "The Golden Year," two poets, Lycidas and Moeris, meet on the road. They recall the poetry of Theocritus as they sing snatches about their goats. But they also discuss serious issues of the day, including the unjust seizure of property and their hope in the rule of "Olympian Caesar's star." Tennyson's poet Leonard, in his effort to fashion a poem which foresees the shape of things to come, the "Golden Year," also works in the tradition of an even more famous Virgilian eclogue (IV) which uses ambiguous, hyperbolic imagery to outline a coming era of justice and happiness. Leonard's poem is self-evidently a Tennysonian rewriting of that prophecy in modern terms.

Virgil's poets (in Eclogue IX) voice the traditional writer's questions about the power of art. They fear that "this poetry of ours . . . can do no more against a man in arms than the doves we have heard of at Dodona, when an eagle comes their way." Tennyson's poet is similarly uneasy. He feels "tongue-tied" in these "feverous days." He has been "born too late: the fair new forms, / That float about the threshold of an age, / Like truths of Science waiting to be caught— / Catch me who can, and make the catcher crowned— / Are taken by the forelock" (ll. 15–19). The writing here is eccentric. Leonard expresses his aesthetic unease in a string of colloquial idioms. This has satiric bite, replicating the unconsidered slang of daily speech and so mocking the ways ignorant readers talk. The passage may also represent for Tennyson a modern replication of Theocritus' "hyper-Doric," the practice of "overindulging colloquial realism until it becomes artificial."[9]

In setting, then, in character types, in use of language, even in dominant themes, Tennyson's relentlessly contemporary poem about Victorian issues such as the reallocation of wealth, foreign trade, and future hopes for world government turns out to be a meditation on the present cast in the forms of Theocritus and Virgil. The consequence is an uncanny kind of doubleness, in which the reader notices not only the particularity and immediacy of Tennyson's scene, but also the faint but clearly discernible echoes of an ancient tradition. Those echoes sometimes function as ironic comparisons, sometimes reinforce and deepen what is already present. But whatever their influence in a specific passage, the net effect of the whole is something like the phenomenon of pentimenti in oil painting. Through the dominant surface image one senses another, submerged layer, a shadowy, background image which is only half present but which continuously modifies the effect of the picture as a whole. For a writer like Tennyson so fascinated with history, time, and change, this manipulation of medium and tradition must have seemed utterly appropriate.

Schur's book is interested in the tension between past forms and Tennyson's nineteenth-century use of them. He takes a late twentieth-century view of this tension, seeing it in terms of power and restriction on the one hand, and individualistic rebellion on the other. So, he argues, "pastoral rhetoric in Tennyson and Hardy exerts inhibitive pressure on their poems. Pastoral forms assume a formulaic or programmatic character in the narrowest sense" (p. 1). And so the poets react rebelliously; they "deliberately subvert the forms of pastoral by means of the genre's traditional rhetoric. Out of this subversion, the two poets create a renewal of forms, new forms of pastoral poetry" (p. 2).

The term *subvert* comes from Latin words which describe something that, from beneath (*sub*) turns over something which is above it (*vertere*). In Webster's Second (1934) we learn the conventional senses of the word: "1. to overturn from the foundation . . . to ruin utterly . . . 2. to pervert or corrupt (one) by undermining his morals, allegiance, or faith; to alienate . . . 3. To destroy completely the existence, potency, soundness, etc. of; to render futile, void, inoperative, or the like . . . ." The term has become popular recently, especially with critics who adopt a feminist and/or Marxist approach, because it encapsulates both their sense of an unjust supervening power structure erected on the wills of others, and of the forces gathering to overturn that structure from beneath. If the term has, in the past, sometimes carried with it the suggestion that subversion, because it comes from within, requires deception, evasion, trickery, lying, even betrayal to achieve its ends, then so much the better. The moral shading of the term feels appropriate in situations where an unjust system of authority has determined the moral code from the start. Subversive heroes and heroines break laws to achieve a new order of morality and justice. The destruction of the existing or the traditional order implicit in the term feels good to critics who would like to see present systems swept away wholesale.

Schur may have decided to adopt this word because it links his work with these current trends in theory and in political attitude—though there is little of feminism or Marxism in his own readings of Tennyson and Hardy. However, the term "subversion" doesn't actually fit very neatly within the actual history of the poetry he discusses. The art of pastoral poetry began—insofar as the surviving texts permit us to perceive its inception—in a highly self-conscious Alexandrian literary culture. Theocritus and his successors were keenly aware of the various ways in which they were using subject matter, modes of treatment, metrical forms, and so on, from the past and reconfiguring them to create a subtle, sophisticated, and highly artificial new kind of poetry. Which is to say, that from its inception pastoral was into the business of taking from a tradition which had become formulaic or programmatic elements which are to become a part of a renewal of forms. This inherently innovative element within the tradition appears emphatically in the efforts of Augustan Latin poets to write new, and yet canonic, poetry—lots of it, as things turned out, within the pastoral tradition. They began with the intent, as James E. G. Zetzel argues, to create a "highly derivative literature" but found themselves, in spite of this intent, shaping their various works in "whatever way [they] chose . . . ." Virgil, more than all the rest, created in his *Aneid* a "sense of ambiguity, [a] doubleness of vision that is the direct result of the Alexandrian deconstruction of poetic genre."[10]

All this suggests that when Tennyson, in a poem such as "Mariana," takes up elements of the pastoral tradition and fashions them into new forms, he does not feel, as Schur argues, that he is "not a part of the textual community to which he alludes" and he does not feel, as Schur suggests, "a sense of exile from the literature out of which his own poetry originates" (p. 34). In fact, if Zetzel is correct, Tennyson may have felt, as he translated traditional pastoral elements into the striking innovations of "Mariana," that he was at his most Virgilian, that he was closest to an achievement which might parallel that of his beloved Theocritus. As Pattison notes, "If Tennyson is in fact another Virgil, he is so because he treats his sources in the same way the Roman poet treats his: as the evidence of a plastic tradition to be evolved through the cultural process of poetry."[11] Tennyson's project was not to "pervert or corrupt" the traditions in which he worked; he was not interested in destroying "completely the existence, potency, soundness" of Western poetry. Rather, he was keenly aware of the robust appetite for innovation and change which has always been, paradoxically, an integral part of that tradition.

Notes

1. Hallam Tennyson, *Alfred Lord Tennyson: A Memoir by His Son* (New York: Macmillan, 1911), II, 495.

2. Donald S. Hair, *Domestic and Heroic in Tennyson's Poetry* (Toronto: Univ. of Toronto Press, 1981), pp. 24–26.

3. Quoted in Hair, p. 9.

4. Angela G. O'Donnell, "Tennyson's 'English Idylls': Studies in Poetic Decorum," *Studies in Philology*, 85 (1988), 131–32.

Tennysonian Pastoral

5. Anthony Holden, *Greek Pastoral Poetry* (Harmondsworth: Penguin Books, 1974). p. 26.

6. Ibid., p. 24.

7. Robert Pattison, *Tennyson and Tradition* (Cambridge: Harvard Univ. Press, 1979), p. 14.

8. Ibid., p. 90.

9. Ibid., p. 27.

10. James E. G. Zetzel, "Recreating the Canon: Augustan Poetry and the Alexandrian Past," *Canons*, ed. Robert von Hallberg (Chicago: Univ. of Chicago Press, 1984), pp. 109, 124, 126.

11. Pattison, pp. 2–3.

The Return of the Native: Ezra Pound as an American

Robert Casillo

Wendy Stallard Flory. *The American Ezra Pound.* New Haven: Yale University Press, 1989. xi, 246 pp.

This book is riddled with sophistry, misinterpretation, misuse, abuse, and neglect of evidence, historical inaccuracies, dubious psychologizing, causal fallacies, and other errors. It at once repeats and extends arguments which critics have often used to minimize Pound's fascism and anti-Semitism and thus to insulate his life and writing against them. Having been praised by prominent critics, it needs an exacting going-over, lest it be mistaken for the balanced reading of Pound that it pretends to be.

Wendy Flory wants neither to extenuate nor to victimize Pound but to give an "open-minded," objective, and "accurate" portrait of his politics and economics (pp. 2, 3). She also seeks to present an "informed analysis" of his anti-Semitism (p. 131), to explain his moral collapse in the 1930s and 1940s, to explore the question of his sanity, and to show the "coterminousness" of his poetry, economic theory, and radio broadcasts (p. 4). Above all Flory greatly emphasizes the "thoroughgoing, determined, and consistent Americanness" of Pound's "aims and priorities as an artist and as a reformer" (p. 2), insisting that he remained "highly moralistic and characteristically American" (p. 4) even in his radio broadcasts. According to Flory, not only does Pound's political, social, and cultural project continue the "moral imperatives" of the tradition of the American jeremiad as described by Sacvan Bercovitch (p. 6), but Pound is "bound to be misunderstood" unless he is seen in this tradition (p. 5), which links him to the New England puritans and to Emerson, Whitman, James,

Eliot, and Williams. Just as the jeremiah figure castigates America for lapsing from its universalizing moral ideals into materialism and cultural stagnation (pp. 5, 6), so America's failure to conform to his high ideals often plunges him into despair and forces him to "withdraw" from his country (pp. 7, 8). This, Flory argues, is what happened to Pound in the 1930s, when he attacked America not in the interests of *their* fascism and anti-Semitism, as some believe, but in moral outrage against *our* ethical and economic decadence.

Armed with the jeremiad, which enables her to reduce the disturbing historical and ideological specificities of Pound's politics to an honorific generalization, Flory confers redemption through genre. Yet her categories of idealism, decadence, "moral earnestness," and anti-materialism are too vague to be useful. Pound may have begun in the jeremiac tradition, but the "high ideals" he ultimately denounces America for neglecting are those of Italian Fascism and Nazism. This book asks us to find a resemblance between what Bercovitch puts forward as Emerson's idea of "continuing revolution" and Mussolini's idea of "continuing [fascist] revolution," which Pound celebrates (p. 7). What connections—given their separate origins, methods, goals—can there possibly be between them? Where is there anything in Emerson even remotely comparable to Mussolini's characteristic contempt for democratic individualism and the autonomous conscience, or to his doctrine of ruthless natural and social struggle, or to his theory of the totalitarian state? Nor may Pound's broadcasts be defined as an example of merely disapproving jeremiac "withdrawal" from a backsliding America, for unlike the biblical and American jeremiahs, Pound expresses a total alienation from many of the fundamental values and institutions of his homeland. Nowhere is this alienation more evident than in his charges from the late 1930s onward that America is an extension of Judea, that it has virtually ceased to be America. Flory gives no sense of Pound's hatred for a country from which he believed himself in exile, to which he recommended fascist totalitarianism as an antidote to liberal individualism, social inequality, and racial mixing, and which had cause at least to suspect him of treason. Could the same charge be brought against any of the

The Return of the Native

other jeremiahs Flory mentions? She should have ignored Bercovitch's paradigm and relied on more specific historical and sociological categories—the radical right, American fascism, status anxiety, the paranoid style in American politics—in order to show Pound's increasing emargination from America's political and social mainstream. His frequent accusations that America has betrayed itself project an unacknowledged fear that he had betrayed America.

Yet Flory insists upon Pound's "Americanness" not just in his politics but everything else. The term is so vague as to allow her to do whatever she wants with it. Pound's family background extending to colonial times proves his Americanness, as does a grandfather's entrepreneurship (pp. 16, 17), as does an apparent absence of racial prejudice in Pound's immediate family (pp. 21, 136), as does the fact that Jefferson, Adams, Jackson, and Lincoln proposed progressive economic reforms similar to those favored by Pound generations after (when the historical context was entirely different). All of this is trivial by comparison with Pound's fascism and rabid anti-Semitism. At the same time, Flory accepts as proof of Pound's Americanness his assertion that his family, in its diversity of conditions, encapsulates the *entire* social history of the United States (p. 15). But Pound's family included no non-whites, proletarians, recent immigrants, or native Americans, and his claims to representativeness are false. Flory fails to see that Pound's conception of his family as an American microcosm contributed to the radio broadcasts' radical white-wing fantasy of the authentic America as coterminous with the threatened white Anglo-Saxon Protestant middle and upper-middle class to which Pound belonged.[1] By the 1940s he has a highly arbitrary view of what constitutes Americanness: it is anything he says it is, just as a Jew is anybody Pound happens to call a Jew.[2] Instead of applying an amorphous notion of national identity, Flory might have defined Pound within the broad spectrum of American society and politics. Pound emerges far less typical than Flory supposes.

As a bridge to her discussion of Pound and fascism, Flory explores the anti-usurious banking proposals of Major Douglas and the Social Creditors, whose timid reformist program she describes as "visionary economics" (pp. 42–81). Was it "visionary" to think that bankers are responsible for all the ills of capitalism, and that these ills might be eliminated by a few simple financial reforms? Or was it a mere daydream, a new version of a familiar conservative fantasy? Meanwhile, Flory stresses what she sees as the perhaps equal influence upon Pound of A.R. Orage, editor of *The New Age* and a leading Guild Socialist before his turn to Social Credit. Flory's longwinded treatment of Orage's spiritual qualities typifies her testimonial strategy of making Pound look good by setting him among his more virtuous associates (pp. 42–48). For Flory, Orage served Pound from the late teens to the early 1930s as an indispensable counterbalance to the bad influence of Wyndham Lewis, who allegedly tempted Pound, naturally against his true nature, to authoritarianism and misanthropy (pp. 49–50). Flory contends that Orage gave Pound a lasting education in Guild Socialism while reinforcing his instinctive optimism, common sense, basic decency, and love of the common man.

Although Flory notes that Orage shared the Guild Socialists' fear of the collectivist state (pp. 51–52), she implies that he favored democracy. Actually, the Nietzscheian Orage suspected democracy, and *The New Age* usually disparaged it. Orage published J.M. Kennedy's articles on Tory Democracy, a reactionary defense of social hierarchy, and Ramiro de Maeztu's exposition of a functional, hierarchical, anti-parliamentary politics.[3] Orage's elitist conservatism appealed to Pound, whose alleged liberalism does not square with his frequent comparisons of average humanity to animal herds.[4] Moreover, while Flory reports that Orage helped S.G. Hobson to revise *National Guilds,* a manifesto of Guild Socialism, she never mentions Orage's rejection of G.D.H. Cole's genuinely socialistic concept of the encroaching control of workers in industry (p. 51).[5] Orage's concern to preserve existing industrial management, coexistent with guilds, calls to mind Pound, who never favored industrial democracy in Fascist Italy but only pretended that it existed. Amazingly enough, Flory suggests that Guild Socialism and Social Credit shared a similar concern for workers' benefits, and that, insofar as Orage shaped Social Credit, it reflected the Guild Socialist call to industrial self-government—as if Social Credit had, beyond its narrow banking proposals, a deep socialist thrust (pp. 51–52). Major Douglas, the founder of Social Credit, detested socialism and preferred the capitalist system of industrial management. Promoting "economic" not "industrial democracy," he hoped— as Flory notes—that his financial nostrums would obviate the need for major institutional changes (pp. 54–55).[6] Social Credit thus bears little of the Guild Socialist imprint Flory supposes Orage gave to it—as can be inferred from the acrimonious break-up of these movements.

Flory finds two major factors in Pound's turn to fascism. One was the death of Orage, whose "salutary warnings" had supposedly restrained Pound from unquestioning support of Mussolini (pp. 105, 42). This interpretation typifies Flory's view of Pound not simply as a self-assertive personality but, whenever convenient, as dependent on the good or bad influence of others, especially Wyndham Lewis and Orage. The second, more important factor in Pound's fascism was Social Credit. Like many Pound apologists, Flory confines his involvement in Italian Fascism to its economic policies, which he mistakenly thought to resemble Social Credit's anti-usurious proposals (pp. 91, 104). For the rest, Pound remained pro-democratic and anti-statist. This judgment fails to account for Pound's disaffection from the Social Credit movement in the 1930s, evident in his strained relations with the Social Creditor John Hargrave (p. 112). Flory rejects the Social Creditors' conclusion that Pound wanted to combine their economics with the fascist statism and authoritarianism they abhorred.[7]

This failure to recognize Pound's attraction to fascist social and political organization exposes Flory's inability to see the relation between economic and social policies as well as the differences between them. She implies that the state-regulated guilds and corporations of Italian Fascism are only economic phenomena (p. 91). Actually, Pound celebrates Italian Fascism for having supposedly achieved an "organic" society where capitalists and workers each take their allotted place in a functional hierarchy. Not only does Italian Fascism substitute economic collaboration for class conflict, it rejects liberal individualism and parliamentary democracy for a system of "vocational representation" whereby each person's political interests coincide with those of his professional group.[8] Although Flory correctly sees a broad resemblance between Guild Socialism and Italian Fascism, she suggests that Pound admires fascism for having fulfilled the Guild Socialist ideal of industrial democracy. To be sure, the "fascist left" held a similar ideal, and Flory makes much of Pound's travelling in disaffected left-fascist circles (pp. 99–100). Nonetheless, Pound never opposed Mussolini's outlawing of strikes, nor his de facto state control of guilds, nor his banning of non-fascist labor organizations.[9] Flory wrongly argues that he recommends fascism only for Italy (p. 92). In his broadcasts Pound tells American industrialists and financiers to seek a "corporate solution" on the Italian Fascist social and political model.[10]

The need to exculpate her hero leads Flory to justify fascism itself. In the 1930s, she notes, Mussolini was widely admired in America (pp. 101–02). She makes the preposterous claim that Italian Fascism differs from Nazism in not being militaristic (p. 93). This would have been news to Count Ciano, Ambassador Grandi, the Spanish loyalists, the Albanians, the Libyans, the Abyssinians, and the Greeks.[11] An imperialistic component figured in Italian Fascist ideology from first to last, shaping Mussolini's rhetoric and policies. Flory also relies on A. James Gregor's dubious attempt to legitimate Italian Fascism as the very type of modern "developmental dictatorship," an intellectual rival of liberalism and socialism (pp. 93–96).[12] It is not clear, though, why Flory needs Gregor to legitimate fascism, since she holds that Pound was no "follower" of Mussolini anyway, that he "saw Italian fascism from a distance," that "any attempt to categorize" his "highly independent" and eccentric politics is "bound to falsify them," and that fascism itself is virtually amorphous in its ideological variations (pp. 134, 98, 97). She finds proof of Pound's political originality in the fact that fascist officials regarded his arcane broadcasts with suspicion (pp. 98, 132). As is evident, Flory covers all bases, throwing contradictory arguments willy-nilly at her readers: Pound wasn't fascist, but just in case he was, the fascists didn't think so, and fascism wasn't that bad after all.

It is wrong to imagine, as Flory does, that the many varieties of fascism render the term hopelessly vague as a political concept—as if Pound's politics could be salvaged by a kind of political nominalism. Zeev Sternhell defends the "generic" interpretation of fascism in pointing out that no major political ideology achieves perfect consistency and that each permits many variations within a basic pattern.[13] Thus the gravest weakness of Flory's book is its failure to demonstrate Pound's essential congruity with fascist ideology. She underemphasizes his support of fascist corporatism and finds him uninterested in its rhetorical corollary, the "parades, uniforms, and rousing speeches" (p. 92) whereby fascism mobilized the masses. Flory's acknowledgement of these aspects of Italian Fascism incidentally undercuts her view of it as non-militaristic. Pound celebrates its collective rituals in the Monte dei Paschi *Cantos*, where festivities in eighteenth-century Siena on the occasion of anti-usurious legislation allude to similar events under Mussolini's regime. In the Cavalcanti essay Pound honors Gabriele D'Annunzio, perhaps the originator of Italian Fascist style, as the "only living author who has ever taken a city or held up the diplomatic crapule at the point of machine guns."[14] Later, in Canto 93, Pound praises D'Annunzio's ability to move theatrical crowds.[15] In *Jefferson and/or Mussolini* Pound prefers the "ancient Roman legion" to "psychic sessions for the debilitated," this being a typically fascist slap at Freud.[16] The reference in Canto 52 to Simone Martini's painting of the condottiere Guidoriccio da Fogliano alludes to Mussolini, Guidoriccio's avatar. In the Chinese *Cantos*, where Pound portrays Confucianism and fascism as ideologically similar, his favorite Chinese rulers love "drillin' and huntin'."[17] Failing to comprehend Pound's attraction to the phallic aggressiveness embodied in Mussolini, Flory likewise misses the no less typically fascist misogyny which pervades *The Cantos*. Indeed she even claims that Pound was something of a feminist (pp. 28–29).

Since Mussolini's invasion of Abyssinia was more a militaristic than economic event, Flory must explain away Pound's support of it. In her view, his naively optimistic faith in Mussolini's economic programs forced him to "rationalize" the invasion (pp. 83, 102), so that henceforward he justified fascist militarism as a response to usurious monopoly and English, French, and American aggression (pp. 113–14). Nonetheless, she thinks, Pound unconsciously disapproved of Mussolini's policies (p. 102). This is only one of many instances in which Flory, without historical, textual, or psychological evidence, transforms Pound's unconscious into the repository of his highest and most genuine moral impulses, however unacted upon. She also resorts to euphemisms which reappear in her attempt to mitigate Pound's anti-Semitism. Far from consciously *choosing* to support fascist aggression, Pound "rationalized" it and thus "evaded the responsibility of conscious moral choice" (pp. 82–83, 85–86). Flory's argument is itself a rationalization which asks us to accept the incredible notion that Pound secretly detested his actions at every turn. Had Pound felt moral reservations toward fascist imperialism, he would at least have kept a discreet silence. Yet he celebrates it in Canto 40, where Carthaginian Hanno's West African conquests prefigure Mussolini's campaign against the "aethiops." Rather than being undertaken as an onerous task, this canto was written in eager anticipation of the invasion, and Pound's later prose celebrates Mussolini's colonial ventures as a "romance" comparable to the American frontier—such is Pound's "American" side.[18] No one forced Pound to describe Abyssinians as "black Jews," a contemptuous reference to the Falasha tribe.[19]

Yet Pound's supposed rationalization of the Abyssinian invasion had worse consequences. Naively committed to Mussolini's economics, though unconsciously opposed to his militarism, Pound nonetheless accepted Mussolini's participation in the Spanish Civil War, his Albanian campaign, his alliance with Hitler, whose values Pound allegedly despised, and the racial laws imposed by Mussolini as a consequence of the Axis Pact (pp. 103, 116, 118, 164). Flory's correct but labored insistence that Italian Fascism rejected anti-Semitism up to 1938 falsely implies that until then Pound rejected it too (pp. 137–38). Just as, for Flory, Pound's faith in Mussolini's economic policies motivates his anti-Semitism, so his prejudice amounts to a mistaken belief in an international banking conspiracy. She repeats the familiar apologetic that Pound espoused only economic rather than racial and cultural anti-Semitism and harbored no hatred of the Jewish people (pp. 138–39).

Flory traces Pound's anti-Semitism to American Populism and reduces it to a pro-agrarian hatred of the Jewish usurer. Thus it supposedly differs from the snobbish resentment which many upper-class white Anglo-Saxon Protestants felt toward socially successful Jews and which led them to brand the philo-Semitic F.D.R. a traitor to his class (p. 137). Actually, status anxiety probably played a part in Populist anti-Semitism.[20] However, Flory overestimates Pound's connections with Populism and thus ignores his resemblance to such anti-Semitic high cultural figures as Henry and Brooks Adams, who partly blamed Jewish arrivistes for their political and social decline. Contrary to Flory's view that Pound turned against Roosevelt for rejecting Social Credit, the broadcasts strongly suggest that he hated him for giving Jews social and political influence and for undermining an "Aryan" or WASP hierarchy dating to colonial times.[21] The truth is that Pound's prejudice extends far beyond Jewish financiers to the Jews as a whole. In Canto 52 Pound (falsely) attributes to Benjamin Franklin a proposal to exclude Jews from America—Pound's equivalent to the Nazi *Judenrein* idea.[22] Moreover, Pound's support of eugenic breeding in the broadcasts applies to the Jewish race, just as his many references to "bacilli" and "vermin" indiscriminately blame the Jews for social, cultural, and racial deterioration.

This book gives little sense of the origins, scope, psychology, and ideological complexity of Pound's anti-Semitism. In suggesting that Pound may have unthinkingly picked up English prejudices against the Jews (p. 136), Flory ignores the fact that the increasingly intense anti-Semitism in his early writing, including *Mauberley*, "Imaginary Conversations," his translations of Voltaire and Laforgue, the third canto, his letters, and other texts, carries ideological import while considerably exceeding in viciousness the "polite" anti-Semitism of his London milieu. Denying that Pound's anti-Semitism derives from prior anger or hostility (p. 133), Flory fails to see that he displaces upon the Jews his original aggression and resentment toward his many Gentile "enemies": the Hell *Cantos* show that the terms of abuse are often identical.[23] Flory also dismisses Pound's ideological hatred of Jewish culture—for instance his anti-monotheism, his antithesis of Judaism and vitalistic paganism, and his identification of the Jews with demonic femininity, all of which have analogues in fascism.[24] Pound was such a feminist. His portrayal of Jewish Mitteleuropa in Canto 35 as a soft, inchoate realm of intellectual and emotional indeterminacy suggests that, even before the Axis Pact, he hoped for the purgation of what he describes in Canto 50 as the Viennese "bog."

Among Flory's many red herrings is the argument that Pound's friendship with Jews such as Louis Zukofsky absolves him of anti-Semitism. This proves nothing. Wagner liked to have Jews in his entourage in order to humiliate them with the withheld promise of cultural acceptability. In Flory's view, Pound's anti-Semitism is only a "fantasy" or abstraction in which deindividualized Jews resemble allegorical figures in a medieval mystery play or works by Spenser or Bunyan (pp. 172, 153). The comparison is unfortunate, since Pound and the Nazis relied on medieval allegories in demonizing the Jews.[25] Does this make Nazi anti-Semitism a mere literary abstraction? Equally dubious is Flory's contention that, as ordinary life is the seedbed of anti-Semitism, no essential difference exists between the average prejudiced person and the "real" anti-Semite (pp. 132–33). She ignores the distinction between occasional suburban everyday anti-Semitism and the virulent ideological anti-Semitism Pound typifies, whereby the demonized Jews become targets of political violence.[26]

Nor can one accept Flory's contention that Pound supported Hitler only in order to conform to Mussolini's policy rather than out of ideological approval. By the late 1930s Pound's fascism had become inseparable from anti-Semitic racism and advocacy of the removal of the Jews from Western society—a program which, in contrast with Italian Fascism even after the Axis Pact, stands at the heart of Nazism. Had Pound disapproved of Nazi racism he would have remained silent about it, as did many Italian Fascists; for as Flory herself notes, Italian Fascism allowed

The Return of the Native 121

for a certain ideological variety. Instead, Pound hailed Nazism as a "force toward a purgation" and spoke favorably of Nazi eugenics.[27] And why did Pound transform his signature into a swastika? (p. 120). This symbolic personal deformation implies his enthusiastic identification with Nazism. Pound volunteered the observation in the radio broadcasts that history is "keenly analyzed" in *Mein Kampf*.[28] There was no gun at his head.

The best indication of the seriousness of Pound's anti-Semitism in the radio broadcasts is that Flory has to explain it as more than the result of Pound's need to rationalize Axis policies of which he allegedly disapproved. It supposedly derives from the "tension" generated by Pound's "mental conflict" between his desire to justify Mussolini's policies and his unconscious aversion to them (p. 140). Flory never explains how or why such tension led to anti-Semitism rather than to its repudiation. She also claims that anti-Semitism results from Pound's "anxiety" in attempting to "evade the responsibility of moral choice" (p. 134) on the issue of fascist aggression and indeed anti-Semitism itself. It is unclear why such presumed anxiety should have this effect. Again, Flory traces Pound's post-1935 racism to his "repressed guilt" in failing to condemn Mussolini's belligerence (pp. 145–46), or alternatively, to a "fear of loss of mental control" (p. 140). Whether deliberately or not, Flory buries Pound's anti-Semitic ideology in impenetrable conundrums of causation. Hers is a casebook on how not to apply psychoanalysis to literary biography.

The title of the fourth chapter, "The Anti-Semitism of the Broadcasts," implies that Pound's anti-Semitism is confined to these texts or that they exhibit an atypical racist virulence. To strengthen this impression, Flory virtually ignores the deep-founded, developing anti-Semitism traceable in Pound's prose and poetry. She thus affords the latest example of the familiar attempt to sterilize Pound's "literary" works from political contamination. She further maintains that Pound would have broadcast over any microphone (p. 8), for his purpose was not to promote a fascist agenda but only to dispel economic ignorance by means of his idiosyncratic, "completely independent," and "unilateral" theories (pp. 3, 8).

Fruitlessly, Flory has tried to reify Pound's anti-Semitism as a detachable theme. In texts as in individuals, anti-Semitism is always a symptom and displacement of conflicts and impulses first evident in other contexts.[29] Most of the metaphors, images, and themes in Pound's developed anti-Semitism appear earlier in his poetry and prose and without connection with Jews: phallocentrism, castration anxiety, fear of microbes, solar mythology, the swamp, the demonic feminine, horror of the unconscious, anti-usury, crowd hysteria, warnings of Western decadence. Thus coming under the play of language, the relation between the broadcasts and Pound's other writings is fluid and permeable.[30] Moreover, just as the broadcasts constantly intersect with *The Cantos,* so they help to reveal anti-Semitism where the poetry tends to conceal it. For instance, the broadcasts show that Mussolini's draining of the Pontine Marshes in Canto 41 signifies a victory over those "Jewish" evils with which Pound associates the "swamp": disease, anti-agrarianism, undisciplined growth, sterility, the inchoate feminine, and cultural decay.[31] As for the absurd notion that the broadcasts are exclusively concerned with economic reform, in reality they celebrate the fascist corporate state, hierarchical order, totalitarianism, solar religion, and eugenic racism.

Flory advances that the broadcasts touch reality "at almost no point" (p. 143). Not only are they "moved much more by unconscious compulsions than by considered, conscious purpose" (p. 85), but from the 1940s onward Pound's hateful fears of Jewish conspiracy and persecution add up to a paranoid psychosis from which he never fully recovered (pp. 85, 144, 157–58). Flory has thus reversed, without acknowledging it, her thesis in *Ezra Pound and The Cantos: A Record of Struggle,* where the broadcasts are described as too abstractly ideological and detached from Pound's "true" feelings.[32] Although Flory still describes the broadcasts as too "theoretical" (pp. 143, 177), she now prefers to see them as dominated by unconscious emotion. If anything, the broadcasts entangle political abstractions and deep psychological drives. Flory realizes, though, that to describe Pound as psychotic might imply that he has left us the literary legacy of a lunatic; and lunatics rarely produce masterpieces. So she insists that, apart from his anti-Semitic paranoia, Pound

The Return of the Native

preserved what she sees as his customary logic and lucidity and the benevolence of his "basic personality" (pp. 144, 162, 166).

How did Pound fall into this conveniently restricted psychosis? Flory again resorts to enigma. The psychosis results from Pound's "unconscious decision" during the Abyssinian invasion to "deny" and "rationalize" Mussolini's belligerence. Once Pound had taken the "fatal first step of suppressing what he knew to be the truth," an anti-Semitic psychosis inevitably ensued (p. 163). Flory's pure speculation opens up a logically insuperable chasm between cause and effect. Whereas previously she had described Pound's unconscious as harboring reservations against his "rationalization" of Mussolini's belligerence, now his unconscious is making decisions and rationalizing them. It does not seem unconscious. But the last thing Flory can admit is that Pound, plainly speaking, voluntarily and immorally chose anti-Semitism (p. 85).

If Pound's anti-Semitism is altogether an expression of unconscious impulses, then it is primordially non-ideological and he cannot be held accountable for it. This is the upshot of Flory's theory of Pound's psychosis. Yet Pound's insanity seems doubtful when one considers the elements by which Flory defines it. Pound fears that Jewish bankers are plotting to dominate the world; that the Jews already control Communist Russia, capitalist England, President Roosevelt, the Congress, and the American press; that they have fomented World War II; and that the Axis is fighting against Jewish-inspired Allied aggression. These supposedly psychotic delusions were the staples of fascist ideology and propaganda. To be sure, in Pound as in other fascists such beliefs are energized by unconscious impulses, but this is true of any ideology. Moreover, clinically defined paranoia in individuals differs from political paranoia: a person may embrace a paranoid political philosophy like fascism without being clinically paranoid.[33] Flory's argument leads to the false conclusion that fascism is itself a mass psychosis or hysteria rather than the political ideology Pound embraced.

Flory evades or misreads the broadcasts' horrifying content and implicitly violent agenda. Her claim that they contain only "isolated passages of antisemitic ranting" is quite mistaken

(p. 134). She holds as well that Pound, unlike the Nazis, wanted only to blame not to punish the Jews, and that he never specifies actions against them, least of all genocide (pp. 144, 146–47, 150). Pound's anti-Semitism is supposedly harshest when he incautiously imitates true anti-Semites like Carlyle and Céline (p. 155). His general recommendation of Jewish deportation and eugenics should not be taken seriously, since he offers no definite proposals, and indeed he questions the need for an anti-Semitic policy (pp. 149, 151–53, 172). Whenever Pound mentions anti-Semitic violence such as pogroms he always backs away into personal nostalgia, reminiscence, arcane allusion, and troubled questioning (pp. 147, 148, 155). Thus the broadcasts "self-dismantle" as Pound resists the destructive implications of his accusations (p. 146). Never does he resort to the "indirect and calculating arts of persuasion . . . of the deliberate demagogue" (p. 139).

While Flory rightly speaks of Pound's "incompetence as a rabble-rouser" (p. 164)—he is too cerebral and allusive for popular audiences—the broadcasts nonetheless exemplify the oblique, insinuating rhetoric typical of radical right-wing and fascist demagogues.[34] Like other demagogues, Pound understands that overt recommendations of anti-Semitic violence must fail with American and British audiences. And yet, even as Pound decries violence he encourages it by harping on Jewish conspiracy while demonizing the Jews collectively as bacilli, syphilis, rats, lice, and other vermin.[35] When Pound calls for "bug poison" and a "purge," a listener would, in view of his description of the Jews as lower animals, have every reason to think subliminally of expulsion and even extermination.[36] Pound's identification of the Jews with violence against Gentiles likewise foments and justifies anti-Semitic retaliation. Flory misreads a passage insinuating Jewish butchery for cannibalistic purposes as indicating Pound's disapproval of the carnage of World War II (p. 145); in fact he is blaming the Jews for mass slaughter.[37] She errs too in taking at face value Pound's exhortations against assassinating F.D.R., allegedly a Jewish puppet (p. 141). "The American Ezra Pound" undoubtedly realized that assassination—like the pogrom—has never been an acceptable or likely form of political expression in America. His denunciations of violence really aim to promote it.

Evaluating the broadcasts as a moral and personal document, Flory argues the irrelevant point that Pound the collaborationist differs from war criminals such as Adolf Eichmann, who officially participated in the Holocaust (pp. 3, 131–32). Pound need not have been an Eichmann to have committed morally reprehensible acts. Flory further holds that, whereas Eichmann "evaded" moral choice by following orders unquestionably, Pound never advocated violence and retained moral autonomy (pp. 3, 134). And, whereas Eichmann's actions harmed individuals, Pound harmed no one (p. 3). Not only are the broadcasts uncontaminated by external ideologies, they exist entirely outside the sphere of action. And insofar as they ultimately harmed only Pound, they are at worst a self-destructive act (pp. 139, 164).

Flory's contention that Pound preserved his moral autonomy in the broadcasts contradicts her view of him as psychotic. But to the extent that Pound remained morally autonomous—and I believe he did—he sought to incite, however ineffectually, anti-Semitic violence. Flory's notion that the broadcasts are not *an act* falsely dissociates writing (and speaking) from action and implies the triviality of politicized literature. The federal government recognized the broadcasts' status as action when it charged Pound with treason, and it makes no difference to the argument that he was never tried. To characterize Pound's broadcasts as self-destructive requires awareness of their disastrous effects on his career. However, they would not have been self-destructive had the Axis won the war, which is what Pound seems to have expected in 1941.

The light thickens as Flory finds the later *Cantos* comparatively free of fascism and anti-Semitism thanks largely to Pound's return to a Confucian belief in the goodness of man, nature, and light (pp. 176–77). But the later *Cantos* identify Confucian and fascist order and frequently encrypt fascist and anti-Semitic themes. The demonic Buddhists and Taoists mirror the Jewish pariahs of Pound's fascist utopia.[38] Flory refuses to accept the fact that the axe used for "clearing" in Canto 97, far from being innocent, tallies with the fascist axe in *Jefferson and/or Mussolini* (pp. 183–84). She claims that four references to the Confucian project of "building light" in the later *Cantos* occur in proximity to "regretful references" to Mussolini (p. 179). In reality these contexts are rife with fascistic and anti-Semitic themes covertly introduced through such texts as *The Sacred Edict of K'ang Hsi,* the Byzantine *Book of the Eparch,* and L.A. Waddell's Aryan supremacist writings on ancient Sumeria.[39]

While the text of *The American Ezra Pound* is often mind-boggling in its argumentation, its dust-jacket blurbs are even more incredible. According to Christine Froula, Flory's "courageous" and "intelligent" work "takes the difficult case of Ezra Pound beyond hero-worship and scapegoating to serious, informed analysis." In exploring Pound's "collaborationist accountability," it does a "valuable service to all those who would face such questions rather than foreclose them." It is impossible to recognize in this description Flory's compound of thin scholarship, evasion, distortion, and special pleading. For A. Walton Litz, this "wise" and "courageous" book "confronts with absolute honesty the most disturbing evidence that can be brought against the poet." Urging "no extenuations," and presenting a "closely reasoned account" of Pound's mental development, Flory "inaugurates a new era in Pound criticism by showing that previously tabooed issues can be discussed openly and responsibly." In fact, Flory has simply added to a long tradition of apologetics which has attempted either to ignore Pound's anti-Semitism and fascism or to reduce them to more or less harmless aberrations and curiosities of his literary corpus. For Louis L. Martz, Flory provides the "first reasonable and convincing explanation" of Pound's "political views and state of mind . . . during his middle years." By what standard could one describe as convincing and reasonable the psychological confabulations which pervade this book?

It is evident that some critics are not yet willing to confront Pound's politics with the logic and objectivity they demand. After all, Pound's anti-Semitism raises the inescapable issue of the relation between his politics, life, and poetry. The question of Pound's collaborationism has become even more urgent in the last two years, during which Heidegger's Nazism has been reexamined, Paul de Man's controversial wartime writings have come to light, and the opening of the T.S. Eliot Library in Boston was marred by reminders of Eliot's anti-Semitism. From this perspective *The American Ezra Pound* is a missed opportunity to elucidate one of the exemplary moral issues of modern times.

Notes

1. Ezra Pound, *"Ezra Pound Speaking": Radio Speeches of World War II*, ed. Leonard W. Doob (Westport, Conn.: Greenwood Press, 1978), p. 153.

2. On this point, see my *The Genealogy of Demons: Anti-Semitism, Fascism, and the Myths of Ezra Pound* (Evanston: Northwestern Univ. Press, 1988), p. 37.

3. For the politics of Orage and *The New Age*, see Alan Robinson, *Symbol to Vortex: Poetry, Politics, Painting, and Ideas, 1885–1914*, pp. 90–107 (New York: St. Martin's, 1985), pp. 90–107; Wallace Martin, *The New Age under Orage: Chapters in English Cultural History* (Manchester: Manchester Univ. Press, 1967), pp. 212–34; G.D.H. Cole, *The World of Labor* (London: G. Bell, 1913), pp. 51–52; Orage, quoted in John Finlay, *Social Credit: The English Origins* (Montreal: McGill-Queens Univ. Press, 1972), p. 69.

4. Pound, *Pavannes and Divagations* (New York: New Directions, 1958), pp. 59, 92, 147; *Selected Prose of Ezra Pound; 1900–1965*, ed. William Cookson (New York: New Directions, 1973), p. 430; *"Ezra Pound Speaking,"* pp. 206, 287, 409; *The Cantos* (New York: New Directions, 1972), p. 443. See also *The Genealogy of Demons*, p. 178.

5. Niles Carpenter, *Guild Socialism: An Historical and Critical Analysis* (New York: D. Appleton, 1922), pp. 27, 212, 217.

6. *Guild Socialism*, pp. 127–28, 218–19.

7. Charles Norman, *Ezra Pound* (New York: Macmillan, 1960), p. 326.

8. *The Genealogy of Demons*, pp. 195–97.

9. Ibid., pp. 197–200.

10. *"Ezra Pound Speaking,"* p. 22.

11. Has not Flory heard of the Pact of Steel? The notion of Mussolini's "nonbelligerency" would have seemed laughable to King Victor Emmanuel, Von Ribbentrop, Serrano Suner, Sir Percy Loraine, William Phillips, the Italian generals and admirals who participated in his Ethiopian and Spanish campaigns, and Count Galeazzo Ciano, Mussolini's son-in-law and foreign minister (1936–43), whose private journal provides abundant evidence. Against the advice and the "unanimous will of the Italian people," Mussolini drove Italy into Hitler's arms in 1940. Mussolini: "To make a people great it is necessary to send them into battle even if you have to kick them in the pants" (11 April 1940); "Five generals are prisoners and one is dead. This is the percentage of

Italians who have military characteristics and those who have none. In the future we shall create an army of professionals, selecting them out of twelve or thirteen million Italians—those in the valley of the Po and in part of central Italy. All the others will be put to work making arms for the warrior aristocracy" (14 Dec. 1940); "The people must know that life is a serious thing and that war is the most serious thing in life" (10 Jan. 1941). In his entry for 8 Jan. 1943, Ciano says of Mussolini: "As usual, he hurled bitter words at the military men who do not make war with the 'fury of the fanatic, but rather with the indifference of the professional.'" See *The Ciano Diaries*, ed. Hugh Gibson (New York: Doubleday, 1945), pp. 122–23, 127, 160, 202–3, 228, 230, 236, 320, 323, 327, 334, 369, 373–74, 416, 502, 568, 581–82. Mussolini's belligerence is also amply attested in F.W. Deakin, *The Brutal Friendship* (New York: Harper and Row, 1962), pp. 15, 20–22, 35. According to Mussolini, it is necessary to keep the Italians "disciplined and in uniform from morning till night. Beat them and beat them and beat them." Again: "Have you ever seen a lamb become a wolf? The Italian race is a race of sheep. Eighteen years are not enough to change them. It takes a hundred and eighty, and maybe a hundred and eighty centuries."

12. See Gregor, *Fascism and Developmental Dictatorship* (Princeton: Princeton Univ. Press, 1979).

13. Zeev Sternhell, *Neither Right nor Left: Fascist Ideology in France*, trans. David Maisel (Berkeley: Univ. of California Press, 1986), pp. 28–29.

14. Pound, *Literary Essays of Ezra Pound*, ed. T.S. Eliot (London: Faber and Faber, 1954), p. 192.

15. *The Cantos*, p. 630.

16. Pound, *Jefferson and/or Mussolini* (New York: Liveright, 1935), pp. 100–101.

17. *The Cantos*, p. 291.

18. Pound, *Selected Prose*, pp. 177, 337.

19. See E. Fuller Torrey, *The Roots of Treason: Ezra Pound and the Secret of St. Elizabeths* (New York: McGraw-Hill, 1984), p. 148.

20. See Seymour Martin Lipset and Earl Raab, *The Politics of Unreason: Right-Wing Extremism in America, 1790–1970* (New York: Harper, 1970), p. 93; Victor Ferkiss, "Populist Influences on American Fascism," *Western Political Quarterly*, 10 (June 1957), p. 354.

21. "Ezra Pound Speaking," pp. 223, 257, 345–46; *The Genealogy of Demons*, pp. 350–51n, 355n.

22. *The Genealogy of Demons*, pp. 53, 260.

23. Ibid., pp. 157–67.

24. Ibid., pp. 77–78, 79–81, 129, 392n.

25. Ibid., pp. 81–83.

26. Leo Lowenthal and Norbert Guterman, *Prophets of Deceit: A Study of the Techniques of the American Agitator* (New York: Harper and Row, 1949), p. 69.

27. Pound, quoted in Noel Stock, *The Life of Ezra Pound* (New York: Avon, 1970), p. 478; "Ezra Pound Speaking," pp. 132, 140, 155.

28. *"Ezra Pound Speaking,"* pp. 133, 140.
29. Ernst Simmel, "Anti-Semitism and Mass Psychopathology," in Ernst Simmel, ed., *Anti-Semitism: A Social Disease* (New York: International Universities Press, 1946), p. 55.
30. *The Genealogy of Demons,* pp. 16–18.
31. Ibid., p. 93.
32. Flory, *Ezra Pound and* The Cantos: *A Record of Struggle* (New Haven: Yale Univ. Press, 1980). See my remarks on this book in *Review,* 6 (1984), pp. 276–80.
33. See G.M. Gilbert, *The Psychology of Dictatorship* (New York: Ronald Press, 1950), pp. 270–71.
34. *Prophets of Deceit,* pp. 5, 99.
35. *"Ezra Pound Speaking,"* pp. 27, 74–75, 79, 86, 157, 194, 196, 199.
36. Ibid., pp. 194, 196, 62.
37. Ibid., p. 331. Pound insinuates that "Jewish butchers" treat "American meat" as "long pig," the term used by South Seas cannibals to describe human flesh.
38. *The Genealogy of Demons,* pp. 123, 125, 127, 129, 262–64, 325.
39. Ibid., pp. 122, 95–105, 262–64, 386n.

Poetic Theorizing in Chaucer's Dream Visions

Michael D. Cherniss

Robert R. Edwards. *The Dream of Chaucer: Representation and Reflection in the Early Narratives.* Durham: Duke University Press, 1989. xvi, 181 pp.

Robert R. Edwards's *The Dream of Chaucer* is an extended critical study of the early dream narratives, the *Book of the Duchess,* the *House of Fame,* and the *Parliament of Fowls,* "a cohesive ensemble" in which Chaucer explores the themes of love and poetic art (p. xi). Edwards develops the primary thesis that these poems operate as mimetic art to convey visionary experience and at the same time self-referentially "represent a sustained reflection on the nature and devices of art" (p. xvi).

In the first three chapters, about two-fifths of the text, Edwards discusses certain elements of the aesthetic and intellectual background from which Chaucer's dream visions emerge. Early in the introduction, Edwards observes that the dream poems are conspicuously literary in character and that their "self-conscious textuality" constitutes a mode of "practical theorizing" in which Chaucer through his narratives dramatizes "the problem of the knower rather than the impossibility of the knowable" (p. 2). These points are developed in later chapters. The three poems "examine a common set of aesthetic problems . . . in dialogue with one another" (p. 3). Chaucer's aesthetic speculation is organized upon the theory of medieval faculty psychology, outlined briefly by Edwards. This tradition of philosophical and medical speculation deals with the relation of the senses to the faculties of imagination, intellect, and memory; it offered Chaucer a way to comprehend or interpret human experience and to discuss the nature of poetic creation. In the *Book of the Duchess* and the *House of Fame*,

> Chaucer uses imagination and memory . . . as topoi for aesthetic speculation. The two categories provide a critical language which allows him to reflect on the nature of poetry and to write his reflection into the poems as part of their narrative action. It is not that Chaucer programmatically reproduces these categories, nor does he shape the poems merely as allegories of imagination and memory. Rather, the poems use the functions of these two internal senses to formulate a series of questions about the truth conditions of the writer's craft. . . . The epistemological problems for the philosophers are taken over as the aesthetic problems of the poet. [pp. 8–9]

Edwards believes that Chaucer's speculations about cognition and poetry lead him to an impasse at the end of the *House of Fame* which he resolves in the *Parliament*. Edwards argues further that Chaucer is developing a poetics that applies to narrative, as opposed to lyric, and so his "critical reflection is embedded in literary representation," whether such narrative be history or fiction (p. 14).

Edwards's next chapter elaborates his idea of Chaucer's "practice of theory": as a self-conscious poet Chaucer raises questions about the aesthetic conceptions of his poems within the narratives themselves. For Chaucer, "thinking about poetry is inseparable from writing poetry; reflection is inscribed in creation" (p. 18). Self-referential, intertextual citation and the use of poetic emblems are the two forms this practice of theorizing takes. The unity of Chaucer's vision is suggested by patterns of citation and allusion that reflect his engagement with key issues throughout these early poems and link them to one another, as likewise do narrative elements, "often visual or iconic images," here called "poetic emblems" (p. 23). "The dream itself is the most powerful emblem for poetic creation" (p. 25). Edwards further suggests that Chaucer made use of the doctrines of poetic composition found in late medieval *artes poeticae*, particularly their approaches to invention, in his "deep and thoroughgoing engagement with his sources" (p. 31). Chaucer's "strategy of translation, like that of rhetorical invention, depends upon an interpretive reading of the sources" and "serves the aim of cultural appropriation and definition" (p. 33).

In the following chapter Edwards discusses "how the narrator operates within the textual economy" of these poems (p. 41). He treats first of all the much-debated question of whether, in any or all of the vision poems, Chaucer's narrator is portrayed consistently in order to provide a stable point of view, giving the reader a sense that a central consciousness contains and unifies the dream experience. Edwards's position could be stated more clearly. He cites with apparent agreement recent critics who argue that the narrator is "radically unstable," less a realistic character than a rhetorical device, noting lapses in "consistent characterization" in the poems (p. 43). He qualifies his own view, however: "the persona is artificial, but it is not arbitrary" (p. 45). Chaucer employs his narrator to create a new kind of perspectival art in English verse. He "uses self-conscious presentation as a means to establish a new form of narrative, one based on a sense of poetic indeterminacy. . . . What [the narrator] describes is contained within the figure he presents of himself, and it is contingent to the same extent as the poetic 'I'" (p. 47).

Chaucer's narrator further provides a traditional authenticating voice for his narrative and locates it within a literary, textual tradition. Edwards finds the prototypes for Chaucer's persona in the *Roman de la Rose* and, secondarily, in Machaut's *dits*, poems which combine subjective narrative with a sense of the poem as text. As a court poet, Chaucer participates in the courtly discourse of social life, but "in the guise of the failed lover who still remains a poet. His persona at once achieves inclusion and distance—a definition of self that allows the poet to participate in society and at the same time a sign of his difference from the circles in which he travels. . . . The roles of initiate and outsider interpenetrate" (pp. 58–59). In the dream narratives, then, Chaucer manages through his persona to dissociate his role as poet engaged in his craft from the traditional social role of the poet as courtly lover.

It is important at this point that we understand clearly Edwards's view of the nature and function of Chaucer's narrative persona and his reasons for adopting this view. To this end, I should like to consider briefly a recent essay on Chaucer's narrator by John Finlayson.[1] Finlayson argues against what he considers (inaccurately, I believe) to be the prevailing critical view that Chaucer's dream narrators are dramatic characters with distinctive, realistic personalities. Recognizing the influence of the *Roman de la Rose* upon Chaucer, he examines the various roles and functions of that poem's narrator-Lover and concludes that they are indeed multiple and discontinuous. Thus, the consistency of the Lover is clearly subordinate to his shifting allegorical functions. Likewise, Finlayson finds that Chaucer's narrators play a variety of roles, disappear for long stretches during their narratives, serve linear and disjunctive functions, and so should not be understood as consistent characters in whom one might find the "sentence" of the poems. Finlayson, I would argue, has simply formulated the "problem" of the narrator badly. He is probably right to reject as inappropriate modern notions of "character" in dealing with medieval dream narrators, but that is not the important point. He has somehow conflated the idea of a "realistic" narrator with the largely unrelated idea that a first-person narrator might be the centrally important unifying consciousness in the poem he narrates. The Lover in the *Roman* functions as its central focus from beginning to end, despite dramatic inconsistencies. There is no good reason to assume, on the basis of an absence of dramatic consistency or "realism," that Chaucer's personae cannot be the central consciousness through which meaning is conveyed. Whether these narrators are autobiographical or dramatically consistent are questions of a different order.

Edwards, like Finlayson, acknowledges inconsistencies in function and tone in Chaucer's personae, but he cannot reject the persona as the central consciousness through which we receive the substance of the narrative. Rather, he appears to want it both ways: the narrator is neither a simple mimetic device who retells a dream as an autonomous fiction nor is he "a thoroughly consistent narrator whose performance is the metafiction that the poem represents, . . . the object of representation and therefore the source of artistic unity" (p. 44). Nonetheless, this narrator is presented by Edwards as a persona who has certain clear connections to the historical Geoffrey Chaucer. In the discussions of the dream poems in the following chapters Edwards quite clearly treats the persona as, at least to some degree, the central mediating consciousness between poem and audience, and so as the subject of the poems. Moreover, given his thesis that these poems contain the poet-narrator's speculations upon the art of poetry, Edwards must treat this narrator, in all three poems, as some version of the same poet, Geoffrey Chaucer.

In the next three chapters Edwards discusses Chaucer's dream visions in their probable order of composition. Historically, Chaucer's first long narrative poem, the *Book of the Duchess,* is clearly connected to the death of Blanche of Lancaster in 1368, but whatever its specific public purpose might have been, the "indwelling and complementary purpose is to examine and reflect on the poet's art" (p. 66). Chaucer's use of his poetic sources here implies "an active poetic dialogue with his contemporaries and predecessors" in which "Chaucer stresses poetic subjectivity, for it is both a technique for point of view narrative and a starting point for aesthetic creation" (pp. 67–68). The opening of the poem, derived from Froissart to express the narrator's mental state, reflects both poetic subjectivity and authority. The narrator's "'Ydel thoght' represents a process of imagination isolated from the external world and specifically isolated from questions of good and evil" (p. 70). He seeks a remedy for (or escape from) this subjective isolation in the fictional world of the narrative; as Edwards interprets this passage (lines 44–61), the function of the "fables" is "to introduce a formal order of imagination that supplants the 'sorwful ymagynacioun' . . . and 'fantasies'" (p. 72). Chaucer portrays "the book as a means of psychological and moral rescue" and as "a means for reorganizing subjectivity, for abandoning the circularity of purely internal images in favor of a richer source of imaginative power" (pp. 72–73). But despite Edwards's claims, Chaucer's lines at this point do not appear to suggest that his "mased" narrator either understands his confused condition or expects his book to provide the sort of therapy Edwards posits.

Ovid's tale of Ceyx and Alcyone "describes a bond of love particularly suited to the rhetoric of elegy and the social occasion of

Chaucer's writing. It is a story of faithful married love, and it dramatizes the need for comfort which brackets the *Book of the Duchess* in the figures of the narrator and the bereaved knight" (p. 74). Edwards's discussion of the intertextual relations of Chaucer's story to its sources, however, focuses upon its implications concerning the nature of poetic representation rather than its thematic content. Thus, the realm of Morpheus becomes "the poetic emblem of self-enclosed imagination" (p. 77) and Morpheus himself the product of (Alcyone's ?) aesthetic imagination. "Morpheus represents the capacity to create an independent fiction within a social and literary language" (p. 82). Edwards ignores the narrator's response to the story he has read (lines 221–90) to focus the remainder of this chapter upon the exchanges between the narrator and the man in black which, he argues, "combine the language of narrative description and aesthetic speculation" (p. 82). He takes the narrator's attempt to "fynde a tale/To hym" (lines 536–38) as an attempt to divert the knight from his sorrow by stories, formal structures of the imagination, while the knight refuses "to displace sorrow through imaginative equations" (p. 83). The dialogue "has to do with the relation of language to experience" and within it "the adequacy of discourse remains at issue" (pp. 83–84). Courtly discourse fails both figures, and finally any pattern of consolation appears unfulfilled. The knight "remains in the present, constrained rather than animated by the realization of death," in a state of moral and emotional stasis which "derives from the very ethical quality that White embodies. She is a paragon of social virtue and conduct, but by defining her through the resources of Machaut's *dits* Chaucer inevitably leaves her bound by human contingency" (p. 91).

At the beginning of the following chapter, on the *House of Fame*, Edwards reviews his observations concerning the *Duchess* and in doing so provides clear links between the two poems. Chaucer "represents the beginnings of his narrative art in the play of imagination and memory." The *Duchess* "defines and reflects on aspects of its narrative art in the very process of creating it." Chaucer "seems to be suggesting from the outset that sense and imagination must lead toward a form of rational memory, memory which preserves the impressions of imagination and subjective experience according to ontological categories and ethical qualities. But Chaucer's first narrative poem does not make a complete shift from sense to intellect." The portrayal of White is "constrained artistically by the limits of courtly language," and "Chaucer's objective at the end of the poem is that of the courtly maker," to make a poem of his dream experience (pp. 93–94). The "strategy of indirection" through which issues emerge in the *Duchess* "is largely abandoned" in the *House of Fame* as "Chaucer brings the poetic issues into the foreground. His concern is to explore the nature of language, the relation of signs to truth, the functions of memory and authority as determinants of aesthetic representation." In *Fame* "poetry itself emerges as an act of memory" and "the hypotheses about language and poetry that Chaucer develops . . . are irresolvably problematic," amounting to "a poetic dead end" (p. 94).

The discussion of the narrator's mental state at the beginning of the *House of Fame* "implicitly develops the analogy between dreams and poetry" (p. 95). His inability to determine the cause of his dreams reflects the general problem of knowledge as Chaucer focuses "on discrepancies and discontinuities within perception, hence on the truth value of aesthetic representation" (pp. 95–96). The "Proem" raises questions which intentionally go unanswered, and the narrator's prayer for some "goode" (lines 1, 58) which will supersede his confusions, a "sublimation of sense to intellect" (p. 99), cannot be attained within the poem. The uniqueness of the narrator's dream (lines 59–63) implies that there can be "no firm ground at all"; the dream itself "exists poetically as a structure of memory" (p. 99). The glass temple in which the dreamer finds himself is a sort of theatre of the memory where the past is in some measure transformed as it is recalled in the present. In the desert outside, the narrator discovers "the extent to which vision and sound are convertible" and he "prays to escape what the imagination has created: 'Fro fantome and illusion/Me save'." "Chaucer's aesthetic concern is with the experience of mental life through images and sound" (p. 102). At this point his means for escaping the aesthetic impasse of the desert are expressed by the eagle and the apostrophe to "Thought." Chaucer adapts these figures from Dante in such a way as to treat memory as the source of poetic invention, as a storehouse of images.

The ostensible goal of the journey with the eagle—to learn about love—gives way to the prior task of examining how one comes to learn about love. The teaching here "concerns itself with the conditions of knowing, and poetic discourse is both the instrument and object of inquiry" (p. 107). The eagle's discourse outlines a physics of speech as he proposes that the design of Nature governs language, whose conservation depends paradoxically on increase. The speech arriving at Fame's palace "marks the radical separation of signs from what they signify.... It escapes further into a realm of autonomous discourse" (p. 108). The eagle's account of language is "a consciously rhetorical gesture ... a mode of imaginative discourse where natural philosophy supplies the materials of poetic invention" (p. 109). Moreover, the narrator finally "suggests that empirical knowledge ... is embedded in imagination and texts" (p. 110). Geffrey's destination, Fame's palace, is a "poetic emblem of memory and image-making" where "abstract concerns about the truth value of language and poetry take literal shape" (pp. 111–12). Memory has a crucial function in this world where names come to stand for language and poetry, and where the mutability of language and poetry is emphasized.

Fame's palace "overtly connects memory and poetry" (p. 114); in this memory house, poetry is given physical presence and conserved by multiplication. Chaucer emphasizes the flux within memory: "language and story are amplified by the physics of speech, but this distortion only magnifies a prior and essential disjunction between words and things" (p. 117). Fame's judgments, like dreams, have no particular causes; they are capricious. The House of Rumor likewise connects the propositions that "language, including poetry, operates under a law of transformation" and that "there is a radical separation of words from things" (p. 117). Edwards apparently finds no important conceptual or thematic difference between the two emblematic houses. Throughout the poem, he says, Chaucer has been working toward a formal definition of poetry based upon imagination and memory:

The definition, *consciously or not*, has been working all along within an incomplete model. Imagination and memory are inadequate by themselves; their power extends to images and sensation, and they require a third element—namely the intellect, which provides an access to ontological categories and ethical values and thereby offers a way of connecting words and things. . . . *Chaucer discovers* that if language and poetry are to foster a knowledge of things, they must embody the same faculties as the mind itself—imagination, memory, and intellect. In other words, he learns the need for a symmetry between the mind and poetry, between the locus and instrument of knowledge. [p. 118, italics added]

Chaucer's formalistic account of aesthetic creation lacks a "differential of exclusion," "a poetic equivalent to the intellect," leaving linguistic representation "arbitrary and problematic" (p. 119). The ending of the poem follows logically from Chaucer's developing hypothesis: the man of great authority is an ironic figure "because anything he might say within the system of discourse that Chaucer has conceived would necessarily be subverted" (p. 120). Chaucer has arrived at a philosophical dead end; "no linguistic utterance, discursive or poetic, can claim a truth value; linguistic representation has no ontological status in Geffrey's dream" (p. 120). But by locating poetry within nature, by recognizing that it is part of the world it seeks to describe and is founded upon a direct perceptual acquaintance with experience, Chaucer points the way beyond his impasse.

Chaucer's *Parliament of Fowls* represents the first consolidation of his narrative art and poetics, according to Edwards. The self-defeating line of aesthetic speculation in the earlier narratives explores the ways in which memory and imagination create images that function as mimetic equivalents to experience. Their formalistic approach "amounts to a poetic thought-experiment conducted within the resources of subjective, courtly narrative" (p. 124). Imagination and memory do not determine the status of poetic creation "as an act of knowing or establish images as reliable modes of representation. Chaucer's experiment . . . is to try to define poetic creation through an *intentionally* defective model of cognition" in which "something equivalent to the intellect is suppressed" (p. 124, italics added). The *Parliament*, however, addresses the problem of the intellect through its narrator's search for literary authorities in order to define the thematic substance of his poetry and through his discovery of the relationship between poetic creation and erotic desire. In the *Parliament*, the intellect becomes "a topos for poetic matter and critical reflection alike" which runs through the entire narrative (p. 125). The narrator's reading of old books is "a symbolic and reflective search for a precise referent, an order of knowledge outside the observer, 'a certeyn thing'" (p. 128). Following A. C. Spearing and J. A. W. Bennett, Edwards argues that this quest for knowledge about love unifies the sections of the *Parliament* and leads to a point of synthesis and an expression of harmony, by examining Chaucer's handling of his sources.[2]

Chaucer's summary of Cicero's *Somnium Scipionis* is a revision of the original dream narrative in which Chaucer's omissions and emphases accent a providential outlook and suggest "an inclusive notion of government and divine ordering" (p. 133). However, he does not find the "certeyn thing" he seeks here. In the traditional garden of love the narrator next encounters the figure of Venus. Chaucer's treatment of this figure from Boccaccio "foregrounds the erotic description in a common viewpoint of human experience," but offers no overt moralizing. Venus' temple "is an object of inquiry for Chaucer" (p. 135). The goddess Nature, whom the narrator next encounters, is "a version of the heavenly Venus" found in Alan of Lille's *De planctu naturae* and like Venus "is the object of knowledge and not a simple projection of desire" (p. 136). "Chaucer discovers in Alan's presentation of Nature a framework for grasping the nature of love..., a substantial unity that contains and makes intelligible the diversity of erotic experience" (p. 137). He adopts the figure of Nature from Alan rather than from Jean De Meun; her work proceeds from reason, she is situated within a precisely defined hierarchy, and she recognizes "the abiding difference between divine simplicity and the multiplicity of creation" (p. 139). "Nature's multiplicity, as Alan articulates it, responds to the lesson that the *Parliament*'s narrator learns through observation and reading—namely, that human behavior is diverse yet intelligible" (p. 140).

Thus, Alan's Nature offers a way to define the narrator's "certeyn thing." Alan's doctrine of love is "a category of experience that both informs and resides in creation" and "the universal that renders the particulars of appetite and desire intelligible." The abstract principle of Nature gives coherence to the particulars of experience, "the accidents of natural desire" embodied in the social order of the birds (p. 141).

Finally, Edwards observes that Chaucer found in Alan the theme of the equivalence of procreation and writing, "a model for connecting erotics and poetics" (p. 143). A language of creation and fertility informs poetic invention as well as love in the *Parliament.* The "intuition of congruence and continuity . . . marks the conceptual breakthrough of Chaucer's early narrative poems. Chaucer has been able to formulate a general theme for his narratives out of the particulars of subjective experience and antecedent texts. In the theme of love his poetry locates an object of knowledge that remains intelligible despite the variety of its formations" (p. 145). He has also "discovered the powerful analogy between this subject matter and his own art" (p. 146).

In his final chapter, "A Chaucerian Prospect: From 'wonder thynges' to 'olde appreved stories'," Edwards attempts in brief compass to trace the impact of Chaucer's critical position, developed in the early narratives, upon his later works. Chaucer's early narratives evolve "from a poetry based on radical subjectivity toward one founded on what can be described as a modified, pragmatic realism" (p. 148). Edwards finds this shift in the poet's outlook signaled in his own reading of the last lines of the *Parliament,* a reading, it must be said, open to serious objections. He then traces some of the transitions he perceives as occurring from the early to the middle and later poems. Chaucer's shift from dream vision to sequential narrative embodies a move "from a poetics of interiority toward an understanding of social context and a grounding in historical experience" (p. 153). The past itself becomes "an object of practical reasoning" which Chaucer understands "through categories and particulars" (p. 154). The space which opens between past and present thus becomes "a domain of moral speculation." History is "a realm of ethical deliberation" independent of any particular doctrine (p. 156). Chaucer's early theorizing leads him to "a deepened and enhanced sense of the way poetry inhabits the world" (p. 158).

As the foregoing commentary should suggest, Edwards has produced an extended, sophisticated analysis of a well-defined segment of Chaucer's poetry. He is to be commended for the overall coherence of a series of close readings and carefully developed arguments, and for the clarity of his presentation of each point in his larger thesis. His chapters and subdivisions of chapters are clearly defined; strategically placed summary statements, reformulations, and reiterations of previous lines of argument (and outlines of what is to follow) provide valuable guidance through the book's complexities. *The Dream of Chaucer* is certainly not easy reading; Edwards's consideration for his reader helps to keep the path reasonably clear. Evidence drawn from medieval sources to provide background and support arguments is carefully selected and apposite. Edwards's citations of modern critics, more often to corroborate his own views than to suggest opposing or alternative ones, demonstrate his extensive familiarity with a growing body of material.

Edwards's narrowly controlled focus upon certain related aspects of Chaucer's earlier dream visions, while obviously not a bad thing insofar as brevity and coherence are concerned, may cause the reader, and especially the specialist reader, moments of discomfort. His predominant concern remains throughout Chaucer's practice of aesthetic reflection, his "practical theorizing," and secondarily his assimilation of his literary sources, his "textuality." At the outset Edwards asserts the inadequacy of earlier approaches through literary convention and genre, and in practice he leaves questions about thematic and structural aspects of the poems largely unaddressed, unless these coincide with or overlap his primary concerns. Thus Edwards consistently offers the reader provocative, often original readings of the poems as reflections of Chaucer's aesthetic preoccupations, but otherwise leaves gaps which the reader might wish filled. For example, he apparently agrees with earlier critics that the *Book of the Duchess* might in some way be intended as a poem of consolation, but he never directly considers consolation as a primary theme. Again, the *Parliament*, it is generally agreed, presents "love" as its subject, and Edwards concurs, but he offers little that has not already been said about Chaucer's treatment of this subject. Whatever it may be that the poet wishes to express about love tends to be buried under Edwards's discussion of love as a topic in Chaucer's "practical theorizing" about poetry. The shifting of emphasis toward Chaucer's aesthetics, in other words, at times results in a sense that Edwards is not addressing the central issues in the poems under consideration, and that he is building upon earlier interpretations rather than offering wholly new ones.

In practice, Edwards does not entirely ignore insights into Chaucer's poetry based upon literary convention and genre, but his focus (and some preconceptions related to it) tends to push such considerations to the peripherae of his discussion. His title is significant: it declares his subject to be Chaucer's "early narratives" rather than "early dream visions" or something of the sort, and he devotes a subdivision of his introduction to distinguishing the aesthetics of medieval narrative from those of lyric (pp. 11–15). He deals with dreams and dreaming where this topic is germane to his argument, most obviously where Chaucer raises it, as he does in the Proem to the *House of Fame*, but in general he ignores questions about dream vision as a specific kind of poetry with its own conventions and assumptions. For example, questions concerning the shared assumptions of poet and audience when a poem is presented as the account of a dream receive little attention, as do conventions of the portrayal of the dreamer-narrator. Relationships between dreamer and dream receive superficial treatment, and Edwards never really considers the possibility of dream as visionary experience or revelation, as privileged inner illumination. He treats Chaucer's dreams, it is true, as part of the narrator's "experience," but dream and waking experience are scarcely distinguished in the discussion; qualitatively they seem all of a piece. But if waking experience, dreams, and reading books are all equally fodder for the imagination of Chaucer's narrator, one wonders why Chaucer has chosen the dream vision form and why he manipulates his materials outside and within the dreams as he does.

Edwards's focus upon the aesthetic implications of Chaucer's dream poems produces omissions and occasional distorted readings of lines and passages. For example, and as mentioned earlier, in the *Book of the Duchess* the narrator's jocular response to the story of Ceyx and Alcyone (lines 221–69) is passed over in silence, as are the hunt, the whelp, and the forest landscape in the dream (lines 344–442). Are these details mere coloring? In the same poem the narrator, after his initial exchange with the knight, says "Anoon ryght I gan fynde a tale/To hym" (lines 536–37); Edwards comments, "The narrator attempts to discover the source of sorrow in terms that recall his own shift from distraction to formal structures of imagination" (p. 83). He must here take "tale" to mean "story"; either the narrator wishes to tell or be told a formal story like the one he sought out in his distracted waking state. But the Riverside Edition (Edwards's standard text for this study) glosses "tale" here as "something to say."[3] These lines probably mean no more than "I tried to find something to say to him in order to find out more of his thoughts."

In the *House of Fame*, Edwards treats the narrator, "Geffrey," as an observer of the operation of imagination and memory as these faculties, through language, create poetry. Midway through his tour of the land of Fame and Rumor someone ("oon") asks Geffrey if he has come to "han fame," and he denies this in emphatic terms: "Sufficeth me, as I were ded,/That no wight have my name in honde./I wot myself best how y stonde" (lines 1876–78). This passage perhaps has no bearing on Edwards's argument, but one would like to know whether he thinks it irrelevant, and why. Edwards takes the final lines of the *Parliament* to signal "a shift in the narrator's object" from a search for absolute knowledge to one for practical, ethical action. "Chaucer gives up the 'certeyn thing' for a kind of partial knowledge ('som thyng') with moral consequences lived in experience ('to fare/The bet')" (p. 149). This of course supports Edwards's argument, but these few words (and the surrounding lines) cannot support the burden placed upon them. The phrases "a thing" and "som thyng" might both mean "any thing," and "moral consequences" are nowhere implied here. One might with equal plausibility read these lines as an indication that the narrator has returned to his original objective, reading to find something that will help him to understand love better.

Neither one nor all of the above examples could, of course, refute Edwards's carefully wrought argument; they are offered here only to demonstrate that the poems or parts of them may at times have become the servants of their thesis-master. Edwards is scarcely unique among Chaucerians in sifting and selecting from the poems to make his own case. Such details raise small questions, but Edwards's larger argument raises a larger question which I would pose here. He has presented a scenario, a sort of inner biography, of the development of Chaucer's poetic theory, according to which Chaucer employed the topic of medieval faculty psychology to write his way toward the resolution of certain epistemological and ontological questions about the nature, function, and validity of poetry. In the *Duchess* and *Fame* he both presents and speculates about a poetry based upon imagination and memory. Such poetry turns out to be inadequate, problematic, and incapable of attaining "truth value" because it lacks the faculty of intellect or its poetic equivalent. Chaucer thus tries "to define poetic creation through an intentionally defective model of cognition" (p. 124). Chaucer resolves this problem by writing the intellect into the *Parliament;* embedded in the narrator's search for knowledge about love, the intellect discovers the unity behind the diversity of experience.

This seems a very neat, orderly thesis—perhaps a bit too neat. Why, we may ask, should Geoffrey Chaucer have devoted more than ten years of his poetic career to worrying over a set of aesthetic and cognitive problems that he must from the beginning have known the answer to? For if Chaucer in the two earlier poems employed an *intentionally* defective model of cognition, then surely he knew that it was defective, and why it would prove defective in its application, and what was needed to render it effective. Chaucer did not invent the model of faculty psychology he appears to be using, and one doubts that he got it from a book with a few crucial pages missing. Edwards would argue that as a poet Chaucer was somehow compelled to arrive at the resolution to his speculations by incorporating them into his poems; "thinking about poetry is inseparable from writing poetry," as he says

(p. 18). But such a formulation seems evasive; it makes Chaucer's critical speculations sound rather like automatic writing. Edwards's individual discussions of the early poems seem more plausible and more satisfactory than his book taken as a whole.

Finally, it would be well to mention a few recent works which might profitably be read along with Edwards's book. As noted earlier, Edwards appears to have considered most of the relevant criticism available to him as he wrote this book, which bears the date 1989 but must have been completed somewhat earlier. I would judge from the citations in the text and in the endnotes that work on the printer's copy of this book was probably completed early in 1987.[4] My own book, *Boethian Apocalypse: Studies in Middle English Vision Poetry* (Pilgrim Books, 1987), is cited in a note; I shall risk the appearance of immodesty to mention that, although my approach to medieval vision poetry is rather different from his, my chapters on the *Duchess* and the *Parliament* do offer views which either complement or coincide with his arguments. Kathryn Lynch's *The High Medieval Dream Vision: Poetry, Philosophy, and Literary Form* (Stanford University Press, 1988) deals extensively with the influence of faculty psychology on selected vision poems of the twelfth and thirteenth centuries, as well as on Gower's *Confessio Amantis*. Lynch does not discuss Chaucer's dream visions, which she mentions as being "significantly different" in their views of the world and art from the works she does discuss, but anyone interested in Edwards's subject would want to read her book as well. J. Stephen Russell's book *The English Dream Vision: Anatomy of a Form* (Ohio State University Press, 1988) offers a quite unusual approach to the dream vision, but interestingly his discussions of the *Duchess* and *Fame* draw conclusions about their themes which are very close to those suggested by Edwards.

Despite the reservations about *The Dream of Chaucer* expressed above, and also perhaps because of them, one must conclude by recommending this book most highly to all serious students of Geoffrey Chaucer and of the medieval dream vision. Edwards's observations concerning Chaucer's poetics, his transformation of his literary sources, and his compositional strategies are never less than thought-provoking, and they are often quite persuasive. This book is a valuable and exciting contribution to our continuing discussion of the works of our greatest medieval English poet; its conclusions may be challenged, but they cannot be ignored by those who would enter this discussion.

Notes

1. John Finlayson, "The *Roman de la Rose* and Chaucer's Narrator," *Chaucer Review,* 24 (1990), 187–210.

2. A. C. Spearing, *Medieval Dream Poetry* (Cambridge: Cambridge Univ. Press, 1976). J. A. W. Bennett, The Parliament of Fowls: *An Intepretation* (Oxford: Clarendon Press, 1957).

3. *The Riverside Chaucer,* ed. Larry D. Benson, 3d ed. (Boston: Houghton Mifflin, 1987), p. 1296.

4. There are citations to three items dated 1987 and three dated 1986, while the endnotes contain references to a second book by Edwards dated 1989, two other items dated 1987, and three dated 1986. The text cited for Chaucer is the *Riverside Chaucer,* noted just above, which appeared early in 1987.

Periodical Verse of the American Revolution

J. A. Leo Lemay

Martin Kallich. *British Poetry and the American Revolution: A Bibliographical Survey of Books and Pamphlets, Journals and Magazines, Newspapers, and Prints 1755–1800.* 2 vols. Troy, New York: The Whitston Publishing Co., 1988. xxxviii, 746; 747–1731 pp.

Martin Kallich's important contribution to our knowledge of American Revolutionary verse lists and gives more reprintings of Revolutionary periodical poems than any other single bibliography. It contains a wonderful amount of basic information. The arrangement is chronological by year, with three subdivisions within each year. First Kallich registers books and pamphlets of verse, then chronicles verse within periodicals, and finally lists verse in prints. The arrangement within the three divisions is alphabetical by author, or, if the author is unknown, by title. The arrangement makes sense for books and pamphlets, where the authors are usually known and titles are invariably present. The arrangement is foolish for periodical verse (which comprises approximately eighty percent of the total bibliography), for the authors are rarely known and titles are often vague ("A New Song" appears dozens of times). For periodical verse, either an alphabetical arrangement by first line or a chronological arrangement would have been superior.

Within the individual entries, the catalogue number is given first; then the author, if known—but most items are anonymous. Next comes the title, but, as Kallich points out on page xxxiv, occasionally the same poem has different titles; and occasionally poems have no title. Kallich notes that first lines are the best method of identifying poems. (The first line can, however, in the case of songs, simply indicate the tune.) The first line and the number of lines are then listed. Next to last comes the source(s) in which the poem has been found. Alas, when newspaper dates give two choices (e.g., April 17–24), Kallich misleadingly gives the first date rather than the second (the second is when the newspaper actually appeared and is the standard short reference); fortunately, newspapers in the late 1770s and in the 1780s just give the latter date. If a poem appeared in more than one periodical, Kallich lists the periodicals alphabetically, though a chronological listing would have been more useful. Finally, Kallich provides the meter of stanzaic pattern, and he gives a brief summary or the poem, usually naming the important people and topics that appear therein.

Surprisingly, Kallich makes few references to previous standard bibliographies and anthologies. The only bibliography that appears to have been systematically used is Stephens/George (for the prints). Kallich includes Bristol, Evans, and Sabin in his list of references (pp. xxxii–xxxiii), but he evidently checked them only for separately printed items. Perhaps he did not realize that periodicals often reprinted poems from broadsides, pamphlets, and books. He appears not to have used the *National Index* (NI) or Ford (all brief references in this review are supplied in the appended bibliography). Only sporadic references to the standard anthology, Frank Moore's *Songs and Ballads of the American Revolution* appeared. The most famous poems and songs were usually not identified as such. No references to Anderson, Crum, Gaston, or to my own *Calendar* appeared. Either Kallich prepared his bibliography in innocence of almost all previous scholarly work on the subject or he did not want to acknowledge the previous scholarship. Though existing scholarship frequently supplements Kallich, in many cases Kallich adds excellent information to the materials published by Frank Moore, James C. Gaston, and others. Too bad that Kallich does not point out his scholarly advances.

I wish Kallich had also given occasional notes about the quality (or lack thereof) of the verse. Kallich frequently omits the author's initials or pseudonym, and he often omits the poem's dateline. These bits of information are essential clues for identi-

Periodical Verse of the American Revolution 151

fying a poet and should have been included. Kallich also is careless regarding the tunes for songs. Sometimes he omits tunes and sometimes omits key refrains (like "Derry down") that identify tunes.

Kallich provides three indices: an author index, pp. 1504–40; a subject and theme index, pp. 1541–1704; and a genre index, pp. 1705–1731. Amazingly, he omitted a first-line index. Since titles vary from printing to printing, since many poems have no title, and since almost all poems were published anonymously, the most reliable way of finding a poem is by a first-line index. The omission of a first-line index of poetry greatly lessens the value and usefulness of Kallich's bibliography.

Reproduced from a typescript, the bibliography measures an unwieldy 8½ x 11 inches, but the type occupies only 6½ x 7½ inches. Some 2½ inches of space on the bottom of every page and nearly an inch at the top are blank. The layout wastes space and paper. If well-designed, the book would have been a substantial single volume. The numbering system makes good sense: the year, a hyphen, and then the item number (e.g., 77-1 refers to the first entry in Kallich for the year 1777). Kallich examined all of the most famous magazines of the period, and a good selection of the newspapers from England, Ireland, and Scotland. He ignored, however, some important newspapers. Iona and Peter Opie found an early song to the tune of "Yankee Doodle" in *The Bath Chronicle* for 21 November 1776, thereby identifying that paper as one to be examined for its periodical verse, but Kallich did not include it (see p. xxxvi).

"The Liberty Song," one of the best-known American Revolutionary songs, turns up as Kallich no. 68-95 (hereafter I will use the abbreviation "K," plus the number, to refer to Kallich items). Kallich valuably lists seven English printings, notes that the song was written by John Dickinson, says it first appeared in the *Boston Gazette* for 18 July 1768, and claims that it was "the first American patriotic song." He rarely gives references for his information. I suppose that an English printing gave its source as the *Boston Gazette,* and I suppose that he recalled that the song was by Dickinson. Had, however, he consulted Frank Moore's standard *Songs and Ballads of the American Revolution,* 36-40, Kallich would have seen that two of the nine stanzas were written by Dickinson's friend, Dr. Arthur Lee, and that a "revised" version of the song appeared in the *Pennsylvania Chronicle,* 11 July 1768—earlier, of course, than the supposed "first" publication he cites from the *Boston Gazette.* I might add that the earliest version of the poem appeared originally in the *Pennsylvania Chronicle* for 4 July 1768, and that Justin Winsor published a good account of the song and its imitations in his *Narrative and Critical History of America,* 6: 86-87. Kallich does not cross-list K74-173, a reprint; the latter, however, cites the former. I cannot imagine why Kallich calls it the "first American patriotic song." In his well-known note on songs as patriot propaganda, Arthur M. Schlesinger lists numerous earlier songs. Perhaps Kallich believes that no patriotic American song could exist before 1765, when Revolution against England became a possibility; but Schlesinger lists several before this one. My own nominee for the "first American patriotic song" would be "New England's Annoyances," a New England folksong of approximately 1643.

"Come Shake your dull noodles, ye pumpkins, and bawl," is the first line of a Loyalist satire (K68-96) of "The Liberty Song." Kallich cites two English printings and points out that it first appeared in a *Supplement* to the *Boston Gazette* of 26 September 1768. He does not note its appearance in Frank Moore's *Songs and Ballads of the American Revolution,* 41-43. No one has previously pointed out that the *Boston Gazette* of 26 September published a letter from Henry Hulton to Edes & Gill, the *Gazette*'s editors, saying that he had heard they intended to publish a parody of "The Liberty Song" under his name and that if they did so, it would be "at your peril." Publication of the letter asserted his authorship. Henry Hulton, a well-known writer and commissioner of customs, wrote the excellent Loyalist parody of "The Liberty Song."

Kallich's annotation for "The Liberty Song" (but not for Hulton's parody) notes that a parody of Hulton's parody appeared. K68-85, "The Parody Parodized; or The Massachusetts Song of Liberty," locates six English reprintings, and says that it originally appeared in the *Boston Gazette,* 6 October 1768. Kallich does not note its reprinting as a broadside by Nathaniel Coverly,

Periodical Verse of the American Revolution 153

Jr. (see Ford, "Isaiah Thomas Collection," no. 167) or its reprinting in Frank Moore's *Songs and Ballads*, 44-47. John Adams's diary entry for Monday, 14 August 1768, reveals that the author was Benjamin Church, a Harvard graduate, who later became an English spy.

Church's *Massachusetts Song of Liberty* is not to be confused with *The New Massachusetts Liberty Song* (Boston: 1770), E42135, NI 579B, which begins "That Seat of Science, Athens, and Earth's great Mistress Rome." Since Kallich has seemingly done no research in the archives or manuscript depositories of England or America, I would not expect him to know that a parody of it circulated in manuscript: the "Massachusetts Liberty Song Parodized," beginning "In Bedlam's lofty Numbers discordiant Yankies sing." A copy at the New York Historical Society is written on the back of *The New Massachusetts Liberty Song*, and another manuscript copy exists in the Historical Society of Pennsylvania.

I was chagrined to find that K75-25, though citing Oscar Sonneck and Samuel Foster Damon, nevertheless said the song "plainly demeans the Yankee New Englander as a coward." Kallich misread Sonneck (1909) and Damon (1959), and he clearly did not read my piece on Yankee Doodle (1976). Since Kallich knew that the song dated back to the capture of Louisburg in 1746, he should have realized that the verses are ironic and satirical. K78-247, the supposed epitaph for the regicide John Bradshaw, is actually by Benjamin Franklin and concludes with the lines that Jefferson adopted as his personal motto: "Rebellion to Tyrants is Obedience to God!" It first appeared in the *Pennsylvania Evening Post*, 14 December 1775.

Though I recognized perhaps one hundred poems in Kallich and could furnish random notes on them, I decided to see what information would be revealed if I compiled a first-line index to Kallich's volume I and looked for the poems in a fairly systematic way, as I had done for the poems appearing in my *Calendar*. (If I ever finish a "Calendar of Revolutionary American Periodical Verse," I will want to use Kallich's volumes systematically; and there is no way to do so without compiling a first-line index to his bibliography.) My examination of the Kallich poems was, however, comparatively cursory, for I did not examine the primary works of the Revolutionary authors, nor did I examine most of the anthologies cited in my *Calendar*. On the other hand, since I have been working (if desultorily) on a continuation of the *Calendar* for the Revolutionary period, 1766–1783, I have analyzed several manuscript commonplace books of Revolutionary verse and added their first lines to my ongoing first-line card index of colonial American poetry.

Despite not availing himself systematically of the scholarship, Kallich sometimes identifies the authors of the anonymous poems because he has read their collected verses.

The most important category of information revealed by comparing first-line indices concerns the authorship. K59-14 is the same poem as *Calendar* 1669, which identifies the author as Valentine Nevel and lists three reprints. K64-81 is the same poem as *Calendar* 161, where I suggested that Benjamin Franklin wrote the poem. It originally appeared in Franklin's *Pennsylvania Gazette* for 24 September 1730. In *The Canon of Benjamin Franklin: New Additions and Reconsiderations*, 46-47, I gave hesitant reasons for concluding that the poem was "probably" by Franklin. K65-29 is the same as *Calendar* 2039, which identifies the author as Richard Peters and gives other earlier printings. K74-99 is the same as Crum T 727 where the author is revealed as "H. Hall of Hereford." K75-138 is Crum I 1671, which identifies Dr. Robert Vans Hart, of All Souls, as the author.

K76-166, the first popular song on George Washington, is by Jonathan Mitchell Sewall. It was printed as a broadside: Ford 2038; NI302A; E43158; Bristol 4361. Its appearance in James M. Lincoln, *The Papers of Captain Rufus Lincoln*, 89-90, and in McConnel's commonplace book, 89-90, attests its popularity. K77-47, an epigram on Benedict Arnold, is said by Stone, 67, to be by Arnold himself. K77-76 is by Col. John Parke and was reprinted in H. H. Brackenridge's *The Death of General Montgomery*, 61-63. K77-86, an epigram on Franklin's electric rods ending in a point, reprinted as Gaston, 171, is sometimes attributed to Horace Walpole. K77-172, a "Monody to the Memory of the Officers who Fell in the Storming of Forts Clinton and Montgomery," is attributed to Francis, Lord Rawdon, in Hobart's manuscript, 3–5.

Information, such as pseudonyms and places of composition, that might lead to the author's identification sometimes appears in the standard bibliographies. K59-37 lists the same source as *Calendar* 1658, but the latter notes that the author's initials were "J.M'P." K60-41 is the same poem as *Calendar* 1813, which reveals that it first turned up in the (London) *General Evening Post* and that the author's initials are "J.W." K62-41 is the same poem as *Calendar* 1891 which cites a reprinting in the *Pennsylvania Journal* for 30 December 1762, gives the author's pseudonym, "Eugenio," and cites another printing in the *New Hampshire Gazette*. K69-252 is reprinted in Gaston, 62, who cites the author's initials as "W.G.E." K74-32 = Gaston, 69–70, signed from "Ayrshire." Gaston, 148, reprints K77-38, giving the author as "Etoniensis." And Gaston, 147, reprints K77-218, where the author is given as "Maria."

Numerous earlier printings of Kallich items are revealed by a check of the standard bibliographies and scholarship. K55-2 is the same poem as *Calendar* 1274 and 1277, which reveals that B. Y. Prime's poem (listed in Kallich from Prime's 1764 collection) appeared in the *New York Mercury* for 8 September 1755, and was reprinted in the *Boston News Letter*, 18 September 1755. K58-2 is the same poem as *Calendar* 1529, which reveals that B. Y. Prime's poem (again listed in Kallich from a 1764 collection) first appeared in the *New York Mercury* for 18 December 1758, and was reprinted six times in the colonial periodicals. *Calendar* 1475 reveals that K59-28 originally appeared in the *New American Magazine* 1 (August 1758): 201. K66-25 is the same poem as *Calendar* 2089, recording its appearance in the *Boston Gazette*, 30 December 1765. K74-207, a travesty of Gage's Proclamation of May 1774, appeared as an American broadside, Ford no. 1767, and was reprinted in Moore, *Songs and Ballads*, 65–69, from the *Virginia Gazette*. K75-143 appears in Moore's *Songs and Ballads*, 92–94; and in Pickering, 182–83; an abbreviated version is in Gaston, 105; Anderson comments on the music and the reprintings, 115, 447, 620, 750, and 1192. K75-203 appears to be *Calendar* 592; and K75-223 is *Calendar* 1628. K75-288, a popular parody of Gage's Proclamation declaring martial law in Boston, is the broadside Evans 14527; NI 830B; it appeared, among other papers, in the *Pennsylvania Journal*, 28 June 1775; and is reprinted in Moore's *Diary of the American Revolution*, 1: 93–94. K76-95 is evidently a partial reprint of *Calendar* no. 1535, which appeared in the *New American Magazine*, 1 (December 1758): 310, and there contained 22 lines. K76-308 may be identical with *Calendar* no. 1701, which appeared in the *Boston Gazette*, 21 January 1760.

A comparison of the first lines of different poems will sometimes suggest a source, though an examination of the two poems is necessary in order to be certain. K75-106 seems to imitate Matthew Prior; see Crum F 319.

Reprintings of the entire poem that Kallich lists, usually with introductions and notes, occur in a number of standard anthologies. I checked only a few of the most obvious anthologies. Though Kallich occasionally lists the reprintings in Frank Moore's *Songs and Ballads of the American Revolution* (1855), he often omits, as the inventory below testifies, even that classic old anthology. On rare occasions, he cites Winthrop Sargent's *Loyal Verses of Joseph Stansbury and Doctor Jonathan Odell* (e.g., K77-187), but, as the following list demonstrates, he seldom cites even the most standard anthologies. K66-59 = Gaston, 48–49, containing one of the few verse predictions of American independence: "America quickly will shake off its yoke, / And of Empires will soon be the prime." K66-60, a poetic version of William Pitt's satirical epithet for Grenville as "The Gentle Shepherd," is reprinted in Moore's *Songs and Ballads*, 27–32, with a good introduction. K66-134, the best English poem satirizing the Stamp Act's repeal, is reprinted in Moore's *Songs and Ballads*, 33–36; in Gaston, 44–46, and in E. S. Morgan's *The Stamp Act Crisis*, 156–57. The satire may have inspired Franklin's "The Mother Country," which uses similar imagery to present an American view (cf. *The Papers of Benjamin Franklin*, 12: 431). K74-114, a good American song on the Boston Tea Party, appears in Frank Moore's *Songs and Ballads*, 55–58; in Gaston, 66–7; in Moore's *Ballad History*, 307, in the *Paul Jones Pine Tree* (Philadelphia, [1845]), 68–69; in the *New England Historical and Genealogical Register* 11 (1857): 337, and in Pickering, 95–96. K75-61, a major satire on George Germain, Secretary of State for the American Colonies, 1775–1782, is reprinted in Gaston, 107–110. K75-80, a squib on

Lord Sandwich for calling the Americans cowards, is Gaston, 78. K75-107, "Fish and Tea," a delightful English song supporting the Americans, is reprinted in Moore's *Songs and Ballads*, 106–08; in Gaston, 80–81, and in Anderson, 272 and 1362. K75-108, a satirical versification of the resolves of Congress, is complete with a reference to Cotton Mather: "And good Doctor *Mather* at large does relate, / What Quakers and Witches, for Conscience's Sake, / We've tortur'd, and brought to the Gibbet or Stake." It is reprinted in Gaston, 111–14.

K75-110, "The Conquering Hero," satirizes General Gage (though one would not know this from Kallich's note). It is reprinted in Moore, *Ballad History*, 326. K75-135 is reprinted in Moore, *Songs and Ballads*, 108n; Gaston, 83; Anderson, 1118. K75-151, containing a good note about a reply to the poem, is reprinted in Gaston, 97. K75-154, an excellent hudibrastic parody of the Massachusetts legislature's address to George Washington, appears in Gaston, 95–96. K75-262, a nice appreciation of an English Naval officer killed at the beginning of the war, turns up in Gaston, 106. K75-264, a delightful satire on Gage's circumlocution for hanging, "destined to the cord," is reprinted in Gaston, 98. K76-214, a popular, amusing and American song, on Admiral Peter Parker's attack on Sullivan's Island, Charleston, appears in Moore, *Songs and Ballads*, 135–38; and in Gaston, 133–34. K76-276, Thomas Paine's famous "Song on Liberty Tree," is reprinted in Moore's *Songs and Ballads*, 18–21; in Pickering, 98–99; and in Anderson, 1074, etc. K77-99, on Benjamin Franklin as the "new Prometheus," reflecting an epithet Immanuel Kant coined for him in 1756 (see *The Papers of Benjamin Franklin*, 20: 490), is reprinted in Gaston, 145. K77-120 = Gaston, 165. K77-129, which Kallich speculates "could be by Jonathan Odell," was reprinted in *Poems Serious and Sarcastical* (New York: Rivington, 1779), 9–10; E16326.

K77-144, an English satire on the present administration, is reprinted in Moore's *Songs and Ballads*, 200–03; in Stone, 69; and in Gaston, 174–76, who questions both Moore's attribution of the poems to Arthur Lee and Stone's attribution to Horace Walpole. K77-186 is reprinted in Winthrop Sargent's *Stansbury and Odell*, 11–12; since the manuscript exists in "Loyalist Rhapsodies," ll. 10v–11r, Manuscript Division, Library of Congress, Pastora San Juan Cafferty edited it in "Loyalist Rhapsodies," 115–16. K77-187 cites the reprinting in Sargent's *Stansbury and Odell,* but omits the reprinting in Gaston, 151; Anderson, 1002; and Cafferty, 139–41. I should note that Stuart-Vincent, no. 805-49, records a later reprinting, K77-189, Jonathan Odell's *Song for St. George's Day,* was separately printed: E43322; Bristol 4548; NI609A. Cafferty reprints it with good notes from "Loyalist Rhapsodies," 111–14. K77-240 appears in Stone, 68.

Here follows a list of additional reprintings of Kallich items: K62-36 is in Rivington's *Songs, Naval and Military* (1779), 64–65. K63-133 = Gaston, 31 (with music in Anderson 1080). K63-134 = Gaston, 33. K66-19 = Gaston, 41–43; and Ford, "Isaiah Thomas," no. 250. K66-49 = Gaston, 50 (which discusses and reprints the second of four epigrams on Pitt, "Mourn England"). K66-52 = Gaston, 47. K66-108 is in Moore's *Ballad History,* 9. K67-13 = Gaston, 56. K67-38 = Gaston, 53, with music in Anderson, 940. K67-38 cites a reprinting at K75-219, but does not cite the reprinting at K72-78. The song appears with music in Anderson, 940, and the text is in McConnel, 243–45. K68-30 = Gaston, 58–9. K69-118, an American song, = Gaston, 63–64. K74-8 is in Moore's *Ballad History,* 350. K74-34 = Gaston, 72. K74-71 = Gaston, 68. K74-86 is in Moore's *Ballad History,* 321. K74-90 is in Moore's *Ballad History,* 334. K74-103 is in Moore's *Ballad History,* 313. K74-152 is in Moore's *Ballad History,* 311. K74-183 = Gaston, 65. K74-209 is in Moore's *Ballad History,* 365. K75-34 is in Moore's *Songs and Ballads,* 88–89. K75-37 = Moore's *Ballad History,* 134–35. K75-44 = Gaston, 76. K75-68 = Gaston, 88 and Anderson 696. K75-77 = Gaston, 77. K75-79 = Gaston, 100. K75-87 = Gaston, 87. K75-115 = Moore's *Ballad History,* 70, and Crum I 14. K75-157 = Gaston, 93; and Anderson 1368. K75-185 = Gaston, 101. K75-204 = Gaston, 82. K75-238 = Gaston, 103. K75-251 = Gaston, 90–92, who mentions a *Pennsylvania Ledger* printing of 20 May 1775, and in Anderson, 171, 757, 1068, 1440. Though Kallich says that it appeared originally in the *Pennsylvania Ledger* (no date given), the *London Evening Post* printing listed by Kallich is earlier. K75-253 = Gaston, 115–16. K75-282 = Gaston, 119. K76-57, in Brackenridge, *Death,* 81. K76-77, in Hobart's MS, 30–31. K76-86 is reprinted in W. Sargent, *Loyalist Poetry,* 86–90. K76-99 = Frank Moore, *Ballad History,* 79, quoting a text from the *Pennsylvania Journal,* 4 October 1775. K76-126 = Gaston, 137. K76-130 = Gaston, 128. K76-157 = Gaston, 139. K76-162 is reprinted in W. Sargent, *Loyalist Poetry,* 107–08. K76-165 = F. Moore, *Ballad History,* 98. K76-175 = Moore, *Songs and Ballads,* 153–55; Anderson 47, etc. K76-190 = W. Sargent, *Loyalist Poetry,* 77–79; Crum C 780 records its earliest printing. Jeremy Belknap copied it into his manuscript "Collection of Poetry" at the Massachusetts Historical Society. K76-203 = Moore, *Songs and Ballads,* 141–43; Gaston, 126; Anderson 521. K76-210 = Gaston, 132. K76-211 in Brackenridge, *Death,* 79. K76-280 = Gaston, 129–30. K76-282 = Moore, *Songs and Ballads,* 90–91, Anderson A514, etc. K76-366 = Reprinted in W. S. Sargent, *Loyalist Poetry,* 36–57, from Rivington's *Gazetteer.* K77-42 = Gaston, 153–54. K77-49 = Carey 152–53. K77-84 = Gaston, 169. K77-87 = Gaston, 168. K77-141 = Gaston, 159. K77-192 = Gaston, 158. K77-193 = Gaston, 156. K77-200 = Gaston, 155. K77-206 = Gaston, 152. K77-231, "On the Intended Rejoicings for the Taking of Philadelphia," is reprinted by Gaston, 173. K77-234 = Gaston, 146.

The music for the poems can often be found in standard reference works, especially Anderson, Crum, and Simpson. K60-50 is Crum A 741, which gives the music for Whitehead's "Ode of the New Year, 1760," by Benjamin Boyce, and notes that it was reprinted in Whitehead's *Poems,* 173–74. Indeed, most of Whitehead's official poetry (he was poet-laureate) was set to music and may be located in Crum, together with a specific reference to its appearance in the 1774 or 1790 editions of Whitehead's collected *Poems:* K61-50 = Crum S 1197, which locates music by Boyce and a reprinting in Whitehead's *Poems* (1774), 2: 273. Similarly, K62-66 = Crum G 285. K63-170 = Crum A 1823. K67-50 = Crum W 1059. K70-108 = Crum H 127. K70-237 = Crum D 324. K71-135 = Crum A 738. K72-107 = Crum A 1821. K73-62 = Crum D 44. K73-110 = Crum B 496. K74-210 = Crum H 252. K74-211 = Crum P 59. K75-313 = Crum Y 107. K76-387 = Crum O 1097. K76-386 = Crum Y 155. And K77-328 = Crum D 474, which locates music by Boyce and cites a reprinting in Whitehead's *Poems* (1790), 2: 127.

Gillian Anderson has often identified the music for the American periodical poems: K75-34 = Anderson G 98. K75-65 = Anderson 1449. K75-188 = Anderson 758. K75-316 = Anderson 1077, 1268, and 1365. And Claude Simpson provides the key to the music of some poems: K63-67 = Simpson 385. K75-147 = Simpson 634. K76-40 = Simpson 91. K76-66 = Simpson 297. K76-321 = Simpson 299. K77-15 = Simpson 787.

A few Kallich items provide information useful in placing later poems and imitations. K62-37 evidently inspired an imitation by St. George Tucker, "On George Washington," which appeared in the *American Museum* 7 (June 1790), Appendix, 11–12. Frank Moore, *Songs and Ballads*, 78–80, reprinted K75-256; it also turns up in the Isaiah Thomas collection, no. 181. The parody by Oliver Arnold, 81–82, beginning "'Twas winter, and blue Tory noses were freezing" is also in Moore. The parody alone is reprinted in Pickering, 98. I noticed that Kallich listed a number of poems twice, several times without giving cross-references. A few examples, not mentioned above, are: K73-21 is seemingly identical with K76-98. K74-26 = K76-51, reprinted in Moore's *Ballad History*, 144–45. K76-70 = K75-311.

I must conclude that though Kallich's bibliography is of great value, it is seriously flawed because he did not include a first-line index and because he did not incorporate the available scholarship into his fine primary listings of poems. In this review, I have only begun to do the work with the secondary scholarship that I would have expected Kallich to do. Such standard works as Bruce Granger's on the satire in the American Revolution as well as the major individual authors' writings (Freneau, Livingston, Trumbull, etc.) should also have been consulted and cited.

Bibliography

Anderson, Gillian B. *Freedom's Voice in Poetry and Song . . . Lyrics in Colonial American Newspapers, 1773–1783*. Wilmington: Scholarly Resources, 1977.

Brackenridge, Hugh Henry. *The Death of General Montgomery*. Philadelphia: Bell, 1777. Evans 15249.

Bristol, Roger P. *Supplement to Charles Evans' American Bibliography*. Charlottesville: Univ. Press of Virginia, 1970.

Cafferty, Pastora San Juan. "Loyalist Rhapsodies: The Poetry of Stansbury and Odell." Ph.D. dissertation, George Washington Univ., 1971.

Calendar. See Lemay.

Carey, George C. *A Sailor's Songbag: An American Rebel in an English Prison, 1777–1779.* Amherst: Univ. of Massachusetts Press, 1976.

Crum, Margaret. *The First Line Index of English Poetry, 1500–1800, in Manuscripts of the Bodleian Library.* 2 vols. Oxford: Bodleian Library, 1969.

E = Evans.

Evans, Charles. *American Bibliography: A Chronological Dictionary* [through 1800]. 14 vols. Chicago: Evans et al., 1903–1959.

Ford, Worthington C. *Broadsides, Ballads, &C. Printed in Massachusetts, 1639–1800.* Boston: Massachusetts Historical Society, 1922. (Cited simply as Ford.)

Ford, Worthington C. "The Isaiah Thomas Collection of Ballads." *Proceedings of the American Antiquarian Society,* 33 (1923): 34–112. (Cited as Ford, "Isaiah Thomas Collection.")

Gaston, James C. *London Poets and the American Revolution.* Troy, N.Y.: Whitston Publishing Co., 1979.

Granger, Bruce I. *Political Satire in the American Revolution, 1763–1783.* New York: Cornell Univ. Press, 1960.

Hobart, Henrietta. Commonplace Book, 1779. Manuscript Division. New York Historical Society.

Lemay, J. A. Leo. *A Calendar of American Poetry in the Colonial Newspapers and Magazines and in the Major British Magazines Through 1765.* Worcester: American Antiquarian Society, 1972.

———. *"New England's Annoyances": America's First Folk Song.* Newark: Univ. of Delaware Press, 1985.

———. "The American Origins of 'Yankee Doodle.'" *William and Mary Quarterly,* 33 (1976): 435–64.

———. *The Canon of Benjamin Franklin, 1722–1777: New Additions and Reconsiderations.* Newark: Univ. of Delaware Press, 1986.

Lincoln, James M., ed. *The Papers of Captain Rufus Lincoln.* Cambridge: Riverside Press, 1904.

McConnel, Hugh. Commonplace Book of Revolutionary American Poetry. Barrett Collection. University of Virginia Library.

Moore, Frank. *Diary of the American Revolution.* 2 vols. New York: Scribner, 1859–60.

———. *Illustrated Ballad History of the American Revolution.* New York: Johnson, Wilson: 1876.

———. *Songs and Ballads of the American Revolution.* 1855; rpt. Port Washington, N.Y.: Kennikat Press, 1964.

Morgan, Edmund S., and Helen M. Morgan. *The Stamp Act Crisis: Prologue to Revolution.* Chapel Hill: Univ. of North Carolina Press, 1953.

National Index of American Imprints Through 1800: The Short-Title Evans. Eds.

Clifford K. Shipton and James E. Mooney. 2 vols. Worcester: American Antiquarian Society, 1969.

Opie, Iona, and Peter Opie. *The Oxford Dictionary of Nursery Rhymes.* London: Oxford Univ. Press, 1951.

Pickering, James H. *The World Turned Upside Down: Poetry and Prose of the American Revolution.* Port Washington, N.Y.: Kennikat Press, 1975.

Sabin, Joseph, Wilberforce Eames, and R. W. G. Vail. *Bibliotheca Americana: A Dictionary of Books Relating to America. From Its Discovery to the Present Time.* New York: Sabin, 1868–1936.

Sargent, Winthrop. *Loyalist Poetry of the American Revolution.* Philadelphia: [Collins], 1857.

———. *The Loyal Verses of Joseph Stansbury and Doctor Jonathan Odell.* Albany, Munsell: 1860.

Schlesinger, Arthur M. "A Note on Songs as Patriot Propaganda," *William and Mary Quarterly,* 11 (1954): 78–88.

Stephens/George. Stephens, Frederick George, and Mary Dorothy George. *Catalogue of Political and Personal Satires Preserved in the Department of Prints and Drawings in the British Museum.* London: British Museum, 1870–1954.

Stone, William L. *Ballads and Poems Relating to the Burgoyne Campaign.* 1893; rpt. Port Washington, N.Y.: Kennikat Press, 1970.

Stuart, Ross, and Thomas B. Vincent, *A Chronological Index of Locally Written Verse Published in the Newspapers and Magazines of Upper and Lower Canada, Maritime Canada, and Newfoundland Through 1815.* Kingston, Ontario: Loyal Colonies Press, 1979.

Winsor, Justin, ed. *Narrative and Critical History of America.* 8 vols. Boston: Houghton Mifflin Co., 1884–89.

Historical Fictions

Alexander Welsh

James Kerr. *Fiction against History: Scott as Story-Teller.* Cambridge: Cambridge University Press, 1989. ix, 142 pp.

Stephen Bann. *The Inventions of History: Essays on the Representation of the Past.* Manchester: Manchester University Press, 1990. x, 246 pp.

Lionel Gossman. *Between History and Literature.* Cambridge: Harvard University Press, 1990. 412 pp.

As the titles of these recent books suggest, in academic circles it is now common to profess a willingness to cross the boundaries of history and of literature, and indeed to pose the question of whether history can help being anything but another fiction such as that served up in a poem, play, or novel. All three books, appropriately, pay homage to Hayden White's *Metahistory* (1973) or to his essays "The Historical Text as Literary Artifact" (1974) and "Historicism, History, and the Figurative Imagination" (1975). Behind White's thesis of the literary emplotments of historical narrative stand, imposingly, the schemata of Northrop Frye's *Anatomy of Criticism* (1957), which White applied more tellingly than did most of Frye's colleagues in literary studies.

In surveying the two fields as he found them, White rebuked literature professors gently for trusting naively in history, and history professors rather more sternly for trusting that their narratives differed very much from literature. It was customary "for literary theorists, when they are speaking about the 'context' of a literary work, to suppose that this context—the 'historical milieu'—has a concreteness and an accessibility that the work itself can never have, as if it were easier to perceive the reality of a past world put together from a thousand historical documents than it is to probe the depths of a single literary work that is present to the critic studying it." White countered that "the presumed concreteness and accessibility of historical milieux, these contexts of the texts that literary scholars study, are themselves products of the fictive capability of the historians who have studied those contexts" and thus placed himself in the somewhat invidious position of warning against the claims of his own profession. Historical narratives, he wrote,

> succeed in endowing sets of past events with meanings, over and above whatever comprehension they provide by appeal to putative causal laws, by exploiting the metaphorical similarities between sets of real events and the conventional structures of our fictions. By the very constitution of a set of events in such a way as to make a comprehensible story out of them, the historian charges those events with the symbolic significance of a comprehensible plot structure. Historians may not like to think of their works as translations of fact into fictions; but this is one of the effects of their works. By suggesting alternative emplotments of a given sequence of historical events, historians provide historical events with all of the possible meanings with which the literary art of their culture is capable of endowing them.[1]

White's forcible yoking of history and literature obviously did not by itself generate all the discussion that this marriage causes today. Saussurian linguistics, Derridean deconstruction, Barthian paradox, New historicism have all come to the wedding, so to speak, with their mixed blessings for the pair. As with many corrective insights in the passage of ideas, the spirit of correction now seems in danger of carrying participants away, so that nothing is more commonly heard at conferences or editorial boards than the charge that someone (someone else) has failed to "problematize" history. Particularly among the group less stigmatized by White, the professors of literature, text and context are to be eyed with equal skepticism and usually with a knowingness superior to any knowledge of the facts or the fictions. Though White is scarcely to blame, the knowingness may actually curtail thinking. It seems to call everything in doubt at once, whereas in practice the research in most fields has traditionally proceeded with some variables arbitrarily fixed while others are under investigation. Moreover, the perception that history is fabled is not new, as ancient epic and modern historical novels, or the very sources for Frye's *Anatomy* and White's *Metahistory*, should remind us.

Let me give an example of the "problematizing" of context so seemingly old-fashioned that nearly everyone would now agree it is counterproductive. For such problematizing, literary history is notorious—I think of the question of authorship of Shakespeare's plays, for example, but more immediately of the composition of Scott's historical fiction, since the latter is germane to this review. Great writers seem to inspire rival invention in their critics: thus Scott's novels were said (by a few persons) to have been composed in a different sequence from that of their appearance in print beginning with *Waverley* in 1814, because his finest novels could not have been written prior to certain novels that looked more like apprentice work to the critics. This problem of context, momentarily fussed over in some quarters, was then effectively demolished in 1948 by Robert D. Mayo in an article entitled "The Chronology of the Waverley Novels: The Evidence of the Manuscripts."[2] Mayo had consulted the holographs at the Pierpont Morgan Library in New York, held the sheets up to the light, and observed the watermarks, which were dated by the paper manufacturer in a sequence strictly appropriate to the novels as published to all the world. In the following decade, nonetheless, as a student in Edinburgh I found myself face to face with J. C. Corson, an authority on Scott who still wished to believe in the problematized order of composition. Inwardly a little alarmed, I asked Corson if he had read Mayo's article. He confided to me that he had seen it, but that quite possibly Scott had transcribed the novels on selected paper in order to conceal the original order of composition. The novelist, it would seem, intended to share his secret joke with a few percipient critics still unborn. Now Corson's persistence in modifying the context—specifically the chronology of certain texts—seems miles away from White's due cautionings about history. For one thing, White is concerned with the plots or predilections of many participants in a given culture rather than with the inventive scholarship of a few. Still, I would argue, there are often excellent grounds (Mayo's "evidence of the manuscripts" and much else) for preferring wise to unwise emplotments. In all determinations of context one is dealing in probabilities, but some probabilities at least approach certainty; and always an economy of investigation dictates against taking up all the variables at once. Above all, knowingness about these problems should not take the place of history or criticism.

Another difficulty with knowingness is the subtle imputation of ignorance to everyone who has gone before, itself a form of blindness to the past. Needless to say White cannot be charged with this: as a close student of Frye's *Anatomy*, he could not help but appreciate the antiquity of relations between history and literature, and highly conscious relations at that. Frye's entire project can be read as a renewed examination of the fit between fiction—comprising formulae, conventions, shapings of desire—and changing social realities encountered over time. That project is rightly associated by the critical community with the study of romance; in 1975, subsequent to the appearance of White's *Metahistory*, Frye devoted his Norton Lectures at Harvard to romance. The lectures, published as *The Secular Scripture*, testified to human imagination "struggling with a world which is separate from itself" and the repeated "adjusting of formulaic structures to a roughly credible context." In other words, the interaction of fiction and history has long been apparent, and the test of probability well known at least since the ancient Greeks, though it may be confronted more directly at some times than at others. Not incidentally, Frye confessed that his lectures stemmed in part from "an abandoned essay on the Waverley novels of Scott."[3] That attribution and various citations in the lectures reveal more interest in Scott, perhaps, than shown by most students of romanticism today. Yet in the nineteenth century, Scott's prose romances served as models both for literary realism and for history. On the former it is still worth consulting Georg Lukacs's *The Historical Novel* (1937); and on the latter, Duncan Forbes's *The Liberal Anglican Idea of History* (1952).

Of the new books under review, none suffers at any rate from knowingness about the relations of fiction and history. The authors, one suspects, would recuperate in one way or another the objectivity of history, if they could. Unfortunately, though I am always ready to hope that fresh understanding of Scott's contribution can help, James Kerr's *Fiction against History* does not take one very far. It is a short book, and too many pages are merely derivative from earlier criticism. While Kerr notably avoids some pitfalls marked by White, he rather hedges in the end on fiction and history. He begins to realign interpretation, for example, by suggesting that the subtext of *Waverley* and others is "English colonialism" but does not provide adequate readings to make the suggestion stick. The thesis that Scott's "novels are fictions written to defer the effects of history, deceptively casual efforts to contain the forces of history by means of story, to alter the past he has evoked" (p. 3), may be unexceptional but remains too general, hardly more than a restatement of what Frye has taught us all to look for. Kerr's book nevertheless is clearly written and provides a decent introduction to *Waverley, Old Mortality, The Heart of Midlothian, The Bride of Lammermoor,* and *Redgauntlet.*

Stephen Bann's essays, collected as *The Inventions of History,* dart all over the place—to art history, historical films, period maps, and above all literature. With one eye on Barthes and the other on White, and side glances at other theorists, Bann still demonstrates his real love for curious texts. One essay, demonstrating both the blurring of history and fiction and this historian's lively curiosity, is "Victor Hugo's Inkblots: Indeterminacy and Identification in the Representation of the Past," handsomely illustrated and presumably written in connection with the centenary of Hugo's death several years ago. Some of these occasional essays seem a bit loosely stapled together, and I have difficulty with the style. In this particular one, Bann writes as follows of the formal pretense that *Quentin Durward* was history:

> It does after all claim in its introductory pages to be the transcription of a genuine manuscript found in a French château. But no one is so unsophisticated as to grasp the possibility of a particular hybrid of truth and fantasy; it accepts the convention of undecidability. We could, of course, spend a great deal more time discussing Scott in this context. [p. 96]

Surely a "not" is missing in the middle sentence, to make a triple negation; and in any event, "it" in the same sentence points tantalizingly to more than one antecedent. Neither these nor the subsequent sentences in this particular digression are "surely clear" as Bann asserts. Because there are nearly as many complimentary allusions to Scott's fiction in the pages of this historian as one might find in the pages of Augustin Thierry, however, my interest is certainly aroused. Bann has written elsewhere of the significance of the building of Abbotsford, and here he remarks how the historical novels "quite genuinely colonise"—not Scotland this time but—"a new and vast region for the historical imagination" (p. 115). Suddenly Scott is accorded the respect he enjoyed in the nineteenth century. Furthermore, with the help of Nietzsche, Bann makes a positive case for precisely the kind of history for which Scott is often condemned. "The 'antiquarian' attitude," he claims, "is not an imperfect approximation to something else—which would be the maturity of scientific, professionalised historiography. It is a specific, lived relationship to the past, and deserves to be treated on its own terms" (p. 102). And here no doubt Bann means to justify as well his own blend of theorizing and curiosity about the past.

Lionel Gossman's *Between History and Literature* is another collection of essays, strictly speaking, but essays so comprehensive and well-made that each one leaves the reader with a sense of completion, of satisfaction such as few books provide. Long magisterial pieces on Thierry and Michelet show how these historians wrote out of their own lives and the political experience of their time, and Gossman brings to these a speculative curiosity about the way in which the image of woman functioned for such writers; so much so that one wishes he would, if he has not already done so, turn his attention to the more extraordinary case of Auguste Comte and the type of woman imaged by the religion of positivism. In a related move, one of the more recent essays in the volume, "History as Decipherment," treats romantic historiography in such a way as to suggest a whole range of reasons why the nineteenth century provided a seedbed for psychoanalysis. Gossman seems ideally situated to expound the relations of fiction and history, since after many years as a pro-

Historical Fictions 169

fessor of French literature he has now devoted this much work to history. In addition, as three of the essays attest, he has made a special study over the years of education in post-Revolutionary France. We are not allowed to forget that one of the most persistent interfaces of literature with history since antiquity is that of the schoolroom; and an accurate knowledge of which texts were prescribed, when and where, provides a further index to this subject.

The essays in *Between History and Literature* are close enough to one another in interest—mainly the focus is on France—that they constitute a coherent book. The effect is too comprehensive to summarize easily, but I can at least adopt the nineteenth-century reviewers' own practice of supplying quotations.

The role of history in the political programs of the first half of the nineteenth century was crucial. By discovering the hidden anonymous history of the nation beneath the outmoded histories of its rulers and its narrow ruling class, historians were expected to provide the legitimation of a new political order, a new state, and at the same time to impose the idea of this state on the consciousness of its citizens. [p. 153]

It is not necessary to agree with all of Gossman's conclusions; they often force one to think whether one agrees or not, because of the care with which they are set forth.

It would not be too difficult to show that nineteenth-century historical narrative also shares important structural features with nineteenth-century fictional narrative, notably the explicit rejection of the clear Enlightenment separation of object and subject, past and present, narrative and commentary or discourse, and the attempt to make them continuous with each other. The dominant feature of both fictional and historical narrative in the nineteenth century is the replacement of the overt eighteenth-century persona of the narrator by a covert narrator, and the corresponding presentation of the narrative as unproblematic, absolutely binding. The nineteenth-century narrator appears as a privileged reporter recounting what happened. The historical text is not presented as a model to be discussed, criticized, accepted, or repudiated by the free and inquiring intellect, but as the inmost form of the real, binding, and inescapable. In the struggle to establish *philosophie,* in other words, the eighteenth-century historian accepted his ideological function proudly; in the nineteenth century the historian's ideological function and the rhetoric he deployed in its service were denied, in the deepest sense, since the historian himself did not recognize them. [p. 244]

These are but two examples of the thoughtful history-writing in the book; and about eighty pages of endnotes enable readers to pursue most of the issues to their sources. Nearly everywhere Gossman is self-consciously alert to what he is doing and to the contemporary metahistorical context. In the last essay, "The Rationality of History," he confronts directly the fashion of the day by remarking, "I am now concerned that the current tendency to conflate 'historical' and 'fictional' narrative and the new emphasis on the 'poetics' of history—which I once welcomed as a salutary release from the smug certainties of historical positivism—may be promoting a facile and irresponsible relativism which will leave many who espouse it defenceless before the most dangerous myths and ideologies, incapable of justifying any stand" (p. 303). That essay concludes with some discussion of how historians actually change their minds in the process of writing history, with the implications of such adjustments for something that may be objectivity after all.

Lionel Gossman's and Stephen Bann's essays argue that nineteenth-century aspirations toward a scientific historiography differ significantly from the claims of historians before or since, and all three books, including James Kerr's, identify strong narrative proclivities with this period. A certain conjunction of science and narrative occurred then: it was, after all, the age of the great narrative sciences, geology and evolutionary biology, and of so-called natural history. None of these books confronts quite directly enough, perhaps, what this narrative idea of proof was like to historians of the time. The following is Thierry's contention in *Récits des temps mérovingiens,* as translated by Bann:

People have said that the aim of the historian was to recount and not to prove; I do not know, but I am certain that in history the best type of proof, the most capable of striking and convincing all minds, the one which allows the least mistrust and leaves the fewest doubts, is complete narration.

Obviously, one has to try to understand Thierry's investment in this proof, even if it stirs misgivings. Then one can have a fuller picture, by comparison, of history's meaning today.

Notes

1. Hayden White, "The Historical Text as Literary Artifact," *Tropics of Discourse: Essays in Cultural Criticism* (Baltimore: Johns Hopkins Univ. Press, 1978), pp. 89, 91–92.

2. Robert D. Mayo, "The Chronology of the Waverley Novels: The Evidence of the Manuscripts," *PMLA*, 63 (1948), 939–49.

3. Northrop Frye, *The Secular Scripture: A Study in the Structure of Romance* (Cambridge: Harvard Univ. Press, 1976), pp. 36, 5.

Barbershop Bravery

Nina Baym

Mark Spilka, *Hemingway's Quarrel with Androgyny.* Lincoln: University of Nebraska Press, 1990. xiv, 383 pp.

The hallmark of Hemingway criticism has long been its fixation on the author's life. The presentations at any academic gathering of Hemingway specialists will always be filled with biographical details. It is no longer deemed necessary to demonstrate that this or that work is autobiographical in nature; it is only necessary to identify the specific life event that Hemingway was writing about.

Hemingway himself strongly encouraged this approach to his writings. From the time he achieved critical success with his short-story collection *In Our Time* in 1925 to the time he committed suicide as the world's most famous author in 1961, he insisted that any good writer's life was one with his work. He fashioned himself for public consumption as a man's man and a man's writer. Writing, as he repeatedly described and depicted it, was a mortally risky, wholly masculine affair, a version of war or blood sport. No doubt this representation appealed to the fantasies of homebound male authors whose lives had little of danger or glamour in them, all the more when Hemingway managed to live in a flamboyant, celebrity-filled and much-publicized manner, consorting with rich men and beautiful women in such world playgrounds as Venice and the French Riviera.[1]

Pursuing his vocation thus publicized, claiming to be a protector of its sacred precincts from writers who were either female or insufficiently male, Hemingway increasingly represented and enacted masculinity itself in the most extreme terms. To the extent that his machismo extreme seemed to follow logically from his definition of writing as a manly thing to do, onlookers increasingly saw that definition as undermined by the ever-more obvious discrepancy between grandiose claims to courage and the limited threat posed by those he identified as the enemy—women, gays, inferior writers, unsympathetic critics, and large animals. Even while he was alive Hemingway's man's man was looking more and more like a bully and a braggart dedicated to silencing every voice except his own, less and less like a culture hero that any self-respecting culture would want to acknowledge.

That there might be immense vulnerabilities concealed behind the machismo—that the machismo was a facade—was also something that critics began to speculate about early on. If the signs of hidden weakness became obvious to all when Hemingway killed himself, the argument that the much-vaunted manhood was a patchy screen had been around in the Hemingway criticism for several decades, certainly since readers like Edmund Wilson and Philip Young had pointed out the degree to which the typical Hemingway protagonist was a mutilated or disabled figure. This observation, although enraging the author himself and quite possibly driving him to more self-parodic and self-destructive displays, also inspired lines of cultural and psychological criticism by which Hemingway was featured in the classroom and the scholarly journals as a major author.

Both the cultural and psychological criticism was inflected by the modernist myths that held sway in the academy in the immediate post-World War II period. Cultural criticism of Hemingway focused on how his work articulated an updated code of manly behavior that preserved heroism and integrity in a world whose traditional codes had been shattered or discredited by World War I. Psychological criticism centered on Hemingway's presentation of manhood as a perilous journey, on the maintenance of manhood as a task requiring constant vigilance. The two critical lines came together in a mythic vision of the protagonist as hero, and of society (to borrow Emerson's words) as a joint stock company in conspiracy against the manhood of every one of its members. Emerson might not have meant to limit his reference by gender; Hemingway certainly did.

Inevitably, therefore, he became a prime target of feminist

criticism when such criticism emerged in the academy during the 1970s. The chief points scored against him by early feminist critics were that his representation of the female was restricted to strong hateful women or docile adorable slaveys; and that his women in any case were not realistic but mere constructs of male fantasy. Many traditionalist Hemingway critics saw the feminist critique as a perfect validation of Hemingway's own supposed claim that manly men were always under attack from man-hating women. Dealing with the feminists, Hemingway critics initially counterattacked; more recently they have been claiming that Hemingway has been badly misunderstood, at least partly because of the ways in which critics have interpreted him. Among recuperative efforts, the re-investigation of his highly gender-specific sexual representations is proving especially productive. The force of the feminist critique along with the previously neglected evidence of gender-anxieties in the author's work and life suggests that careful rereadings might easily recuperate Hemingway for a critical moment more attuned to the victims of masculinist abuse than to the inflictors of it.

Such rereadings could in principle take many forms, and they have in fact already done so; but the chief form that they have taken is that which presents the author as himself a victim of pernicious ideologies of the masculine as well as of a bad upbringing that, by producing extreme inner confusion about his own sexual identity, drove him into reductive and brutal forms of masculine self-display. His writing may now be seen as the record of attempts to defend himself against such confusion, to bring order out of his inner sexual chaos, to connect with women whom he desired, needed, and feared. The 1986 publication by Scribners of a Hemingway novel called *The Garden of Eden*, concocted from a long manuscript he was working on when he died, as well as scholarly study of the manuscript itself, have added considerable weight to this new biographical approach. For the work is composed of numerous transsexual episodes showing an interchangeability of male and female that is simultaneously seductive and destructive to the protagonist, a Hemingway-like writer named David Bourne. From the retrospective vantage point afforded by this work, the idea that the clamor Hemingway was attempting to silence was within rather than outside him has clarified and complicated our understanding of his earlier writings.

The two most ambitious revisionist studies of Hemingway in this vein are Kenneth S. Lynn's 1987 *Hemingway* and Mark Spilka's recent *Hemingway's Quarrel with Androgyny*. Although Lynn's book came out three years earlier than Spilka's, Spilka had published several relevant essays before that, and one sympathizes with his rather mournful complaint that he ought to have received some of the credit for originality that went to Lynn's book. Both critics work within the conventional biographical mode of mainline Hemingway criticism, Spilka much more so than Lynn even though Lynn's book is the one that is formally designated a biography. Both books are testimonials to the author's heroism. Lynn writes in his preface that a reconsideration of Hemingway's life "can show that while his faults were terrible he was also a more truly heroic figure than even the gaudiest version of his myth could grant him."[2] Spilka finds in his conclusion that Hemingway came "remarkably, even heroically, close to affirming it [his androgyny] before tragically betraying it as his life neared its grim conclusion" (p. 336). For both of these critics, Hemingway's chief topic is not war, the modern world, the decline of the west, or men without women; it is men and women, and in particular the destructive effect on male-female relations of a masculinist ethos—the very ethos, that is, that Hemingway went around promulgating to newspaper reporters. That Hemingway in fact found it impossible to live without women (and seldom if ever lived only with men) suggests to both writers that unless Hemingway was altogether self-deluded (which they agree cannot be the case since he was a great writer, and great writers are not wholly self-deluded) the discrepancy between his preachment and his practice would have to enter his writing in some central way.

Yet the two books, although they overlap, approach their shared topic quite differently; neither book makes the other redundant. For Lynn, the single source of Hemingway's many life problems was his mother—more specifically, his mother's early overriding of Hemingway's true sexual identity as a boy by dressing him as a girl like his slightly older sister Marcelline. And Lynn sees Hemingway as a hero because he managed to overcome his lifelong battle against his mother and her feminizing traces and write "some of the most memorable fiction of the century."[3] By memorable fiction Lynn means stylish, well-crafted work in which Hemingway analyzes and criticizes his compensatory machismo (rather than merely replicates it) with a surprising degree of subtlety and insight. Lynn declines to speculate on how widespread or representative Hemingway's sexual malaise might have been, and his close focus on the presumed uniqueness of Hemingway's case suggests that he thinks of the writer's problems as very likely *sui generis*. Lynn thus anchors Hemingway's writing in his life while granting it a crucial degree of autonomy from that life. His view of Hemingway's significance requires such autonomy, for in his view writing is not coterminous with biography—or, more accurately, writing that is coterminous with biography has not achieved artistic distance and is therefore of little aesthetic value. To Lynn, Hemingway matters not because he had problems but because his writing overcame them.

Spilka, by contrast, is far less interested in Hemingway as a conscious artist and does not expect Hemingway to transcend his problems by writing about them. Spilka provides none of the full-dress formal readings of specific Hemingway works by which Lynn demonstrates Hemingway's excellence; rather he treats each work as a biographical source. In each text Hemingway registers the symptoms and progress of his malaise, and Spilka praises him for psychological honesty rather than for transfiguring artistry. At the same time, Spilka interprets Hemingway's dis-ease as a cultural rather than a personal malaise. Hemingway is "our" recorder as well as his own. "We" are all infected—as he writes in his preface, "none of us can afford to be holier than Hemingway. He too is our brother" (p. xiii).

But this recuperative gesture ought perhaps to be resisted, if not by those whom Spilka includes with his pronouns, then at least by those whom he leaves out. The first person plural formations here and throughout *Hemingway's Quarrel with Androgyny* make it crystal clear that, notwithstanding the occasional and approving invocation of feminist writing (work by Elaine Showalter, Patricia Meyer Spacks, Sandra Gilbert and Susan Gubar, and others is cited) and notwithstanding the welcome traces of feminist critique in his analysis, Spilka values Hemingway in the old way—as a man writing for other men, with membership in the category "men" further restricted to those whom Hemingway himself admitted to be such: males who are white, middle-class, heterosexual, Christian, of Anglo-American descent. Spilka's work, like Hemingway's, is that of a man writing to other men. Readers who are not members of the favored group would seem to have the chance to substitute a compassionate and enlightened understanding for our previously uninstructed hostility to Hemingway's male chauvinism (or his ethnocentrism, racism, or the various other -isms with which he so much likes to decorate his writing).

For the "men" reading the book, however, Hemingway figures as a monitory figure demonstrating not the damage that men of his type do to others, but the damage they do to themselves. In Hemingway's "shortsighted denial of his mother's influence, he continued to deny also those emotional resources—fearless friendliness with women, manly courage in domestic relations—which might have strengthened his own relations with women, enriched and expanded his art, and preserved his life and sanity in old age" (p. 64). With such a payoff, a man would be crazy not to adopt androgyny. To bring about change in (white, Anglo, middle-class) men is very much an aim of the new men's movement and of the related academic field of men's studies; *Hemingway's Quarrel with Androgyny* clearly belongs within this field, but Lynn's book has no place in it at all.

Whereas Lynn explains Hemingway's confusion solely by maternal behavior, and attributes it in particular to Grace Hemingway's dressing her son like a girl for many years, Spilka places her behavior in a much larger cultural context with babywear playing only a minor role. To Spilka, Hemingway's problem was not that his mother tried to make him into a girl, but that the traits of girls and boys, men and women, were not clearly or consistently distinguished in either the Hemingway family's behavior or the cultural texts that inspired them. Through a series of lengthy readings that occupy the first half of the book, Spilka analyzes various English Victorian works that Hemingway is known to have read in his boyhood or that the Hemingway family is known to have valued. These include Diana Mulock Craik's *John Halifax, Gentleman*, Frances Hodgson Burnett's *Little Lord Fauntleroy*, several sea novels by Captain Marryat, various imperial and boy stories by Rudyard Kipling, Emily Brontë's *Wuthering Heights*, and poetry by John Masefield. All are read with an eye to their gender representations, and the conclusion is that masculine identity figures as something far more fluid and less homogeneous than the masculinist creed that Hemingway later adopted—a creed, it begins to seem, that he adopted as a defense against all this inchoately gendered material.

For example, John Halifax, though an aggressive Victorian entrepreneur, was also a modernized eighteenth-century man of sensibility and benevolence; Little Lord Fauntleroy, though he loved his mother, was also a sturdy independent little scout; Brontë's Heathcliff was at once intensely masculine and indistinguishable from Cathy. From these readings Spilka argues for the existence of a pervasive androgynous ideology of the masculine in the culture of Hemingway's childhood. The Hemingway parents themselves could not be classified neatly as masculine man and feminine woman; Hemingway girl and boy children were equally instructed in domesticity, outdoor life, and genteel culture. It is not, then, that Hemingway was inscribed with the *wrong* sexual identity, but that to the extent that such identity is defined through difference from another sexual identity he had been inscribed with *no* sexual identity at all. Thus, sexually speaking, he was "androgynous."

Putting aside Spilka's failure to distinguish between biological sex and cultural gender, I find several problems with this analysis. One is that Spilka does not show what happened to instill in young Hemingway any felt need to counteract this androgynous cultural shaping—yet this need is taken to be the driving force of his entire adult life. Just as Lynn fails to identify any source from which Hemingway might have drawn his countermaternal "will to be a boy"[4] or even acquired the knowledge that he *was* a boy or what it meant to be a boy, Spilka does not identify any source for

Hemingway's apparent feeling that something was wrong about his sexual makeup, that he *ought* to be more neatly compartmentalized than he experienced himself to be. Spilka writes: "One could at least define androgyny in his life and works as a mixture or exchange of traditionally male and female traits, roles, activities, and sexual positions" (p. 4), but this definition resolves nothing. What led Hemingway to quarrel with this androgyny? And even more, since Spilka has shown at great length that "traditionally male and female traits" did not exist in the cultural context by which he believes Hemingway to have been shaped, from what ground might Hemingway have been able to interpret any given traits, roles, activities, or sexual positions as inappropriate to him?

Another problem with this analysis is that the most important of Hemingway's "androgynous" traits by far to Spilka turns out to be his enjoyment of the supine position in heterosexual intercourse. This is a problem since it is quite impossible that any of the adduced cultural sources could have served to inform him that such enjoyment disqualified him as a true man—the appropriate positions for men and women during sexual intercourse is not a topic that Emily Brontë, Frances Hodgson Burnett, or even Captain Marryatt deal with. Missing from Spilka's analysis, then, is evidence that would enable us to make a connection on Hemingway's behalf between any specific sexual practice and a given sexual identity.

Also missing from Spilka's analysis, notwithstanding an appreciation of Hemingway's mother that improves greatly over most accounts, is consideration of what the father's role in creating this (apparently) sexually mixed-up son might have been. I am not talking here about a conventionally passive or "absent" father. Spilka refers a few times to inconsistent and severe "parental" punishments instead of to (as other biographers make clear) specifically paternal brutality and irrationality. He does not allude to the father's depressions, even though they eventuated in suicide (as they also did in Ernest Hemingway's own case and those of two of his siblings and one of his children). The paternal suicide is rationalized as a response to physical disease and business failure rather than as manifesting a mental illness that might have victimized his children—both through his behavior and through their possibly inheriting his chemical predisposition to illness—far more than the mother's flaky experiments in child costume. "Though Ernest would never quite assimilate that tragedy [the father's suicide], he loved his father much and could forgive him many things. But his bitterness about his mother's disapproval . . . stayed with him" (p. 134); "Hemingway, of course, had the most trouble with his mother. He knew his father loved him, and for some things loved him back, but had good reasons to disrespect him and resent him. But it was his mother's sufferings . . ." (p. 194). These sentences seem faithful to Hemingway's own silences and noisy grievances, but if the whole point of Spilka's work is to read through what Hemingway wrote to understand what he was really saying, then Hemingway's attitudes toward his father should not be protected from scrutiny and rereading.

I question, finally, Spilka's inconsistent use of the concept of androgyny. At times he seems to mean the total reservoir of human attributes and potential deeds as they exist prior to cultural gender-marking; at other times he seems to imply individuals in whom specifically male and female traits are "really" mixed—hermaphrodites rather than androgynes. It could be argued that the persistent overlapping of traits in Hemingway's male and female characters implies that he himself had an androgynous (in the first sense) view of human potential; it could be argued contrariwise that his poorly concealed (indeed often proudly flaunted) homophobia displayed a very strong need for firm sexual boundaries. However that may be, when Spilka writes of Hemingway's "curiously androgynous makeup" (p. 328) or of one character's imposing "her androgynous and lesbian needs" on another (p. 307)—these are two of hundreds of possible examples of his practice—we seem to be working with a rather crude concept.

To summarize my critique: Spilka's book relies on interpretations of Hemingway's childhood reading for conclusions that such interpretations cannot support; though somewhat liberated it still remains partly in thrall to a view of Hemingway's childhood as dominated by a mother whose strength prevented him from attaining healthy manhood; and it adopts a crude model of what, at best, is a highly problematic concept—androgyny. It also suffers from an excessive admiration for the *Garden of Eden* manuscript that eventuates in pure bathos—as for example when Spilka writes that the work is

> a novel about a writer's bravery—about Hemingway's bravery as he saw it in the daily struggle to transcend his own terrible dependencies and passivities.... The traveller's daily record of meals, bars, beaches, beds, and barbershops is there because that is how he chiefly lived, under the "softening feminine influence" of married love that he sorely needed to exist at all; and his bravery consists mainly of stripping away his daily portion of manly sports (save one marvellous fishing scene and much androgynous swimming [sic]) and of collapsing the essential isolation of his post-Hadley marriages into a single honeymoon year of touring, tanning, eating, drinking, and making androgynous love—as if to force the lonely essence of the writer's inner life into felt existence for us, while at the same time indicating, indeed demonstrating, the power, range, and varied richness of his writing. [p. 300]

Despite all these far from minor concerns, I still find scattered in this enterprise, and particularly in the second half of the book where Spilka works through the Hemingway corpus with a view to uncovering the workings of androgyny, some superbly jolting insights. Generally speaking, Spilka views Hemingway's work as evolving from an initial openness to his own androgynous nature, through a sexual hardening and coarsening during the 1930s and after, until *The Garden of Eden* returns with some degree of self-consciousness to the question of androgyny, with the writer belatedly aware of how much he has lost through his lifelong attempt to achieve sexual certainty. As he delineates this progress, or regress, Spilka offers many suggestive readings. Naive and parochial as he might seem in our *fin de siècle* moment, a "man" who really believes that only "women" enjoy the supine position in heterosexual intercourse and then finds that he enjoys it too may become seriously disturbed. If he finds himself attracted to women who like the "dominant" position, which he believes that only "men" should enjoy, if he covets "women" who cut their hair short while still believing that they should grow their hair long, he may well become confused about what or who they are and he is. The most striking analysis in *Hemingway's Quarrel with Androgyny*—marred only by the exclusionary "we"—occurs in chapter 8, which analyzes *The Sun Also Rises* and *A Farewell to Arms*. "What if Brett is the woman Jake would in some sense like to be?" Spilka asks provocatively (p. 204); "she may well be the woman we vulnerable males, we antiheroes of the modern age, would all like to be, even as Catherine Barkley in the next novel is the healing woman whose ministrations we might all like to command" (p. 210). The idea that the Hemingway males would like to be women (as they imagine women to be) and that if they were women they would continue to love women—that, in some sense, the vaunted Hemingway hero is an (imaginary) lesbian woman—truly marks an epoch in Hemingway criticism.

Not, of course, that it says much or does much for "real" women, lesbian or not. Some of the strength of Spilka's readings resides in his fairly consistent and humane refusal to approach Hemingway's women figures as though they were meant to be realistic depictions. The best they can be, given the protagonist's struggle for sexual sanity, is a multiply mediated figure of his confused desire. When Spilka writes something like the following: "As he grew older, Papa Hemingway badly wanted a daughter through whom he might express those feminine feelings, and for this reason I think he addressed all women as Daughter—which suggests, not incidentally, that he might never have committed suicide if he had had one" (p. 252), he falls into the very trap that he usually rescues Hemingway from, the trap of confusing "real" women with male fantasy. A daughter might have saved Hemingway from committing suicide, but I wouldn't put money on the survival chances of that daughter.

It is clear that for Spilka, Hemingway is a better writer when he is more open to his own sexual multiplicity, a lesser writer when he gives in to his need for sexual certainty. How to judge literary quality is problematical, but it makes sense to think that writers will do better work when they are less intent on defending themselves. We all know that the two first short-story collections, the two early novels, and the two African stories—"The Short Happy Life of Francis Macomber" and "The Snows of Kilimanjaro"—are Hemingway's best writings. Their quality may have little to do, or everything to do, with Hemingway's sexual uncertainties. But that Spilka has developed a new and potentially more complex approach to these uncertainties—even though the approach needs to be rescued from the terminology within which he has developed it—is certain, and for those interested in sexual politics, the construction in culture of sexual differences, or the life and work of Ernest Hemingway, this book is necessary reading.

Notes

1. For an excellent account of Hemingway's self-publicizing activities, see John Raeburn, *Fame Became of Him: Hemingway as Public Writer* (Bloomington: Indiana Univ. Press, 1984).
2. Kenneth S. Lynn, *Hemingway* (New York: Simon and Schuster, 1987), p. 11.
3. Lynn, *Hemingway,* p. 11.
4. Lynn, *Hemingway,* p. 44.

Self-consuming Discourse: Spenserian Poetics and the "New" New Criticism

Richard A. McCabe

Harry Berger, Jr. *Revisionary Play: Studies in the Spenserian Dynamics*, introduced by Louis Montrose. Berkeley, Los Angeles, and London: University of California Press, 1988. xi, 483 pp.

Objecting to the pastoral conventions of *Lycidas*, Dr. Johnson contemptuously dismisses Milton's portrayal of innocent academic friendship as radically insincere: "We know that they never drove a field, and that they had no flocks to batten . . . . He who thus grieves will excite no sympathy; he who thus praises will confer no honour."[1] It might justly be replied that it is precisely through the use of pastoral conventions that Milton succeeded in exciting sympathy for, and bestowing considerable honor upon, an otherwise unremarkable young man. The efficacy of pastoral, whether personal or political, was one of the primary lessons he learned from his moral and aesthetic mentor, Edmund Spenser: "Let the novice . . . not therefore give himselfe to God, that hee may close the better with the World, like that false Shepheard *Palinode* in the Eclogue of *May*, under whom the Poet lively personates our Prelates, whose whole life is a recantation of their pastorall vow . . . those our admired *Spencer* inveighs against, not without some presage of these reforming times."[2] By slyly alluding to the prelates' "pastorall vow" Milton deftly assimilates Spenserian form to Spenserian theme, literary convention to ecclesiastical convention. The ensuing dichotomy between prelatial practice and apostolic injunction subverts the bishops' claim to spiritual descent from the first great author of pastoral: "The Lord is my shepherd; I shall not want./ He maketh me to lie down in green pastures" (Psalms 23:

1–2). The very landscape of literary pastoral satirizes bad ecclesiastical pastors, the acknowledged artificiality of the convention serving to expose the hidden artifice of outwardly conventional Christians. Acutely aware of both the traditional and "re-visionary" components of Spenserian pastoral, the Miltonic variety cultivates the potential coalescence of literary revision and the ecclesiastical reform it appears to adumbrate: a meticulous revision of traditionally unalterable texts and conventions was central to the endeavour of the great Reformers. What Spenser "presages" Milton sees. Thus it would seem that an intense awareness of convention is essential to its effective use, and it is this sense of awareness, this knowledge that "they never drove a field" which constitutes the central preoccupation of Harry Berger's *Revisionary Play: Studies in the Spenserian Dynamics*.

The work divides into two sections, the one a substantially new interpretation of *The Shepheardes Calender,* the other an anthology of Spenserian essays written in the wake of *The Allegorical Temper* (1957) before the onset of the New Historicism and its related disciplines.[3] The "revisionary play" of the title, therefore, is not solely the "play" of Spenser's creative imagination as it fashions and refashions its accumulated literary inheritance into ever more sophisticated and "reflexive" structures, but also the revisionary play of a "reconstructed old New Critic" practising a form of "close reading" characteristic of his school but discarding "its basic commitment to the ideology of *the work* as a self-contained fictive representation" (p. 460). Despite the apparently heterogeneous nature of its material, the resulting book achieves a surprising coherence since Berger's concerns remain similar while his methods develop. Because he is himself an obsessively "reflexive" critic, the evolution of his work remains one of its own major concerns, the conventions of criticism receiving almost as much attention as those of poetry. At times *Revisionary Play* seems more involved with itself than with Spenser. Anyone contemplating a history of New Criticism will ignore it at their peril.

In a remarkable afterword designed as a personal *apologia*, Berger provides a trenchant critique of the numerous unchallenged assumptions underlying contemporary critical theory and in particular of the notion that any reading "not explicitly

Self-consuming Discourse

accompanied by a critical credo" may be dismissed as purely subjective. By focusing attention upon the often haphazard subjectivity of the theorists themselves—together with the somewhat "thin results" of "their critical self-reflection"—he neatly reverses the argument, taking a forceful, if polite, offensive (pp. 458–59). The difficulty with all of this, however, lies in the implication that close reading of the type Berger himself champions is to be regarded merely as a critical method rather than a critical creed, a tool rather than a theory. This is debatable to say the least, and when Berger asserts that he can find "no necessary connection" between the quality of a literary reading and "the degree of self-reflection preceding it," the irony is unfortunately palpable.

Berger's account of his personal development speaks of his attempt to "de-aestheticize New-Critical practice" by questioning "the autonomous status of 'the work' in Renaissance literary discourse" (pp. 453–54), thereby establishing a reciprocal relationship between "aesthetic" and "political" approaches to texts (p. 456). Crucial to this decision was the influence of, amongst others, Roy Strong, Stephen Orgel, Stephen Greenblatt, Jonathan Goldberg, Richard Helgerson, and Louis Montrose, who provides a critical introduction to the volume. But influence is one thing and agreement is another.[4] The distinctive mark of Berger's criticism is that its "aesthetic" character remains paramount. The effort to "de-aestheticize" is also an effort to re-aestheticize "by appropriating the methodological and substantive insights of new historicists and others" (p. 458) to the concerns of New Criticism. Seldom has an act of "appropriation" flaunted itself so brazenly—or so candidly. Thus one detects in many of the resulting readings a circularity of movement from literature to politics and back to literature again which progressively strips the chosen passages of the keen social relevance detected by Milton. By effectively reducing politics, history, and literature to a set of "discourses" appropriate for—or appropriated to—the New Critical practice of close reading, Berger aestheticizes political discourse while pretending to politicize literary discourse. This is only to be expected since he regards Spenser's poems as "discourses of discourses, which is to say that they are discourses about the discourses they represent" (p. 462). The result of such "metadiscursivity" is that all "intertextual citations" function to direct the reader "to the values and interests embedded in the discourse of any genre" (p. 463). Thus Spenser emerges as a sort of New Critical deconstructionist whose major theme is new critical deconstruction. This seems a rather extreme conclusion to draw from the available evidence, tending as it does to diminish the vibrant vitality of Spenserian vision by narrowing its range from the portrayal of life and society to "the portrayal of the portrayal of Life, Society, and so on" (p. 467)—to the mere shadow of a shadow, as Plato might have said. Whereas the former New Criticism merely isolated the work, the new brand would appear to isolate the poet as well. The danger now arises that the pursuit of "close reading" may generate "enclosed" readings, that "close" may degenerate to "near-sighted," obscuring overall design in its concentration upon minute detail. To employ an analogy from the visual arts, one may move too close to a picture to see it.[5]

Berger's argument suffers from a failure to define "close reading" or clearly specify its methods. Is it acceptable, for example, to canvass a word's total range of connotations in a context which seems to demand only the primary one, or to labor its alleged significance by insisting upon an etymological root normally obscured in common usage? Is it permissible to deduce from mere coincidences of sound, conclusions regarding broad issues of authorial intent?[6] Consider the following example designed to lend textual support to the hypothesis that Spenser constructs around the *personae* of *The Shepheardes Calender* an elaborately "metapastoral" framework which sets them in ironic perspective. Since any reader would have to be alerted to this mechanism at an early stage, Berger focuses upon the description of Colin Clout's first monologue as a "plaint"—a conventional component of pastoral poetry and for that very reason a convenient instrument of "metapastoral" wit. *"Playning,"* he asserts, "combines *play* with *payne*" (p. 330). And so it does, but to extrapolate from the combination of sounds an equivalent combination of ideas is another matter. In any case, why should Colin's pastoral "play" prove any less "serious" than Berger's own "revisionary play"—unless, of course, the entire volume constitutes a "metacritical" joke designed to parody itself? Greater caution still must be exercized with "play" and "playne" when we learn some hundred pages later (pp. 442–43) that the whole notion of Spenserian "metapastoral" is to a large extent premised upon the highly contentious psychological theories of Harold Bloom concerning the alledgedly oedipal "anxieties" of creative "influence."[7] Spenser "resists the co-optation of paternity," clearing a space for himself in literary history "by a combination of 'revisionary ratios' that perform a brilliant misreading of the precursor traditions" (p. 443). One suspects that this theoretical "combination of ratios" must itself "co-opt paternity" for the "combination" of "play" and "payne" in "playne." Close reading of the text has become close reading into the text: Spenser provides one word, the critic supplies three.

I am not disputing the imaginative qualities of Berger's suggestion but rather the implications for the critical method he espouses in the light of his own comments upon "theory" and "creed." It is indeed important to keep literature at the heart of literary studies, and I share his dissatisfaction with readings which have "like doughnuts, a hole in the middle where interpretation ought to be" (p. 323). Nevertheless, in attempting to rectify this situation Berger seems to produce interpretations which diminish the relevance of literature to its readers by reducing the concerns of poetry to poetry itself. Struggling to establish the importance of literature, he renders it instead self-important because self-absorbed, and his criticism suffers a fate equivalent to its subject because its revisionary methods are so inextricably linked to its textual theories. Consequently, Berger's study of *The Shepheardes Calender* is fraught with procedural difficulties.

In Berger's view Spenser's attitude to pastoral is circumspect to the point of endeavoring a reflexive critique of the very tradition it simultaneously attempts to employ and develop: *The Shepheardes Calender* is "self-amused pastoral, a critical and comically squint reenactment of attitudes, topics, and norms characteristic of a traditional literary mode" (p. 277). This is to say that Spenser is not merely a pastoral poet but a critic of pastoral poetry producing his criticism as pastoral verse. Such a reading comes perilously close to exposing Spenser to the criticism levelled against Colin Clout—that his "rymes" are more important than his avowed themes (p. 400)—but for the alleged association between literary conventions and states of mind in "showing how an attitude toward art implicates an attitude toward life" (p. 288). Thus the "hard" and "soft" views of pastoral, whose symbiotic relationship has been well explored by Paul Alpers, express different reactions to human experience whether "escapist" or "realistic."[8] Through a critique of conventions, it is argued, Spenser performs a critique of attitudes: "The fundamental object of Spenser's criticism is the longing for paradise as the psychological basis of the pastoral retreat from life" (p. 277). Ultimately this may be regarded as "an attempt to flee from the lessons of experience by forgetting them" (p. 451). Berger differs from Alpers, however, in regarding Spenser as standing at an equivalent critical distance from the pastoral tradition as does Alpers himself with the result that "Alpers's conclusions about the *Calender*, and his evaluation of it, are represented in the *Calender* and have been targeted in advance" (p. 287). What pastoral poetry actually retreats to in its recreative mode, Berger insists, is not rural life but pastoral convention, literary rather than agricultural topography, "a set of *topoi*, of 'places' as well as conventions, authenticated by their durability" (p. 288). Such a movement, he argues, "is by no means apolitical" since "it implicates a pastoral of sexual politics and, by the same token, a political critique of paradisal poetics" (p. 386). It would therefore follow that, within such conventions, criticism of mental attitudes necessarily involves critical reassessment of the conventions themselves: "Romantic expectations are the source of failure and premature bitterness. And since poetic conventions are in turn the source of romantic expectations, the pastoral critique is first and foremost a critique of pastoral" (p. 289). By maneuvers such as these the dancer is confounded in the dance even though they are quite distinct as soon as the music stops.

Berger's critique teeters on the edge of infinite regress. To what extent, we might ask, is reflexive critique itself to be understood as a pastoral convention entailing yet further procedures of reflexive assessment and so continuing *ad infinitum*, or *ad nauseam*? Repeatedly the new brand of New Criticism seems to veer away from its own best insights, refusing to engage with the political implications of a form replete with social and religious significance—especially for a poet about to venture into the "hard" pastoral world of Tudor Ireland in the service of its severest critic, Lord Arthur Grey. Berger seems relatively uninterested in the issues examined, for instance, in Patricia Coughlan's anthology *Spenser and Ireland*, but rather transforms all acts of political criticism into acts of literary criticism.[9] Apropos of what he regards as Spenser's "ironic relationship" (p. 336) to his "puppet" Colin Clout, he asks "how genuine or authentic" are "the love and grief that can be proportioned to the demands of poetry and displayed in the mirror of art?" (p. 345). But how authentic, one may ask in return, is a critique exquisitely proportioned to similar demands and displayed in the same mirror? Has the critic been manipulated into accepting conventional critique as a critique of convention? The puppet play in Jonson's *Bartholomew Fair* relies upon the perversion and distortion of heroic conventions, but in order to appreciate the point of such satire one must understand the nature of the puppeteer and his audience. The real explanation lies outside the conventions.

Berger is surely right, however, in insisting that Spenser is not to be *identified* with Colin Clout, a point sometimes overlooked, or at least obscured, in John Bernard's *Ceremonies of Innocence: Pastoralism in the Poetry of Edmund Spenser*.[10] Colin Clout is a *persona*, not a person, as E. K. acknowledges, and his odyssey through the *Calender* may well entail an element of "petulance" as well as "spirituality" (p. 331). Even so, the relationship between Colin and Spenser remains elusive. Convention is not the same as cliché nor puppetry identical to pastoral characterization. It is not at all clear to me that "as *Colin* moves to naturalize his plight, *we* perceive his language to conventionalize it in distortions that denaturalize nature" (p. 334), nor that "Colin's bathos increases together with his increasingly grotesque metamorphosis . . . of nature and man into distortions each of the other" (p. 337). Irony of a sort is certainly present, but whether it be the irony of increasingly detached amusement is debatable. There is also the irony of unrequited desire, the fatal irony of obsessive pursuit and inevitable frustration informing so much of human experience. Perhaps not "petulance," then, but disillusionment. It could well be argued that as the mood of the *Calender* darkens, Colin becomes more sympathetic, not less, as the pains of blighted love come to symbolize those of all finite, linear creatures trapped in the relentless, impassive sequence of cyclical renewal and decay. Not the proportioning of man to nature, but their radical disproportioning would then become the poet's theme as Colin "homeward drove his sonned sheepe,/Whose hanging heads did seeme his carefull case to weepe."

Whereas Nancy Jo Hoffman reads these lines as Spenser's endorsement of Colin's outlook, Berger detects "ambivalence" in "seeme."[11] Ambivalence there is, but not, I think, at Colin's expense. The sheep don't care because pathetic fallacy is, as its name implies, a fiction. The really pathetic thing is Nature's indifference to song and silence, love and hate. Poet, persona, and reader are drawn closer at the very point Berger would have them draw apart. "I find it hard to imagine," he writes, "that Spenser expects me to work up much alarm over the plight or pathology of Colin Clout or to spend much time judiciously castigating his pastoral puppet's flawed character" (p. 390). Such a dismissive attitude is hard to reconcile with the contrary insistence upon the need to assess the psychological motivations of all of Spenser's pastoral speakers. Whereas a distinction between Spenser and Colin Clout provides a salutary corrective to those who would too easily translate Colin's elegies of love into Spenser's elegies of state, their complete dissociation proves counter-productive (pp. 385–89).[12] Spenser can no more be wholly identified with or wholly dissociated from Colin Clout than Elizabeth I can be wholly identified with or dissociated from "fayre Eliza." By identifying Colin as Spenser's "target" rather than his "mouthpiece" (p. 385), Berger reduces Spenser to the level of Zeal-of-the-Land-Busy "judiciously castigating his pastoral puppet's flawed character" in an apparently absurd exercise. As I see it, Colin Clout is not an end but a means, not an object of praise or blame, but a medium through which a variety of aesthetic and political issues are explored, including the relationship of aesthetics to politics.

Self-consuming Discourse 193

By arguing that the "carefull" patterning of Colin's verse renders its sincerity suspect, Berger takes upon him the mantle of Johnsonian disapproval: "Where there is leisure for fiction there is little grief."[13] But what if fiction be a component of grief or a necessary psychological strategy for its containment? Is the Dido elegy inevitably narcissistic because the elegist identifies with his subject, or may his gestures towards transcendence, related as they are to the ancient tradition of *contemptus mundi*, be dismissed as the mere escapism of a self-discrediting "paradise principle" (pp. 414–15)? As Isabel MacCaffrey rightly points out, Christianity necessitates a "paradise principle," a longing to return to the Good Shepherd's "green pastures," which may well be "shadowed" in the pastoral convention.[14] Since E. K.'s "glosse" to the Dido elegy suggests as much, it is difficult to see what Spenser's "target" might be—if not Christianity itself by way of King David's own spurious poetic "devising."[15] This seems unlikely in view of the *Calender's* concern with spiritual pastoralism. Self-pity masquerading as compassion is doubtless repugnant, but the Dido elegy surely demonstrates a contrary principle: "Any Mans *death* diminishes *me*, because I am involved in *Mankinde;* And therefore never send to know for whom the *bell* tolls; It tolls for *thee.*"[16] As some of the best elegies, including Gray's, are based on Donne's premise, I cannot agree that Dido's demise is "*illogically* converted to a paradigm of the hopelessness of the human condition" (p. 407). At moments such as these the textual evidence for Berger's "metapastoral" seems weak, particularly since such an enormous proportion of the *Calender's* lines are actually assigned to pastoral speakers (p. 286). Despite the fact that the poem is such an early Spenserian work, Berger assumes that relatively uninspired passages are designed to display "conspicuous triteness" and must therefore be deliberately flat (p. 411). Furthermore, he assumes that readers must be aware of this in order to appreciate the debilitating social and poetic effects of the "paradise principle" occasioning the "triteness" to be such as it is. This is questionable from whatever point one approaches it and makes many of the alleged convolutions of "metapastoral" seem increasingly arbitrary. I think it not unfair to say that Berger reads *The Shepheardes Calender* through *The Faerie Queene* even though Spenser could never have written it from such a perspective. The critic's final "Spenserian" work was virtually Spenser's first. As a result the interpretation is more sophisticated than the text.

The difficulty is that, whereas man remains locked in the "green cabinet" of nature, not art, Berger will allow of no "nature" in pastoral that is not primarily "a cultural category . . . an abstraction selectively defined according to the norms of any particular culture." Accordingly, "the primary referents of nature terms in pastoral are literary conventions and contexts . . . it is not, then, the book of nature that causes the fall but the nature of books" (p. 353). None of the denizens of pastoral is allowed any concept of nature not born of reading pastoral, even though the "pastors" who discuss the fall in the moral eclogues have clearly been reading a different set of texts—or at least are so presented. On balance the subject of nature is better handled by John W. Moore and Isabel MacCaffrey, as indeed by Berger himself in an earlier essay which argues that "Spenser presupposes not only a matrix of 'nature' but also a matrix of convention" (p. 111).[17] The limitations of nature constitute a major theme of Spenserian pastoral analogous to the chilling pastoral vision of Poussin: "Et in Arcadia ego."

Berger is on much surer ground in his treatment of pastoral misogyny where his subject is less the pastoral of political power than the "psychocultural" power of pastoral itself in determining attitudes towards gender.[18] "Misogyny," he argues, "is the dark side of recreative narcissism" (p. 393). The absence of woman "as a person" from the pastoral landscape—as distinct from her ubiquity as "Idea, Grace, Goddess, Muse, fairy, Queen, tormentor" and so on (p. 359)—he attributes to the shallow stereotypic fantasies of male desire, a frequent theme of his earlier Spenserian essays. On this basis he produces a highly provocative reading of the *March* eclogue designed to demonstrate how the perception of love as a predatory hunt with woman as the prey "provides the recipe for frustration and bitterness whether the hunter fails or succeeds, though the deferred bitterness of success-induced failure is the more interesting of the two possibilities" (p. 371).

As such a reading might suggest, the major benefit deriving

Self-consuming Discourse 195

from Berger's insistence upon reflexive "metapastoral" is that, when handled with restraint, it enormously heightens the psychological complexity of the bucolic drama presented before us in twelve intriguing acts. By dissociating the motives of individual speakers from the traditional attitudes they espouse, he helps us to appreciate the suggestive ambivalence of the dialogues (pp. 283–84). Thus we find that the "hard" pastoral attitude of the elder shepherds is actually a disenchanted product of its "soft" counterpart, since the callow innocence of the youthful lovers provokes as much envy as moral concern: "*Januarye* shows how the plaintive *puer* is *senex* in being imprinted with conventional expectations derived from the culture of the literary elders he imitates, while *Februarie* shows how the moral *senex* is *puer*—how the so-called wisdom of the elders thinly veils the bitterness born of nostalgia for lost youth" (p. 369). In this manner Spenser distances both himself and us from the apparently insoluble polarity of the debate by creating a complex relationship between the speakers indicating "how the two opposing viewpoints contaminate each other" (p. 371).

This insight is greatly developed in the chapter entitled "An Hoor Heed and a Grene Tayl" which provides, in relation to the sexual politics of the invariably acrimonious dialectic between youth and age, one of the most stimulating expositions of the *Februarie* eclogue to have appeared. Berger rejects the notion that Thenot's aphoristic home-truths enunciate Spenser's own dismissal of "soft" pastoral attitudes positing "an idyllic congruence between man and nature, microcosm and macrocosm, that experience belies" (pp. 419–20). Instead he suggests that Spenser depicts a measure of "self-dividedness" in Thenot attributable to his unconscious "membership in the devil's party of youth" (p. 417). As a result, "we do not seriously question Cuddie's insight that envy and the loss of virility make Thenot a killjoy" (p. 418). Thus the moral potency of age is undermined by its sexual impotence—in fact, moralizing is its last vicarious sexual pleasure. The "breme winter" of which Thenot warns Cuddie, "drerily shooting his stormy darte," is no less than "a wintry Cupid . . . a figure of the persistence of desire in old age" (p. 422). In so far as Cuddie's view of love is motivated by a hollow "paradise principle" which views the attainment of women as a mere "test of masculinity" ensuring his place in male society, he will in time become Thenot, an ironically appropriate punishment for his dismissal of the old man's advice (p. 429). The two shepherds "are more in agreement than they know" (p. 429) since their respective positions are "dialectically inter-involved in a single complex attitude" (p. 430).[19] Such interpretations seem to me to represent "close reading" at its best, and the Spenser revealed to us is a master of intricate dramatic monologues. The drama of his pastoral poetry is no longer confined to the opposition of antithetical viewpoints but extended to embrace such internal ironies and contradictions as render the viewpoints themselves ambivalent.[20] Many of the inconsistencies noted and complained of by former critics reveal surprisingly problematic facets of their speakers' characters.[21] Apparently inconsistent stereotypes become complex *personae*.

Such ideas are not entirely original to Berger but may be found, for example, in the work of Patrick Cullen.[22] But Berger departs from Cullen in that his vision of an almost obsessively reflexive pastoral disallows any suggestion that Spenser's literary technique was intended to analyze human nature. Rather, he asserts, its target is "*literary* comedy, human *traditions,* and *artifice* . . . received opinion sedimented into the institution of literature operative in his time" (p. 425). This is unfortunate since it demonstrates the alarming tendency of New Criticism's "hoor heed" to emulate the fabled *uroboros* by swallowing its own "grene tayl." Spenser's concerns are wider than literary tradition because he is more than just a literary critic. As I have attempted to show elsewhere, his acute assessment of the social and political implications of "tradition" in *A View of the Present State of Ireland* indicates a clear awareness of the relationship between "re-vision" and reform, between poetics and politics.[23] Indeed, the logic of Berger's own argument seems to point in the same direction.[24] The ironic portrayal—or exposé—of Thenot's morality has important implications for the censorial attitude to cultural achievement which exercises Spenser elsewhere, particularly in the proem to the fourth book of *The Faerie Queene*.[25] The censor's desire for a poetry of moral imperatives excluding "anything ambiguous or problematical" renders Spenserian art impossible. Ironically it would impose upon him the very strictures he himself wished upon the Celtic poets whose technique he admired even as he deplored their politically "licentious" love for a form of heroism antipathetic to the fashioning of Elizabethan gentlemen "in vertuous and gentle discipline."[26] Berger notes that "the Poet is a budding Censor" because "the Censor is a closet Poet" (p. 444).

Through their use of literary conventions the eclogues do turn our attention to human nature and the turbulent history that is its product. That "Redde rose medled with the White yfere" in the face of the shepherds' queen bespeaks an intricate relationship between the pastoral and the political, fairy myth and Tudor myth-making. But Eliza plays a subordinate role in Berger's "personal *Calender*" (p. 442). And "personal" it certainly is since it appropriates Edmund Spenser to the party of the New Critics while revising the New Critics' self-image through the reinterpretation of Spenserian texts. Critical "re-vision" becomes personal reform. Berger has absorbed both Colin Clout and Edmund Spenser into a "metapastoral" construct as artificial in its own way as that of William Browne who, in the "revisionary" landscape of *Britannia's Pastorals* (1613–16), exploited the coincidence of Colin's senescence and Spenser's death to confront public conscience with an image of the poet, not as Berger's "parricidal" slayer of ancestral conventions, but as the pathetic filial victim of the social, political, and cultural evils lamented by Cuddie in the *October* eclogue.[27] As one mask is replaced by another, the face beneath remains elusive.

Notes

1. Samuel Johnson, *Lives of the English Poets*, ed. George Birkbeck Hill, 3 vols. (Oxford: Clarendon Press, 1905) I, 164.

2. John Milton, *Works,* ed. F. A. Patterson, A. Abbott, H. M. Ayres, et al., 18 vols. (New York: Columbia Univ. Press, 1931–1938) III, 165–66.

3. Berger, *The Allegorical Temper: Vision and Reality in Book II of Spenser's "Faerie Queene"* (New Haven: Yale Univ. Press, 1957).

4. See especially Stephen Greenblatt, *Renaissance Self-fashioning: From More to Shakespeare* (Chicago: Univ. of Chicago Press, 1980); Richard Helgerson, *Self-Crowned Laureates: Spenser, Jonson, Milton and the Literary System* (Berkeley: Univ. of California Press, 1983); Jonathan Goldberg, *James I and the Politics of Literature: Jonson, Shakespeare, Donne and Their Contemporaries* (Baltimore: Johns Hopkins Univ. Press, 1983); Louis Montrose, "Of Gentlemen and Shepherds: The Politics of Elizabethan Pastoral Form," *ELH*, 50 (1983), 415–59; Stephen Greenblatt, ed., *Representing the English Renaissance* (Berkeley: Univ. of California Press, 1988).

5. It is an analogy Berger himself endorses: "Spenser is never fully or realistically caught up *within* his imaginary world; he stands before it as a painter before a panel, looking at it, adding touches, interpreting to observers, displaying rather than expressing his responses" (p. 59).

6. See, for example, *Revisionary Play*, pp. 45, 118, 161, 345.

7. Bloom, *The Anxiety of Influence: A Theory of Poetry* (New York: Oxford Univ. Press, 1973).

8. Alpers, "The Eclogue Tradition and the Nature of Pastoral," *College English*, 34 (1972), 352–53.

9. Coughlan, ed., *Spenser and Ireland: An Interdisciplinary Approach* (Cork: Cork Univ. Press, 1989).

10. Like Berger, Bernard too is much concerned with the "reflexive" and "revisionary" components of Spenserian poetry—sometimes to the extent of treating it as fictive autobiography. Bernard, *Ceremonies of Innocence: Pastoralism in the Poetry of Edmund Spenser* (Cambridge: Cambridge Univ. Press, 1989), pp. 11, 69–70, 107, 163–85.

11. Hoffman, *Spenser's Pastorals: "The Shepheardes Calender" and "Colin Clout"* (Baltimore: Johns Hopkins Univ. Press, 1977), p. 52

12. Annabel Patterson, "Re-opening the Green Cabinet: Clement Marot and Edmund Spenser," *ELR*, 16 (1986), 44–70.

13. Johnson, *Lives of the Poets*, I, 163

14. MacCaffrey, "Allegory and Pastoral in *The Shepheardes Calender*," *ELH*, 36 (1969), 104–5.

15. According to E. K., the "Elysian fieldes" were "devised of Poetes to be a place of Pleasure like Paradise, where the happye soules doe rest in peace and eternal happynesse." *The Poetical Works of Edmund Spenser*, ed. J. C. Smith and E. De Selincourt (London: Oxford Univ. Press, 1912), p. 463.

16. John Donne, *Devotions upon Emergent Occasions*, ed. Anthony Raspa (Montreal: McGill-Queen's Univ. Press, 1975), p. 87.

17. Moore, "Colin Breaks His Pipe: A Reading of the 'January' Eclogue," *ELR*, 5 (1975), 12–17; MacCaffrey, "Allegory and Pastoral," 93–101.

18. See Louis Montrose, "'Eliza, Queene of shepheardes' and the Pastoral of Power," *ELR*, 10 (1980), 153–82.

19. Applying this principle to the larger world of *The Faerie Queene*, Berger concludes that "the contradictions that perpetuate this dialectic convert the

Self-consuming Discourse 199

delusion to its antithesis; the proffered exemption from reciprocity and death generates the false consciousness of childhood, and the subsequent disenchantment of the naked babes only reproduces in their generation the bitterness from which the elders tried vainly to escape" (p. 452).

20. Particularly provocative are the arguments for the "fictional autonomy" of the character Thenot throughout the *Calender* (pp. 396–99).

21. Alpers remarks that "Colin's dramatic speeches, in 'June' and 'December,' are full of inconsistencies of rhetoric and attitude. Only in the elaborate stanzas of 'Aprill' and 'November' . . . does Spenser find a way of making divergent modes and stances seem at home in the same poem." See "The Eclogue Tradition," p. 367. See also Hoffman, *Spenser's Pastorals,* p. 65.

22. Cullen, *Spenser, Marvell, and Renaissance Pastoral* (Cambridge: Harvard Univ. Press, 1970), pp. 31–34.

23. Richard A. McCabe, *The Pillars of Eternity: Time and Providence in "The Faerie Queene"* (Dublin: Irish Academic Press, 1989), pp. 43, 191–93, 202–3.

24. "For Spenser . . . vision must be bounded and shaped by the sense that it is not reality; and it must yield to reality at last" (p. 242). See also pp. 268–69.

25. "The stern morality of the Tudor fathers is imitated or glanced at in statements made by E. K., as well as in other corners of the *Calender,* not only to anticipate and disarm it but also to expose its roots in motives that are not reducible to a concern for virtue and public morality" (pp. 446–47).

26. Richard A. McCabe, "The Fate of Irena: Spenser and Political Violence," in *Spenser and Ireland,* ed. Patricia Coughlan, p. 123.

27. Browne, *Britannia's Pastorals,* 2 bks. (London, 1613–16), Bk. 2, pp. 26–27.

Canon or Sixshooters?

Keen Butterworth

A. Carl Bredahl, Jr. *New Ground: Western American Narrative and the Literary Canon.* Chapel Hill: University of North Carolina Press, 1989. 195 pp.

An Easterner traveling into the American West for the first time is struck with openness—vast stretches of landscape, distant horizons, an overwhelming sky. There is a communion with space and distances that is seldom possible in the East. If one allows himself to be drawn out by this landscape, the ego attenuates in a way that can be both frightening and exhilarating. The feeling is expressed by Jim Burden in Willa Cather's *My Ántonia:*

> There was nothing but land.... I had the feeling that the world was left behind, that we had got over the edge of it, and were outside man's jurisdiction. I had never before looked up at the sky when there was not a familiar mountain ridge against it. But this was the complete dome of heaven.... If we never arrived anywhere it did not matter. Between the earth and that sky I felt erased, blotted out. I did not say my prayers that night: here, I felt, what would be would be.[1]

At times the feeling can be oceanic. The painter George Catlin said of the high prairies during his travels of the 1830s: "Here you are out of sight of land." And A. B. Guthrie, who grew up in northwestern Montana, has denominated the region the land of "The Big Sky."

It is Bredahl's contention that Western landscape has shaped not only the character of its inhabitants but also the forms of its art. This is not an original perception, as Bredahl himself recognizes. Charles Olson, in *Call Me Ishmael,* observed that space has always been a central fact to the American mind. Bredahl, however, wishes to distinguish between the Easterner's response to space and that of the Westerner. Easterners are concerned with taming the land and making it serve the needs of man, whether to create the City on the Hill in the North or enclose and preserve Eden in the South. Westerners, on the other hand, find their vast landscapes intractable; thus, they adapt themselves to the processes and rhythms of Nature rather than attempting to impose theirs on the land. The Eastern sensibility consequently finds value in enclosure, in traditional literary forms; the Western sensibility resists enclosure and finds value in surfaces and processes. Because, Bredahl maintains, the major publishing houses and the critical establishment are dominantly Eastern, Western writers have been misunderstood and undervalued. It is his purpose in *New Ground* to explain and illustrate the nature of the Western sensibility with the hope that readers will see Western writing as different from but not inferior to the work of canonized writers of the East. Thus, Bredahl's purpose is much the same as that of John R. Milton in *The Novel of the American West,* a work to which Bredahl acknowledges his considerable debt.[2] Bredahl, however, does not limit himself to fiction; he treats both fiction and non-fiction prose, and ends the book with a chapter on the films of John Ford and Sam Peckinpah. Nor is the book a systematic study like Milton's. It is, after the first two chapters, which establish East-West polarities, rather a series of discrete essays about representative writers of the region—a region which he defines broadly to include such midwesterners as Hamlin Garland, Sherwood Anderson, and Ernest Hemingway.

Bredahl's first chapter does a credible job of establishing the importance of enclosure to the Eastern sensibility by tracing attitudes toward the new land from colonial times to present. Bredahl ignores, however, the anti-enclosure implications in Emerson's writings and, most importantly, the emphatic "open-ness" of Whitman. His attempts to place Melville and Faulkner among the proponents of enclosure seem to me misdirected. *Moby-Dick* is certainly one of the most spacious books in our literature. And Ahab does not become "demonic to the extent that he resists enclosure" (p. 14). He becomes demonic to the extent that he resists the natural human values represented by Queequeg—precisely because he attempts to enclose the cosmos with his mind. And Faulkner's attitudes toward landscape and wilderness are more akin to those of Western writers like Cather, Guthrie, and Stegner than to Hawthorne, James, and Updike. A minor matter is Bredahl's use of W. G. Simms's fiction to illustrate the Easterners' lack of attention to surface. He uses *The Yemassee,* one of Simms's first novels, for illustration. Yet Simms's later novels, particularly *Eutaw* and *The Forayers,* are filled with realistic details of the flora and fauna of South Carolina forests and swamps. Also, Bredahl's discussion of traditional captivity narratives would have been more effective if he had compared modern novels, such as Thomas Berger's *Little Big Man* or Benjamin Capps's *A Woman of the People,* which are based on—but subvert—the tradition, with Mary Rowlandson's seventeenth-century narrative.

Bredahl's second chapter, "The Demands of Space: The Westering Imagination," is the best in the book. Taking his cue from John R. Milton, Bredahl compares Francis Parkman's *The Oregon Trail* with Lewis Garrard's *Wah-to-yah and the Taos Trail.*[3] Both men had travelled into the mountain west in 1846, but their reactions to and reflections upon their experiences are strikingly (and tellingly) different. Parkman, the Bostonian, remained detached from the world he travelled through, and attempted to understand his experience in terms of the cultural attitudes of his native New England. Garrard, on the other hand, was a midwesterner, an Ohioan, who opened himself to his experiences and tried to understand the land, the mountain men, the Indians, and the Mexicans on their own terms. He immersed himself in and relished his adventures, whereas Parkman retreated into the safety of a critical Eastern superiority. Bredahl's comparison of these two men makes clearer than any of his other discussions the differences of attitude between East and West.

The remaining eight chapters of *New Ground* are discussions of the works of Sherwood Anderson, Mary Austin, Ernest Hemingway, A. B. Guthrie, Walter Van Tilburg Clark, Harvey Fergusson, Wright Morris, Ivan Doig, John Ford, and Sam Peckinpah. Bredahl manifests his appreciation and understanding of the works that he discusses; but he has a tendency to isolate individual works and take them to represent the author's entire vision, when, in fact, they may not do so. A case in point is *The Big Sky,* A. B. Guthrie's best-known novel. Bredahl's emphasis is on the disjunctions of the novel's structure and the thematic emphasis on the impulse to break free of enclosures. But to separate *The Big Sky* from the other two novels of the trilogy can be misleading. *The Way West* is about the Oregon migration of the 1840s, and *These Thousand Hills* about the establishment of cattle ranches in Montana during the latter decades of the century. They are about the settling and enclosing of the West. Boone Caudill of *The Big Sky* is only a partial expression of Guthrie's vision: it will take Lat Evans of *These Thousand Hills* to complete it.[4]

The chapter on Hemingway also suffers from similar distortions. First, it seems odd to consider Hemingway a Western writer. His childhood was spent in suburban Chicago, except for those periods at Walloon Lake, which is northwoods, not much different from Maine and parts of New York, Vermont, and New Hampshire—certainly not a Western landscape. And the shaping of his intellectual life was largely cosmopolitan. There are Western elements in Hemingway's writing, due mainly to the influence of Twain and Sherwood Anderson. But to take *Green Hills of Africa* as an example of Hemingway's Western-ness seems misdirected.[5] Bredahl's point is that *Green Hills* is a book about process, purification, finding oneself through interaction with the physical world. But these are not themes peculiar to writers of the American West. One finds the same structures and themes in Thoreau's *Walden,* Marjorie Rawlings's *Cross Creek,* Horace Kephart's *Our Southern Highlanders,* Henry Beston's *The Outermost House* and even Annie Dillard's *Pilgrim at Tinker Creek.* Bredahl makes interesting, fresh observations about Hemingway's work, but they are only peripherally related to the concerns of the rest of the book. And his statement that Hemingway's literary star has fallen during the 1970s and '80s is not borne out by fact: In the mid-eighties, full-length studies by Kenneth S. Lynn, Jeffrey Meyers, and Peter Griffin, and the publication of *The Garden of Eden* and the *Finca Vigía* edition of Hemingway's short stories would indicate that Hemingway's literary star is still ascendant and shines very bright.[6]

Bredahl has an excellent chapter on what he calls the "Divided Narratives" of Mary Austin and Sherwood Anderson. The treatment of Anderson is limited to a short analysis of *Winesburg, Ohio;* but it is illuminating and cogent, illustrating how George Willard's impulse to function physically in the environment correlates with his desire for verbal expression. The treatment of Austin is extended and also illuminating. Using the arguments of Austin's *The American Rhythm*—that jazz and Native American music provide rhythms closer to the American experience than do the imposed rhythms of European music—Bredahl analyzes the structure and themes of Austin's classic *The Land of Little Rain,* a book that deserves more attention and a wider audience than it has attracted in recent years.[7] The thesis of the chapter, however, that the divided narrative—the ordering of a narrative into discrete individual units, rather than sequential units—is a result of the Western experience and a strategy to escape enclosure is unconvincing because Bredahl does not consider a larger context. He traces the form to Hamlin Garland's *Main-Travelled Roads.* However, James Joyce would use the same methods in *Dubliners* spontaneously, and this tendency toward disjunction became an identifying trait of modernism—evident also in the poetic-sequences of *The Waste Land,* Pound's *Cantos,* and, later, Warren's *Audubon: A Vision.* Artistic disjunction, whether it be in literature, music, or painting, is an expression of modern man's philosophical perception that experience is not continuous and that attempts to present it as such are remnant manifestations of eighteenth- and nineteenth-century mind-sets. Although a few western and midwestern writers like Garland, Austin, Cather, Anderson, and Hemingway were among the first to experiment with the form, divided narrative does not set Western writing apart from Eastern American and European art of the twentieth century.

Bredahl's analyses of Walter Van Tilburg Clark's *The Ox-Bow Incident* and Wright Morris's *The Home Place* are very good; and even though neither of the two seems to me definitively Western—not formally different from, say, Faulkner's *Light in August* on the one hand and the Agee/Evans collaboration *Let Us Now Praise Famous Men* on the other—I cannot argue with Bredahl's perceptions and conclusions. His discussion of Harvey Fergusson's *The Conquest of Don Pedro,* however, seems forced into the framework of this study. Fergusson's novel is about an outsider's attempt to penetrate, understand, and alter an established culture. It is an ancient theme: in American literature we find it prominently in such works as Henry James's *The American,* G. W. Cable's *The Grandissimes,* and Kate Chopin's *The Awakening.* To isolate Fergusson from the tradition is to deny a continuity in European and American literature that is obvious and valuable.

Bredahl's final chapter on a literary figure discusses the work of Montana-born writer Ivan Doig. The chapter is a perceptive and sensitive treatment of Doig's work to date. Anyone who has visited the valley of the Smith River, both summer and winter, can understand the tremendous impact landscape has had on Doig's sensibility. Surrounded by mountains—the Little Belts to the north, Big Belts on the west, the Bridgers stretching southward, the Castle hills on the east—the village of White Sulphur Springs seems isolated from the rest of the world, yet open to the universe. It is obvious why Doig titled his autobiography *House Made of Sky: Landscapes of a Western Mind*—a book that must stand with Wallace Stegner's *Wolf Willow* as the best accounts of childhoods spent in the northern Rocky Mountains region. My appreciation of the book is not so unqualified as Bredahl's, however. An egoism creeps into its final pages, a self-indulgent egoism that leaves a sour taste in the mouth after the wonderful evocation of a childhood spent in that harsh and beautiful landscape. Nevertheless, Doig is a talented and powerful writer who deserves a place among the most respected writers of his generation, and Bredahl is to be commended for recognizing his importance and attempting to gain Doig a wider audience. And, perhaps, Doig is more Western than any of the other writers Bredahl discusses. Certainly his attitudes, formal concerns, and themes are more purely Western—without apology to the East— than are his predecessors'.

Bredahl's final chapter, on the films of Ford and Peckinpah, is more difficult to assess than his other chapters. First, all competent film directors are concerned with surfaces and so are "Western" by Bredahl's definition. There are, however, differences in thematic interest, form, and technique which can be contrasted to illustrate "Eastern" or "Western" attitudes; and this is Bredahl's approach. For him Ford's theme is the conquest and enclosure of wilderness to make it safe for women, children, and, thus, posterity; Peckinpah's films, on the other hand, are about men attempting to escape enclosure, or ones already outside who strive to remain so. Here, Bredahl is most convincing in his analyses of Peckinpah's best films—*Major Dundee* and *The Wild Bunch*, and of Ford's worst ones—*Fort Apache, She Wore a Yellow Ribbon*, and *The Man Who Shot Liberty Valance*. His attempt to give Peckinpah's conventional and cliché-filled *Ride the High Country* the respectability of serious art is unconvincing. His insights into the visual devices and thematic development of *Major Dundee* and *The Wild Bunch*, however, are excellent. Conversely, his observations about Ford's cavalry films and *My Darling Clementine* are accurate but superficial. Furthermore, his treatment of *Stagecoach* is distorted and inaccurate: the enemy to be fought is not the Indians—it is the evil in American society. The Indians are merely an externalization of the savagery of the white men themselves. Lordsburg (America's ideological destination?) is dominated by outlaws and filled with saloons and houses of ill-repute. Ringo must kill Luke Plummer and his brothers and rescue Dallas from her fate as whore by whisking her away to his ranch across the border in Mexico, away from the prison and brothel where society has held them in captivity. *Stagecoach* is not an entirely successful film because its melodrama and hackneyed acting are at odds with its dark underlying vision, but it is a much more complex and "Western" film than Bredahl's treatment suggests. Bredahl's interpretation of Ford's best western film, *The Searchers*, is also distorted because he deflects the meaning of the film away from Ethan Edwards and fails again to see the symbolic importance of Indians (particularly Chief Scar[8]) as projections of Ethan's (and the other whites') own savagery; for the film is ultimately about Ethan's search for himself, and that can be achieved only through escape from enclosure—the enclosure of conventional biases and racial hatred.

It seems Bredahl is deceived by the generational differences between Ford and Peckinpah into believing they represent differences in regional attitudes. Peckinpah is more the alienated existentialist, but his themes have all been prefigured in Ford. One must remember as well that Ford's work was affected by the Hollywood studio system which dominated production during most of his career, whereas Peckinpah's career coincided with a period of independent production and unprecedented freedom from censorship. Furthermore, the traits that Bredahl believes make Peckinpah a Westerner—alienation, violence generated by violence, the struggle against enclosure—are common in modern cinema: they are the same themes that Stanley Kubrick treats in his masterpiece *A Clockwork Orange*. And if positive response to one's physical environment is an identifying trait of the Western film, I cite Woody Allen's *Manhattan* as being quintessentially "Western."

New Ground is filled with valuable insights and analyses. Bredahl's purpose—to bring excellent but neglected writers to the attention of a wider public—is commendable: certainly Austin, Fergusson, and Doig deserve more recognition than they have received. In his enthusiasm, however, Bredahl has oversimplified and distorted in order to make his points about Western attitudes, themes, and forms. This is a short book which ignores or treats summarily important writers who figure largely in the development of Western American narrative. There is not enough on Twain, who must be considered central to the subject. Cather is mentioned only twice, yet *My Ántonia* is one of the greatest works to come out of the American West—and perfectly illustrates what Bredahl calls "Divided Narrative." Wallace Stegner, whose *Wolf Willow* and *The Sound of Mountain Water* would illustrate several of Bredahl's ideas, is mentioned only once. A chapter on the best work of Western Native Americans—Scott Momaday, Leslie Silko, James Welsh, Louise Erdrich—would give balance and provide a corrective to the Anglo vision. I miss Loren Eiseley, several of whose essay collections illustrate far better than Hemingway's *Green Hills of Africa* the essential Western sensibility. Also missing is Edward Abbey, whose *Desert Solitaire* is one of the finest narratives to come out of the American West. Finally, I question whether the East, and the American literary public in general, are as closed to the Western narrative as Bredahl believes they are. The whopping success of Larry McMurtry's *Lonesome Dove* in the mid-1980s would seem to belie that contention. The novel has all the qualities Bredahl says define the Western narrative: it is episodic, violent, and concerned with process instead of goals. Its surface is so dazzlingly dense that one would rather linger over its attractions, caressing and savoring them, than attempt to penetrate or enclose them with the critical mind.

Notes

1. Willa Cather, *My Antonia* (Boston: Houghton Mifflin Company, 1918), pp. 7–8.

2. John R. Milton, *The Novel of the American West* (Lincoln: Univ. of Nebraska Press, 1980).

3. See Milton, pp. 75–76, for a comparison of the same two works.

4. Guthrie's *Arfive* and *The Last Valley* would later carry his saga of the West into the twentieth century, and *Fair Land, Fair Land* would return to the days of the Mountain Men.

5. Bredahl chastises critics for referring to Hemingway's book as *The Green Hills of Africa*, yet he himself refers to Twain's masterpiece as *The Adventures of Huckleberry Finn* (p. 33).

6. Kenneth S. Lynn, *Hemingway* (New York: Simon and Schuster, 1987); Jeffrey Meyers, *Hemingway: A Biography* (New York: Harper and Row, 1985); Peter Griffin, *Along with Youth: Hemingway, The Early Years* (New York: Oxford Univ. Press, 1985).

7. A recent paperback edition published by Penguin Books in 1988 with an introduction by Edward Abbey should help to gain the book that wider audience.

8. Bredahl calls him Chief Scarface (p. 153), and he calls Luke Plummer of *Stagecoach* Hank Plummer (p. 150). These are details that could easily have been checked by an author or editor.

Chronicling the Chronicler

Juliet McMaster

R.H. Super. *The Chronicler of Barsetshire: A Life of Anthony Trollope.* Ann Arbor: University of Michigan Press, xvi, 528 pp.

R.H. Super has called his biography of Anthony Trollope *The Chronicles of Barsetshire;* and it would seem that he sees himself as the chronicler of the chronicler. His chapter headings are simply dates: "1815–34" for the first, in which Anthony is born and grows into young manhood; "1853–57" for the one that sees him through the writing and publishing of *The Warden* and *Barchester Towers;* and so on. The biographer's persona, so far as he allows one to appear, is of the patient and meticulous chronological recorder, who will take great pains to check his records and get things right, but who disdains the dangerous generalizations and inspired guesses of the biographer-psychologist. What emerges is a very useful book indeed. If you want to know where Trollope was when, whom he met and what they said about him on which occasion, this is where you will find it. You won't find the kind of psychological detective work and brave speculation that make, say, Leon Edel's multivolume biography of James read like one more serial novel.

Trollope's *Autobiography* afforded plenty of sensational material, especially about his childhood: his "dreadful walks" in muddy lanes between farmhouse and school; his subjection to his brother at Winchester, who daily "thrashed [him] with a big stick"; his painful lessons from his father, who sometimes knocked him down with the folio Bible when he forgot his lesson. Other biographers have been glad to tap this material for the enlivening of their own volumes. But Super distrusts the *Autobiography,* and documents the many points at which it is "not true" (p. 109). In fact he even claims that "*An Autobiography* has heretofore largely precluded any serious attempt at writing [Trollope's] life" (p. vii): a rather sweeping dismissal of T.H.S. Escott, Michael Sadleir, James Pope Hennessy, and C.P. Snow. Super certainly has the advantage over all these, however, of having N. John Hall's admirable and authoritative 1983 edition of Trollope's letters available to him.

He is no doubt right that the *Autobiography* is inaccurate in many ways, and very much a construction of the life (as most autobiographies are) rather than a strict historical record. But of course a novelist's construction of his life has its inherent interest as such; and Super is occasionally inclined to throw out the baby with the bathwater. Are we to believe Trollope's account of his terrible sense of degradation in feeling "I have been flogged oftener than any other human being alive," or Super's bracing dismissal that "the punishment was so commonplace as to entail no humiliation" (p. 7)? I think on such a point I prefer to believe Trollope. The precise number of floggings may be matter for dispute and further historical investigation. But Trollope is surely the authority on how he felt about them.

The *Autobiography* has perhaps been most famous (or most notorious) as a description of Trollope's working habits: all those years of being woken at the crack of dawn by a groom (who was paid extra for the service), so that the novelist could grind out his 2500 words before breakfast; all those arrangements with publishers about how many words per weekly number, how many chapters per monthly number; all those bets with himself as to how fast he could complete how long a novel. Trollope himself explains how, being conscious of having been lazy and incompetent as a young "hobbledehoy" (his term), he rejoiced during later life in a spectacular productivity. He prided himself in giving the public "good measure." He sneered at Victor Hugo for missing deadlines when he himself kept them, and with time to spare. And he claimed that punctuality was an artistic virtue. When he was writing for serial publication, he made it a point of principle to complete the whole novel before the publication of the first number. "An author should keep in his hand the power of fitting the beginning of his work to the end," he asserts, as though he were in the habit of making intricate revisions to his first number after he had completed the last. Super is quite right to be suspicious of such an assertion. Though Trollope claimed never to have broken this self-imposed rule after the emergency case of finishing *Framley Personage* at short notice for the *Cornhill*, Super notes, the boast was "not true," for "*Orley Farm, Small House, Can You Forgive Her?* and *Belton Estate* all began serial publication before their writing was completed" (p. 109). And if one examines Trollope's manuscripts, one finds further evidence that *this* artist never used "the power of fitting the beginning of his work to the end," even if he had kept such power in his hand. Such revisions as appear in the early chapters of his novels seem all to have been made within the first few days of composition. Trollope scorned drafts as a waste of time, and committed himself firmly to a single manuscript that went straight into the hands of the typesetters.

The working calendars that Trollope maintained for nearly all of his novels, and which still survive among his papers in the Bodleian, afford an exact record (such as probably exists for no other writer) of precisely when he wrote any given passage in his many books. And Super has made fuller use of this material than any other biographer. He uses it among other things to refute one of Trollope's most memorable anecdotes in the *Autobiography*, his claim to have "killed" Mrs. Proudie as a result of overhearing some hostile commentary on the chronicles of Barset in a conversation between two clergymen at the Athenaeum. They objected to his reintroducing the same characters into different novels, and dwelt on the egregious Mrs. Proudie, until Trollope interrupted them by introducing himself. "As to Mrs. Proudie," he told the flabbergasted clergymen, who hadn't known the author was within earshot, "I will go home and kill her before the week is over" (p. 210). "Perhaps it didn't happen quite that way," comments Super skeptically. And he uses the calendars to show that Trollope wrote Mrs. Proudie's death in *The Last Chronicle* "about the middle of August, 1866," whereas the novel didn't begin publication until December (p. 211). Thus the clerical readers at the club could not have been talking about Mrs. Proudie's latest exploits, although each had "a magazine in his hand." In fact Mrs. Proudie had not been prominent in any novel since *Framley Parsonage* of 1861. But for me this casts no doubt upon the anecdote, which I feel free to continue to believe. It simply provides evidence of what is very likely: that the Athenaeum kept its issues of *The Cornhill* available in its reading room for several years; and (again, not surprising) that readers found Mrs. Proudie a highly memorable character.

"Trollope loved to refer to events in his own life," Super notes tantalizingly on page 233. Occasionally he catches Trollope in lyric vein, allowing his own feelings to leak through into his characters' lives. When the heroine of *The Bertrams* is married to the sound of the church bells at Hadley Cross, Trollope as narrator recalls his sister's burial there: "I know full well the tone with which they toll when the soul is ushered to its last long rest. I have stood in that green churchyard when earth has been laid to earth, ashes to ashes, dust to dust" (p. 32). Such a passage lives up to the expectations Super creates in his program to document the connections between the fiction and the life (though of course other biographers have noticed it). But for the most part the connections Super records are relatively trivial. The name of a local pub Trollope has visited in life appears in a novel, or a complaint about "those learned societies which are rife in London" occurs in *The Vicar of Bullhampton* when he has been renewing his subscription to the Early English Text Society. On matters more juicy, such as the possible real-life personnel for all those eternal triangle plots, or the ways in which Trollope's erotic attraction to Kate Field finds expression in the novels, Super is cautiously reticent. He quotes Trollope as claiming that "The man of letters is, in truth, ever writing his own biography" (p. 366). But more appropriate to this biography is what Trollope said of George Eliot, that "private life should be left in privacy" (p. 412).

Super does make efforts to get at that "inner life" which Trollope explicitly excluded from his autobiography. He conveys more sense of the Trollope marriage than previous biographers have done, and manages to characterize Rose Heseltine Trollope—always a rather shadowy figure—by substantial quotations from her travel diaries. He provides some material on Trollope's relations with his sons once they were grown men; but

Trollope as the father of young children is as usual scarcely visible. Notoriously, outside the autobiography he has created hardly a single memorable child character in his forty-seven novels, though Dickens, Thackeray, George Eliot and the Brontës were all busy contributing to the great gallery of Victorian fictional children. And perhaps this had something to do with Trollope's being so little amenable to the kind of psychological biographies that the other writers have inspired.

Of the professional life, of course, we hear a great deal, and Super has done more work in this area than have his predecessors. He draws freely on the material in his own book, *Trollope in the Post Office,* and documents the epistolary battles Trollope waged with his colleagues and superiors. Sir Rowland Hill, his long-time official opponent, after his retirement recorded in his diary, "There has, I learn, been a fearful passage of arms between Trollope and Tilley—Trollope, of course, being the aggressor" (p. 173). And Super has much to tell about dealings with publishers, from the princely George Smith, who set Trollope on the road to fame by publishing two of the Barset novels in the *Cornhill,* to the curmudgeonly Norman Macleod, who asked Trollope for a novel for the evangelical *Good Words,* and didn't like what he got.

This book does not purport to be literary criticism, but the content of all the novels and travel books receives attention in turn, with workmanlike synopses. The travel books, which aren't much read nowadays, furnish fine material for the biographer, and Super makes the most of them. I don't know if the passages of autobiography in them are as questionable, historically, as Super finds the *Autobiography* to be; but I'm ready to enjoy them anyway. Here is Anthony's account of roughing it in the bush from his book on *Australia and New Zealand:*

The camping out was, I think, rather pride on our part, to show the Australians that we ... could sleep on the ground, *sub dio,* and do without washing, and eat nastiness out of a box, as well as they could [Crocodile Dundee, look to your laurels!]. ... We lit fires for ourselves, and boiled our tea in billies, and then regaled ourselves with bad brandy and water out of pannikins, cooked bacon and potatoes out of a frying-pan, and pretended to think it was very jolly.... For myself, I must acknowledge that when I got up about five o'clock on a dark wet morning, very damp, with the clothes and boots on which I was destined to wear for the day, with the necessity before me of packing up my wet blankets, and endeavoured ... to wake the snoring driver, who had been couched but a few feet from me, I did not feel any ardent desire to throw off forever the soft luxuries of an effeminate civilization, in order that I might permanently join the freedom of the bush. But I did it, and it is well to be able to do it. [p. 303]

In his discussion of the novels, Super does not purport to dwell on subtleties: Phineas' mental breakdown in *Phineas Redux*, for instance, gets short shrift. But Super is reliable on matters of setting and external action. His critical tastes may surprise some. He finds the sparkling *Eustace Diamonds* "slow-moving and repetitive" (p. 286), and the masterstroke of having Lizzie steal her own diamonds is "clumsy" (p. 289). On the other hand he considers *Ralph the Heir* "almost unsurpassed" (p. 277). These tastes are not mine; but then critics have never agreed about a hierarchy among Trollope's novels.

There is a fine collection of comments by his contemporaries *about* Trollope, particularly on the "two Trollopes" that have become familiar: Trollope the novelist, who was sensitive, tactful, accommodating, with an astonishing delicacy of touch; and Trollope the man, brash and loud, "vulgar, noisy & domineering ... as unlike his books as possible" wrote Lady Rose Fane (p. 205). Lever was surprised he could write them (p. 285). Sala claimed Trollope "had nothing of the bear but his skin" (p. 133). Carlyle denounced him as "irredeemably imbedded in commonplace, and grown fat upon it" (p. 133). While we have such comments coming thick and fast, the biography can't fail in interest. Trollope, with his connections in literature, the civil service, fox-hunting, clubs, travel, and politics, seems to have rubbed shoulders with nearly all the memorable characters of the age, and Super's biography allows us to bask in the company of the great. Indeed, the great themselves did a little basking of their own, as we learn from an anecdote that Super takes from Anne Thackeray. The Trollopes, it seems, went for a walk in Knole Park with Anne and Millais:

They came upon an artist at work in a little wood; Millais, stopped to inspect the work, remarked, "Why, you have not got your lights right. Look, *this* is what you want," and taking the brush out of the painter's hand made a line or two on the picture, then nodded to him and walked away. Trollope, noticing the man's bewilderment, said he should be told who had made those brush strokes, and ran back to explain. Then it became necessary for Annie to run back and point out that this second person had been Anthony Trollope. And finally yet another returned to state that the last messenger was Thackeray's daughter. It is to be hoped that the man kept his painting, if only for its associations. [p. 195]

The reader of biography can for the nonce identify with the bemused painter, and enjoy the privilege of hobnobbing with the stars of the bygone age.

Super's fidelity to his documentary sources has made for a book like its subject, rather overweight in later life. As Trollope gathered fame, more people kept records of him, and the biographer has more to deal with; and the space devoted to the different parts of the life corresponds rather with the amplitude of the record than with the intrinsic interest of the subject. Some readers of Trollope would consider *Barchester Towers* of 1857 as his masterpiece; and for such readers the climax would be reached at page 87, and the following 350 pages would be a long anticlimax. But even for the reader who rejoices in the later Trollope, the relatively slim record on his young manhood is a sad gap, and creates an appetite for a little creative filling-out on the part of his biographer. What *was* Trollope up to in those hobbledehoy years, in which he was establishing the patterns that were to inform all his works? Super is too responsible, too faithful to his sources, to write that piece of fiction. And for that we must thank him, even while we lament its absence.

As Super eschews the sensational in his rendering of Trollope's childhood, so he won't succumb to pathos at his death. Trollope died laughing, almost literally: he had a stroke during the reading of a comic scene in *Vice Versa,* and never recovered. It is in keeping with the *Autobiography*'s tabulation of the "results" of his career as a total of pounds,shillings, and pence that Super records the arrangements of Trollope's will. "The estate was valued at £25,892 9s. 3d." (p. 434). *Requiescat in pace.*

Roethke and Medium

Thomas Gardner

Peter Balakian. *Theodore Roethke's Far Fields: The Evolution of His Poetry.* Baton Rouge: Louisiana State University Press, 1989. xiii, 171 pp.

Peter Balakian's *Theodore Roethke's Far Fields: The Evolution of His Poetry,* appearing as it does almost a decade after the first wave of major studies of this poet was completed and confronting what Balakian calls "the present decline in Roethke's reputation" (p. 1), gives us an excellent chance to ask what remains live and usable in that body of work. From 1974 to 1981 at least nine full-length studies appeared—several quite strong but most, as Balakian asserts, "thesis-oriented" and, as ways of reading and writing have shifted in the last decade, wedded to specific claims that have become less pressing. In response, Balakian, himself a poet, has attempted to sketch "the unique structures and concerns of each of [Roethke's] evolving phases" (p. x)—in a sense wagering that such a "gymnastically eclectic" method of reading might, by uncovering moments of tension and continuity as it moves along, make Roethke's work available again to readers.

Responding sympathetically, Balakian finds the poems of Roethke's first book, *Open House* (1941), often at odds with themselves, "metaphysical in style but ... essentially romantic in theme" (p. 16), but continues on to identify the sources of that tension. Conceiving of the imagination "as something impenetrable, pure, and ultimately inscrutable," Balakian observes, Roethke often turned to the language of paradox and conceit to point toward that source which seemed at once "stalled" and yet "indomitabl[y]" independent of conventional ways of speaking (p. 19). "The Adamant," for example, describes an inner realm which

>   bears
> The hammer's weight.
>
> Compression cannot break
> A center so congealed;
> The tool can chip no flake:
> The core lies seaked.

Other poems refer to a "dignity within, / And quiet at the core" or to a world "sealed honey-tight." Consequently, when Roethke boasts in the volume's title poem that "My secrets cry aloud. / I have no need for tongue," it becomes possible, building on Balakian's observations, to see not simple confidence but a blustery attempt to describe a manner of speaking (not "tongue" but "deed") that might circumvent that seal:

> The anger will endure,
> The deed will speak the truth
> In language strict and pure.
> I stop the lying mouth.

Roethke's breakthrough in 1941–1946 came about, Balakian continues, when he began to develop "an elemental and dynamic language" (p. 36) that, in shying away from the lying mouth, seemed to approach the purity of deeds. One stage of that development can be seen in the "greenhouse poems" published in *The Lost Son and Other Poems* (1948). There, reworking memories from childhood years spent in his father's greenhouses, Roethke discovered a source of imagery, Balakian writes, which took him back to "preconscious experiences and processes" (p. 48). Such experiences, teased from fluidity into language by Roethke's striking engagements with material "not only fertile and generative but uncertain, dark, and dangerous" (p. 51), might be said to offer an opening into what had previously seemed silent, "sealed honey-tight." Read as a sequence, these fourteen poems, Balakian argues, "follow a tortuous journey in which the poet moves from darkness to light, charting the evolution of himself and the development of his consciousness" (p. 49). The second stage in developing a more elemental, deed-centered language can be seen in Roethke's *Praise to the End!* sequence, published in 1948, 1951, and 1953. There, as Balakian clearly shows, Roethke, in three separate passes, charts the process by which a "lost son," stripped of both identity and voice by his father's sudden death, works his way back to "a vital and dynamic contact with the world" (p. 72) and thereby regains access to that "dignity within." Repeatedly gaining and losing "that point of conjunction and fusion at which the fullest part of the self and the most organically complete elements of nature could meet" (p. 74), the lost son becomes a device by which Roethke can put into play both the drive to gain an active, elemental speech and its perpetual frustration as the poet is forced to begin again, over and over.

Although Balakian likely would not phrase the matter in these negative terms, the next stage of Roethke's "growth" as a poet was in fact a reversion to the language of paradox and conceit. This is seen most clearly in a series of "Love Poems" from *Words for the Wind* (1958) where, as Balakian puts it, the "ceaseless struggle to be born" (p. 99) is replaced by a world where "love . . . moves outward, *confirming* some relationship between the self, the lover, nature, and finally the divine" (p. 104; emphasis mine). Content in many of these poems to claim that in giving himself to his lover he has found a medium to fully call forth what had been sealed off—"The valley rocked beneath the granite hill; / Our souls looked forth, and the great day stood still"—Roethke often seems to assert rather than enact a union in which bodies become such transparent recorders that "the whole motion of the soul lay bare." It is no surprise then that Roethke's next major sequence, "Meditations of an Old Woman," in shifting away from the conventional language of the love poems, finds its voice in a woman uneasy with her aging body. "The rind, often, hates the life within," she says, torn between what Balakian calls "the interpenetration she experiences between herself and nature" (p. 120) and the nagging realization that she remains "earthbound" (p. 125), able to approximate that union only through the visible and cumbersome "reality of her bones" (p. 127).

Perhaps the clearest staging of this struggle to unite a bodied-forth expression ("the rind") and "the life within" can be seen in Roethke's posthumously published "North American Sequence"

(1964). There, Balakian convincingly argues, Roethke found an even more extensive medium to encourage what the poet called "the long journey out of the self": the shoreline of Puget Sound, where streams pour into and are pushed back by the ocean's weight, where the boundary between immensity and form is everywhere alive and in doubt, constantly drawn and erased. "On this edge of place," Balakian writes, "the poet finds . . . a primal territory where man can face his 'own immensity'" (p. 134). But, "Although Roethke affirms the necessity of a primal territory where man can confront the dimensions of his being," this particular place, its margins "convoluted and ambiguous" (p. 136), also makes it clear that such a confrontation must be written in the language of "flux and motion" (p. 149). In this poem, then, Roethke shows that "merging [a] sense of his being with the *Other*" (p. 143) necessarily involves a wholehearted giving of himself to "the real web of uncertainty" (p. 139) at the place where they meet.

The strengths of Balakian's work—telling observations about virtually every phase of Roethke's "arc," a quiet highlighting of the poet's investigatory struggles to make himself visible through something other—come from his ability to read sympathetically: as he puts it, "to move with the sensibility of his various stages of growth" (p. ix). But as the book's introduction suggests, a weakness follows from this method as well. Attempting there to make the case for Roethke's continued importance but refusing to rest the argument on the cumulative weight of his book's observations (a "thesis"), Balakian falls back on familiar accounts of American poetry in the late fifties, sixties, and early seventies and argues that Roethke "pioneered" (p. 12) many of its important directions. This may be so. Certainly Roethke was crucial to what became the "deep image" movement, and certainly there are important links between Roethke and what came to be called "confessional" poetry. (The claim, though, that Roethke "intersects" [p. 9], if not anticipates, the "Black Mountain" movement will strike many as forced.) But this sort of argument, that Roethke was "a poet of consequence to the evolving direction of his art" (p. 11), leaves him in the past, visible only if we look backward, intent on certifying influences. Putting to use Balakian's observations, I would suggest much more—that Roethke's dramatized struggle to voice something "quiet at the core" through the "minimals" of a world external to him intersects with a number of problems still at issue in poetry today.

To get a sense of what those concerns are, we might turn to a volume entitled *What Is a Poet?* (1987)—essays delivered at a recent University of Alabama symposium by a group of poets and writers that included Charles Altieri, Charles Bernstein, Kenneth Burke, David Ignatow, Denise Levertov, Marjorie Perloff, Louis Simpson, Gerald Stern, and Helen Vendler.[1] As this list suggests and as the often-exasperating transcript of a concluding panel discussion confirms, the positions taken at this symposium were controversial, often formulated in opposition to the views held by other participants. And yet, if one reads these essays carefully, one can see a number of concerns repeated. Among them—and here is where Roethke fits in—is the question of what to make of a poet's dramatized struggle with the medium he or she works within. Helen Vendler, for example, argues that the "social function of art" (p. 73) comes not from treating events directly—a poet's "means are radically other than reportage" (p. 76)—but from making "hieroglyphs of life" (p. 77). Only through such an arrangement, Vendler argues, "an order [that] bears an algebraic or indicative relation to the order of reality" (p. 77), does the sensual world become socially intelligible to others. Such visible hieroglyphs are prompted, Vendler insists, by an "artist investigating his medium" (p. 69)— "render[ing] transparent language opaque" (p. 215) so that questions about its status and its relation to reality might be put into play. Asking quite another question—is "prose" a proper medium for "poetry"?—Marjorie Perloff, after tracing what she calls "the geography of poetic form" from Goethe to Beckett, similarly emphasizes an artist's investigatory confrontation with the medium itself. Poetry, she concludes, "is no longer any one thing (the lyric, the language of tropes, metered language, and so on) but rather that species of *writing* that foregrounds and insists upon the materiality of the signifier, the coincidence between enunciation and enounced" (p. 103). An engaged materiality, she shows with Beckett's prose, is the primary site where any such "coincidence" occurs. Charles Altieri, to give one last example, thinking about still another question—does "modernism" offer contemporary poetry a way out of its recent tendency to limit itself to "expressions of mood and sensibility" (p. 61)?—also turns toward a notion of a "poetry [that can] fully elaborate its medium" (p. 43). Returning to some of the concerns of modernism, he argues—"giving full play to the energies, tensions, and duplicities that enter the artist's constructive acts" (p. 42), "call[ing] attention to . . . physical properties of the medium, which the poem can then name and in naming create as the poem's basic metaphorical substance" (p. 44)—returning to these concerns, an artist might call attention not to moods but to our capacity to employ (and reflectively evaluate) forms of knowing. For all three of these writers, an investigation or elaboration of medium is the first move, from which all other questions follow.

Within this context, Balakian's observations about Roethke's struggle to bring a "dignity within" into visibility can be fruitfully extended. For Roethke has always been a poet who shows us how one might foreground questions about voice and medium. The breakthrough greenhouse poems, for example, not only chart, as Balakian remarks, the process by which the "preconscious" is brought from "darkness to light," they are also organized as a meditation on the strengths and limits of that linguistic process itself. Thus, the first poem of the sequence, "Cuttings," in which the poet's eye is traced engaging with gradually reviving "sticks-in-a-drowse" cuttings, is followed by a companion piece written "(later)" in which two different ways of reflecting that conjunction of awakening self and greenhouse material are juxtaposed. Should the poet handle this material, this potentially new medium, in the manner of his first, metaphysically inclined book—"This urge, wrestle, resurrection of dry sticks, / Cut stems struggling to put down feet, / What saint strained so much, / Rose on such lopped limbs to a new life?"—or is a new response called for?

> I can hear, underground, that sucking and sobbing,
> In my veins, in my bones I feel it—
> The small waters seeping upward,
> The tight grains parting at last.

That the second response is chosen is, of course, in the context of Roethke's entire career, obvious. Less obvious, perhaps, is the way clearly defined "stations" of the greenhouse—the "rank, silo-rich" root cellar; the concrete benches dividing "black hairy roots" from "everything blooming above"; the flower dump; the roof, where one might reel deliriously out of control; areas outside, where one might reflect back on that "rhythm" within—allow Roethke to explore a number of questions about bringing self to light through this medium. In his veins, in his bones, he feels a rich disgust with this preconscious fluidity, or feels a deep yearning to radically transform fluidity into form, or senses first the dizzying and then deadening limits of momentarily achieved form, and so on. Roethke's "quest for identity" (p. 47), this is to suggest, is prompted by an intricate series of reflections on the aesthetic act itself.

We can similarly extend Balakian's excellent reading of the *Praise to the End!* sequence—that Roethke's fatherless lost son discovers himself in a "struggle between forward motion and assertion of identity, and the necessary regressions to some form of beginning" (p. 68)—by noting that what the sequence does is foreground the problem of singing in what Roethke calls this "in-between" space. If losing a father means that one's identity is no longer guaranteed, that it is forever touched and lost, touched and lost, how might one sing and voice a self in that space? How does an awareness that no single connection between "the particulars of nature . . . and the conditions of the body, mind, and spirit" (p. 73) holds prompt what Balakian calls "a new intimacy between his inner world and the rhythms of nature" (p. 79)—an intimacy which both works with the rhythms of nature and acknowledges that its embrace of that medium will never be complete and full? These, I take it, are questions very much alive for contemporary poets and thinkers, and mark the area where I would locate Roethke's continued claims on us.[2]

We might notice, then, that "Where Knock Is Open Wide," first poem in the sequence, uses the language of a small child singing to himself in an attempt to replace a too-busy-to-sing father—"His ears haven't time. / Sing me a sleep-song, please. / A real hurt is soft"—in order to set up the sequence's central problem. With a guarantee of identity and connection removed by the father's eventual death, Roethke's lost son will have to develop an unsponsored way of touching and singing:

> Kisses come back,
> I said to Papa;
> He was all whitey bones
> And skin like paper.
> . . .
> I'm somebody else now.
> Don't tell my hands.

The hands find out, of course, and one might say that the remaining poems in the sequence, like waves constantly approaching and collapsing, find new ways of handling the world and temporarily approaching that sealed-off core. All of these songs—ranging from an infant's "A deep dish. Lumps in it. / I can't taste my mother" to a teenager's "For whom have I swelled like a seed? / What a bone-ache I have. / Father of tensions, I'm down to my skin at last / . . . I'll feed the ghost alone. / Father, forgive my hands" to an adult's more resigned "The dark has its own light. / A son has many fathers"—all of these songs have about them a striking air of fragility and improvisation. Responding to the impossibility of the father's return, these poems foreground and work through the problematic implications of attempting to re-establish that previously assured identity through tasting or touching an external medium. Unlike the greenhouse poems, which grapple with these issues one "station" at a time, these poems—it's the mark of their genius—are engaged simultaneously on several fronts.

I've argued elsewhere that what is most striking about Roethke's final great work, "North American Sequence," is the way he takes another non-guaranteed connection—this time with the sea—as the impetus to launch a series of far-ranging, meditative responses to the limits of language and indirection raised by what Balakian rightly calls Roethke's realization that, in the "journey out of the self, there is no passage *to*—only a passage ceaselessly unfolding" (p. 133).[3] What is still live in this poet's work, then, I would claim, is the rigor and sheer inventiveness with which he throws himself into showing and evaluating what language can do in what might be called the space between seek and find. Whether one is drawn to the imagistic stationing of this problem in the greenhouse poems, the shifting cascades of language in *Praise to the End!*, the tightening disavowals of the problem in the love poems, or to the patient unfolding of its implications in his last poems, one finds approaches to current questions sketched everywhere in Roethke's work. It is to Balakian's credit that his sympathetic readings have returned us to this poet.

Notes

1. Hank Lazer, ed., *What Is a Poet?* (Tuscaloosa: Univ. of Alabama Press, 1987).

2. One example would be the work of Stanley Cavell, in particular his claim that one might respond to the threat of skepticism—the discovery "that we cannot achieve certainty in our knowledge of existence on the basis of the senses alone"—by realizing that "our relationship to the world's existence is somehow closer than the ideas of believing and knowing are made to convey." Cavell speaks of this unsponsored, improvised relation as a form of "intimacy." Quotations drawn from *Disowning Knowledge in Six Plays of Shakespeare* (Cambridge: Cambridge Univ. Press, 1987), p. 4, and *The Senses of Walden.* (Expanded edition, 1972. Reprint, San Francisco: North Point Press, 1981), p. 145.

3. Thomas Gardner, *Discovering Ourselves in Whitman: The Contemporary American Long Poem* (Urbana: Univ. of Illinois Press, 1989), pp. 78–98.

Stephen Crane and Poststructuralism: Fragmentation as a Critical Mode

James Nagel

David Halliburton. *The Color of the Sky: A Study of Stephen Crane.* New York: Cambridge University Press, 1989. vii, 351 pp.

David Halliburton's new book is a fascinating and frustrating study of the essential canon of Stephen Crane, from his earliest attempts at fiction in the Sullivan County tales to his posthumous novel *The O'Ruddy*, from his journalism to his two volumes of poetry. Throughout the volume, Halliburton's energetic analysis demonstrates a close reading of Crane's works and an extensive intellectual range of reference to modern philosophy, psychoanalysis, social and political thought, literary theory, and historical data about the growth of American cities, westward expansion, racial tensions, and cultural change. Given the broad perspective from which he writes, one would expect Halliburton to present a full assessment of Crane's work from a clearly articulated critical matrix; he does not. Instead, he brings his perspective to bear on isolated passages, sometimes individual words, developing a sophisticated discussion of only certain aspects of a work without attempting to show how those aspects function in context. When it succeeds, this method can be challenging and penetrating; when it does not, it is often elusive and unconvincing. The overwhelming impression the book makes is of a scholar who is impressive in his knowledge of details and isolated facts but has little capacity to understand the literature he is reading. It is not surprising, in other words, that after three hundred pages of discussion, Halliburton offers no conclusion to his book.

The Color of the Sky is divided into nine chapters, each broken into units addressed not to individual stories or novels or poems but to such concepts as "Matters Economic," "The City," "Color," "Marginality," and, in a section on Crane's verse, "Apocalypse." A given section will then offer not a complete exegesis of a work but rather an exploration, sometimes impressively detailed, of one or more isolated matters. For example, the discussion of "The Open Boat," one of the most extensive treatments of an individual work, is divided into "The Group," "The Color of the Sky," "Many a Man," "The Ethics of Their Condition," "By Analogy," "The Correspondent, the Oiler, and the Soldier," and "Meaning," which ought to, but does not, integrate the parts to the whole.

Halliburton sees the group in the boat not in specific terms but as representative of "a larger collectivity," although he never gets around to showing how the four men in the boat are in some way archetypal or what their story would suggest even if they were. What he does do is to explore how the roles of the men are altered by the sinking of the ship, the captain retaining command, the oiler reduced to a lower level of functionality than before: "The correspondent becomes a member of the company in the new vessel, while the cook, remaining subordinate with the others, is effectively unemployed, having no food to prepare, and apparently being unable or unwilling to assist in the rowing" (p. 237). Halliburton, however, draws no further conclusions about the meaning of the group or their roles.

The discussion of color, always a central concern in Crane criticism, misses the simple point that the men in the boat do not know the color of the sky because they are preoccupied with the sea and their precarious position in it. Rather, Halliburton attempts to make the simple complex: "'The color of the sky' suggests the presence of some particular hue or of some combination of such, this being the second OED definition of the noun *color*. At the same time something more general could be at issue if the first sense, 'the quality or attribute in virtue of which objects present different aspects to the eye,' is also implied" (p. 238). He then goes on to list at length all the terms of color in the story and to offer a scansion of the opening line of the story, showing its regularity of rhythm and suggesting that the sea, too, has a regular motion. But this section ends, as do the others, without any attempt to describe the function of color in the story or to synthesize the concept of color into a full reading of the narrative.

In "Many a Man" Halliburton addresses the observation that "many a man ought to have a bath-tub larger than the boat which here rode upon the sea" with comparisons to Dickens and Shakespeare. Halliburton does not explain whose judgment this is, or where it comes from, but he does observe wisely that "we hear a voice saying what the men cannot say because it knows what they cannot know" (p. 242). Later in his discussion he reveals a similar lack of understanding of narrative technique by attributing the "if I am going to be drowned" refrain to the correspondent, whereas it is actually the narrator's projection of the collective attitude of the four men (p. 247). In other sections as well, Halliburton shows little grasp of Crane's complex modes of narration.

In the final section on the "Meaning" of the story, Halliburton equivocates through obfuscation: "In a world of signifiers, a world in which everything seems weighted with sense, no ultimate signifier emerges, but only, if you will, a certain sense of sense" (p. 249). Later, attempting to sum up the meaning of the experience for the men, he says that "ethics of intensity is intensity of ethics, which is to say that the condition in which the men find themselves from beginning to end is extraordinarily felt and felt to be extraordinary" (p. 254). Danny Kaye used to do wonders with lines like that. Halliburton does make the excellent if not original point that the heart of the story rests in the correspondent's contemplation of the poem about the soldier of Algiers, a passage that shows movement from indifference to empathy and compassion. But there is no clear summation of what Halliburton makes of the story, no articulated thesis that draws together the disparate sections of discussion. Although some of the individual remarks are insightful and new, this lack of unifying vision is a problem throughout the book.

Which is not to say that there are not valuable observations. Halliburton is good on the "complex perspectivism" of Crane's narrative technique, even if he lacks the critical lexicon to describe precisely what that is. His point that the position from which something is observed is distinct from the act of observing is well taken: "A locus, as distinguished from a point of view, can remain almost defiantly indeterminate, as may be seen in 'The Open Boat,' where it is easier to locate what the men do not know than to determine who it is that knows that they do not know" (p. 21). He is also good on the concept of "passage" in the Sullivan County tales and on the psychic role of George's dead brothers in *George's Mother:* "Like castles and fortresses, the brothers belong to an anterior, heroic time that lives in the mother's present but not in the son's" (p. 73). He is also insightful about the thematic inversions between *George's Mother* and *Maggie*, pointing out that in one the family rejects the child, and in the other the child rejects the family. In *Maggie*, "*the parent who stays the same lives while the child who changes dies*"; in *George's Mother*, conversely, "*the parent who stays the same dies while the child who changes lives*" (p. 85; italics Halliburton's). Halliburton offers a number of symmetrical observations along these lines.

His best section, however, is on *The Monster*, a story he reads closely and with a particular sensitivity to language. He notes, for example, that animal imagery is used to describe all the characters, not just Henry Johnson, and that an extraction of only the images that describe Henry would give the false impression of racist bias. Dealing with race, he observes that there is a "distinction between the uncontrolled, exaggerated, and submissive behavior of the black characters and the restraint of the white doctor, whose behavior is measured and authoritative" (p. 188). He is equally good on the concept of individualism in the story, developing the central point that the behavior of the characters is not limited by identification in a group: the individual "is free to assert himself or herself through a determinate act of will" (p. 191). Particularly valuable is the section on Dr. Trescott's practice of medicine, as both researcher and clinician, and the irony that society punishes him for his altruism. Halliburton misses the influence of Ibsen's *The Enemy of the People* on this situation, but he is excellent on the nature of the town and on the final impact of the Trescotts' ostracism within it.

But there are also problems with the book on all levels, from style, to evidentiary procedure, to a tendency for rigid paradigmatic reasoning. Surely it is disingenuous for Halliburton, in his fine discussion of *The Monster,* to blame Crane because, on the issue of race, "he is not quite sure what he thinks" (p. 199). This is biographical fallacy of the worst sort, and it exemplifies a critical assumption that serves Halliburton ill, that the works are direct revelations of Crane's mind: "The object of Crane's desire is an ideal, a military fraternal order or society of warriors" (p. 8). Anyone who knows even the outlines of Crane's life, with its iconoclastic undercurrents, would doubt that Crane's ideal was a rigid, military society. Halliburton confuses themes in the works with Crane's personal views: "Crane's attitude toward war in general and heroism in particular is reminiscent of the little man's attitude toward the mountain" (p. 145).

At other times, Halliburton's critical logic is flawed, as when he observes about *George's Mother:* "The novel is decentered because, while readers may identify with the mother, the son is the main character and it is very hard to identify with him" (p. 88), as though only positive characters should serve as protagonists for novels. Another kind of logical error that comes up frequently is the use of nonexclusive categories, as when he divides things into "parody" and "dialect," as though parodic works might not contain dialect (p. 3), or the assertion that "natality" leads to three areas of activity, "labor, work, and action" (p. 77).

More importantly, Halliburton's habits of mind in this study lead to interpretations that are often fragmented, unconvincing, and without critical coherence. In an extended exploration of *Maggie,* he observes, in typical style, "if the family's conflicts are largely due to the father's submission to the bottle, they are also due to his submission to the mother, which derives in turn, circularly, from her submission to the bottle" (p. 39). He is good on the restrictive innocence of Maggie's perspective but misses how that limitation relates to the narrative point of view. There is nothing about how Maggie misinterprets Pete's status in the world, only that she is impressed by his "thereness" (p. 44). Halliburton is excellent in discussing Chapter 17, Maggie's last walk, as action that suffers little if all the speech is removed, but he misses any sense of the history of causality that leads to her suicide; indeed, Halliburton suggests that she was murdered (p. 68).

Beginning an interpretation of the body language of the characters in the Bowery, Halliburton again makes the simple unnecessarily complex: "Erwin Straus has explored the significance for human development of the upright posture, which consists in a vertical axis permitting flexibility of action (e.g., the hand, released from merely supporting the body, is freed for a variety of performances), in contrast with the horizontal or digestive axis of quadrupeds" (p. 50). Many readers will regard such writing as a parody of scholarship, a routine by Professor Irwin Corey, not Erwin Straus. But even more serious is the final conclusion, that Maggie's "fate becomes a parody of the golden rule: Do to yourself what others have done to you" (p. 70). Nowhere in Halliburton's discussion of the novel is there any sense of the irony that pervades the action and the narration, any sensitivity to the self-serving moral posture of Maggie's mother and brother, the culpability of Pete, the thematic importance of Nellie (another girl of the streets, one who thrives, in contrast to Maggie), or even the basic structure of the novel, divided evenly into cause and effect. The failure to deal with Crane's comment to Hamlin Garland that the environment is a powerful force allows Halliburton to ignore the physical and moral degradation of the Bowery and to misread the role it plays in Maggie's death.

The treatment of *The Red Badge of Courage* shares these traits. It is sometimes insightful about details but misses the central meaning of the novel. Halliburton seems more interested in clever word play than in a sensitive response to Henry Fleming: "As there is a letter of the *Letter* and a *Letter* of the letter, there is also a badge of the *Badge* and a *Badge* of the badge: a synecdochic arrangement through and through, yet a metaphoric one as well" (p. 101). The section on Henry's capacity to see himself apart from himself is fascinating, but it does not lead to any observations that ultimately help explain him. Halliburton does little with the famous "wafer" passage, ignoring issues of its literal or figurative meaning, of whether the red wafer represents a symbol or a projection of Henry's mind or a simple description of the sun, in favor of a discussion of how a flat

Stephen Crane and Poststructuralism

surface has two faces and how the image leads nowhere: "This is basically what Crane does too. Like a sublime version of a creature known for fence-sitting, it turns its mug toward a larger meaning and its wump towards undecidability" (p. 132). If so, it mirrors Halliburton's basic strategy of interpretation.

Despite its problems, *The Color of the Sky* is a book that Crane scholars need to know, and not only as a subject for humor. There are individual observations that are bright and provocative and deserve further contemplation, if only to synthesize them into a full reading of Crane's work, something Halliburton does not accomplish. The comments on Crane and music are fresh and valuable (p. 166), as are many of the sections on social context. If the book lacks a comprehensive thesis, it does present challenges to the existing critical record. And it offers an excellent opportunity to assess the relative merits of the insights born of poststructural methodologies against more traditional approaches.

Dear Dialogic Dublin:
Three Joyceans and Mikhail Bakhtin

Thomas L. Burkdall

Zack Bowen. *Ulysses as a Comic Novel.* Syracuse: Syracuse University Press, 1989. xvi, 150 pp.

R. B. Kershner. *Joyce, Bakhtin, and Popular Literature: Chronicles of Disorder.* Chapel Hill: University of North Carolina Press, 1989. xiv, 338 pp.

Michael Patrick Gillespie. *Reading the Book of Himself: Narrative Strategies in the Works of James Joyce.* Columbus: Ohio State University Press, 1989, xii, 250 pp.

In such transfusion just to know twigst timidy twomeys, for gracious sake, who is artthoudux from whose heterotropic.
—*Finnegans Wake*, 252.19–21

Since his emergence on the contemporary critical scene, Mikhail Bakhtin's theories have been employed to analyze a wide range of texts: from Augusto Roa Bastos's *I, the Supreme* to Henry James's "The Jolly Corner," from the self-promotional writings of Benjamin Franklin to the subtle shading of Virginia Woolf's novels, from Samuel Butler's *Hudibras* to Woody Allen's *Zelig*. Bakhtin himself does not consider the fiction of James Joyce, due either to the Soviet political climate or to the critic's aesthetic sensibilities.[1] Yet, as R. B. Kershner asserts in *Joyce, Bakhtin, and Popular Culture: Chronicles of Disorder*, "given his predispositions and methodology, there is an undeniable sense in which, if Bakhtin did not celebrate Joyce, he should have" (p. 17). These three studies help to fill this *lacuna* in Bakhtin's work, each applying the Russian's theoretical concepts to varying degrees and attempting to correct a perceived lack in Joyce criticism: believing that generations of critics have endeavored to suppress it, Zack Bowen wishes to reawaken readers to the comedy of *Ulysses*; R. B. Kershner hopes to introduce voices of popular literature and the principle of dialogism as vital elements in the interpretation of Joyce's early work; and Michael Patrick Gillespie champions the growing role of the reader throughout the evolution of Joyce's canon as a means to appreciate its polyphonic virtues. In *Wakean* terms, they all promote a "heterotropic" view instead of the "artthoudux" perspective.[2]

In his slim volume, Ulysses *as a Comic Novel,* Zack Bowen applies the theory of Bakhtin as only one part of his kaleidoscopic exploration of the comic aspects of *Ulysses*. He intends his study to serve as a corrective to those readers who, like Carl Jung, "emphasize the dark side of the novel," and to those more recent critics who slight the comedy of Joyce's epic in their analyses (p. ix). To this end, Bowen promises to address many facets of comedy: "My attempt is, then, to deal with theory, history, and influences (past and present), in making the case that *Ulysses* is primarily a comic novel," and he is true to his word (p. xiii).

The result is actually a series of brief and related essays on the comic mode, as manifested in the novel. The scope impresses one, even if, as Bowen admits, "the argument only touches briefly upon or omits much of what might profitably be further elaborated" (p. xiii). It amazes the reader that the book considers the comic theories of Suzanne Langer, Francis Cornford, Mikhail Bakhtin, Henri Bergson, and Aristotle (in hypothetical reconstruction) in only forty-four pages. The following three chapters match this pace, exploring comic narration in nine of the eighteen episodes of *Ulysses,* then tracing parallels in the works of Joyce and his comic forefathers—Rabelais, Cervantes, and Sterne—and finally considering the role of the reader, as Bowen compares the comedies of Dante and Joyce.

One of the more interesting portions of the study is the opening chapter in which Bowen fruitfully applies one of Suzanne Langer's essays to *Ulysses*. In "The Comic Rhythm," the philosopher "sees comedy as reflecting a basic biological pattern of life,

Dear Dialogic Dublin

or life rhythm, which when disrupted tries to restore itself and the natural balance of existence"; as a fish assumes "new functions with its other fins when part of its tail is bitten off," so humans compensate for life's travails with comedy (p. 2). In the comic novel then, this homeostatic drive acts to offset the disruptive forces of life. Bowen briefly considers various aspects of *Ulysses* in this light: the tensions between Bloom and Molly and Bloom's status as an outcast in Dublin on the one hand, and Bloom's appreciation of life's smaller joys and "his sense of equanimity" on the other hand suggest the types of disruption and resolutions that establish the comic intent of the novel within Langer's parameters (p. 7). According to Bowen, the efforts of many Joyceans to scour the text for hints of future resolutions to the problems of the Blooms are clearly misguided, making tragic hay out of a comedy:

> If we ever tend to forget that *Ulysses* is a funny book, we need only refer to the comic innovations and devices of Joyce's style, his scores of variations on established motifs and themes, until at last its protagonist becomes the symbol of the vital continuity of life, never destroyed, if momentarily defeated, as nature and process go on. Whatever Molly's "Yes" signifies, it is . . . the final aspect of the comic spirit, because vital continuity begets affirmation of process rather than ultimate answers. [p. 15]

The comic spirit of *Ulysses* may be evaluated not only in Langer's terms, but also in those of Mikhail Bakhtin. In a number of his chapters, Bowen tersely notes how Joyce's novel fulfills the Russian's ideas of comedy. *Ulysses,* especially the "Circe" episode, captures the essence and tradition of the carnival in all the grotesqueness that Bakhtin delineates in the work of Rabelais. Joyce's penchant towards parody, particularly in the latter half of the novel, even more closely allies him to the carnivalized genres, and as Bowen puts it, makes "an unmistakable declaration of comic intent" (p. 46). Bowen also invokes Bakhtin in a discussion of elimination as a source of comedy, again linking Joyce to Rabelais and associating Bloom with Gargantua. Finally, the conceits of creation generated by Stephen (in *Portrait*) and Bloom (in "Calypso"), Shelley's fading coal compared to Bloom's morning session in the outhouse, are contrasted and explicated using Bakhtin, who saw "A pattern of descent images toward truth and the sublime by way of the lower body and its functions: 'Finally debasement is the fundamental artistic principle of grotesque realism: all that is sacred and exalted is rethought on the level of the material bodily stratum'" (p. 100).

By using such theorists to demonstrate that *Ulysses* is indeed a comedy, Bowen affirms and legitimizes the humorous aspects of the work. In addition, this compilation of critics and literary predecessors may serve Joyce scholars as a prolegomenon to future studies in this area. But in Bowen's drive to convince the reader that the novel is comic in a multitude of ways, the definition of comic becomes too elastic. The closing of the chapter "*Ulysses* and Comic Theory" intimates this: "Throughout the research on this chapter, though admittedly undertaken to fit *Ulysses* into prevailing comic theory, I was hard-pressed to find any variation on the theory that would not admit Joyce's novel" (p. 44). No matter how you define it then—in Dantean, Bakhtinian, or Aristotelian terms—Bowen regards the novel as comic. Though I agree with his basic contention, had the focus been narrower and the critical analysis more detailed, Bowen's stated goal might have been more effectively achieved. A kaleidoscope offers many beautiful images, but it does not provide a clear view. Almost any of the essays might have been expanded into a fascinating full-length critical study, thus more powerfully illuminating Joyce's comedic vision.

In *Joyce, Bakhtin, and Popular Literature*, R. B. Kershner attempts to refocus our interpretation of the early work, melding new historical perspectives and old-fashioned historical research with Bakhtin's theories, resulting in a powerful blend. That critics might benefit by altering their perspective is made plain in Kershner's observations regarding *Portrait*:

> Because of our relative ignorance of the popular intellectual ferment of the British Isles in the late Victorian and early Edwardian periods, the contemporary reader ... tends to give the young artist inflated credit as a rebel. We take Stephen's presumption of uniqueness at face value and ignore the degree to which his conversation and thoughts are dialogical participants in—or even products of—a series of culturally mandated discourses of his time. [p. 228]

Dear Dialogic Dublin 241

Bakhtin's notions of heteroglossia and dialogism, Kershner concludes, can help us to pursue the "reinsertion of [Joyce's] writings, protagonists, and—we must suppose—Joyce himself into history" (p. 297). Such research, he convincingly argues, has seldom been pursued previously due to "the power of the overlapping ideologies of Modernism and of the New Criticism, as well as of the more formalist varieties of structuralism and poststructuralism" (p. 297). The number of guides and notes that identify historical and cultural allusions prove that Joyceans have been aware of this material, but Kershner, echoing Cheryl Herr's *Joyce's Anatomy of Culture*, wishes to examine "the structural and functional" aspects of allusions, exploring how popular literature and the discourse of the era form a dialogue with and within *Dubliners, Stephen Hero, Portrait,* and *Exiles* (p. 2).

Pursuing this quest, Kershner has provided a valuable study. Not only has he given us full descriptions and analyses of works like Filson Young's novel *The Sands of Pleasure*, Alfred C. Harmsworth's numerous periodicals, and Arnold Lunn's schoolboy tale, *The Harrovians*, he also explains how these texts relate to those of Joyce. He moves us beyond the identification of allusions to a consideration of the formative and intertextual power of popular literature, allaying the frustration that sometimes results from the helpful (but necessarily brief) entries in Don Gifford's *Ulysses Annotated* or Weldon Thornton's *Allusions in Ulysses*. And by reconstituting the late Victorian and Edwardian ideology, Kershner is not limited to works alluded to by Joyce; texts which would inform the view of Joyce's contemporaries, as *Portrait*, for instance, would undoubtedly evoke comparisons to *Tom Brown's School-Days*, are profitably discussed. (Indeed, Joyce's fiction was relying so blatantly on the traditions of the school-boy novel that an allusion would have been a breach of his aesthetic subtlety.)

Perhaps the best way to encapsulate and evaluate Kershner's book is to consider briefly a selection of his intertextual and dialogic readings. Kershner is at his best when he discusses the relationship of popular literature to Joyce's work. A reading of "An Encounter" benefits much from the background on the Harmsworth publications the schoolboys of the story read (*The Union Jack, Pluck,* and *The Halfpenny Marvel*), but when the "old josser's" actions are viewed against a backdrop of the themes of

Victorian pornography and Bulwer-Lytton's *The Last Days of Pompeii*, the resulting interpretative possibilities reveal the ideological depths of the story. This study may even help to increase the stature of what has frequently been regarded as the weakest of the *Dubliners* stories: "After the Race." Joyce himself acknowledged its imperfections, as Kershner reminds us (p. 71). But when set against the "chivalric/militaristic ideology" of the tradition crystallized by Dumas's *The Three Musketeers* and other conventions of popular fiction, Jimmy Doyle's nostalgic belief system and his inability to participate in it are more effectively exposed (p. 76).

Not all of the protagonists in *Dubliners* are directly portrayed as victims of popular literature's ideology, but all of them find themselves surrounded by conflicting discourses. Kershner argues that the boy in "The Sisters," for example, is trapped by the languages of Old Cotter, Eliza, and his aunt and uncle on the one hand and the priest on the other:

> As Bakhtin insists, the languages that surround him, with their concomitant ideological structures, are the only means of thought and speech available to the boy; he cannot escape them, however alien he feels them to be. They are the world, and they articulate his consciousness.... Whether he will or not, the boy must speak with the overscrupulous priest's voice and with the voices of the unscrupulous adults he despises. [pp. 30–31]

Thus the ideologies and the discourses, whether derived from the language of the press or the voice of the culture, frame the perspectives of the protagonists and throughout *Dubliners* entrap them.

In a similar way, *Portrait* is analyzed intertextually and intratextually. The work's connections with popular literature are explored, including the obscure—Tom Greer's *A Modern Daedalus*, a late nineteenth-century "politically revolutionary fable" of a misfit of an Irish boy who learns the secret of mechanized flight (p. 190)—and not excluding the famous—Dumas's *The Count of Monte Cristo*. The persona of Edmond Dantes, Kershner argues, greatly influenced the creation of Stephen's character, contributing much more to the novel than the *tableau* of the lovely Mercedes and the memorable "sadly proud gesture of refusal" of muscatel grapes.[3] Like the young protagonist of "The Sisters," Stephen is immersed in and struggling with the languages of his environment; Kershner documents the ways in which "Stephen is a product of his listening and reading, an irrational sum of the texts, written and spoken, to which he has been exposed" (p. 162).

The introduction of Bakhtinian criticism to and a deeper exploration of popular literature in Joyce studies bring another dimension to our appreciation of the canon. Though the influence of "sub-literary" texts has always been acknowledged by the Joycean community, Kershner's study causes us to consider the cultures and ideologies which informed Joyce and his writing, or, as the Bakhtinian would have it, to acknowledge "the participation of Joyce's characters and texts in a historically determined, multidimensional dialogical interchange" (p. 298). This strategy takes us beyond allusion to a range of new interpretations, inviting the critic to consider the polyphony of Joyce's texts. This work may serve as both a detailed reference guide to popular literature in Joyce's early fiction and an example of the intriguing readings that a Bakhtinian analysis of discourse may evoke.

Michael Patrick Gillespie's *Reading the Book of Himself: Narrative Strategies in the Works of James Joyce* explores polyvocal aspects of Joyce's canon too, drawing upon the theories of not only Bakhtin, but also those of Roland Barthes, Kenneth Burke, and various reader-response critics. Gillespie analyzes the transforming use of free indirect discourse and the evolving position of the reader as Joyce matures as a writer and the works of his canon metamorphose. Although the subtitle of the book describes the substance of the study, an exploration of the title's subtleties underscores much of its method. In his second chapter on *Portrait*, Gillespie discusses the novel's well-known epigraph as an encapsulation of "the intellectual posture that the novel encourages us to assume" (p. 82). He considers the ambiguity of the pronoun in *et ignotas animum dimittit in artes* ("he turned his mind to unknown arts"): "he" could be the author, the protagonist, the reader, or the mythical Daedalus. Similarly, Gillespie's title can be interpreted in several ways—who is "himself," the reader or Joyce? Who is "reading the book of himself"? Is it Joyce as writer or as reader that the study considers? Since the phrase from "Scylla and Charybdis" alludes to Marllarmé's prose-poem "Hamlet et Fortinbras," and thus Shakespeare's *Hamlet,* and since it occurs in an episode concerning issues of creativity and authorship, then what can Gillespie's reader make of these patterns?[4] As Gillespie writes about Joyce, "the point is not that one choice [or interpretation] is invariably correct and that the other[s] . . . are necessarily wrong but rather that from its first words *Portrait* self-consciously calls attention to the stylistic imperative that it repeatedly addresses to the reader to participate in the creation of meaning" (p. 82). The ambiguity, the involvement of the audience, and Joyce's reading are all examined in this bibliographically informed and critically interesting analysis of all the major works of Joyce. In his examination, Gillespie wishes to

> draw attention to the polymorphous possibilities of any particular artistic impression. This awareness seeks to accommodate both/and rather than either/or thinking, relying on the assumption that one can enjoy completely whatever immediate response one makes to the aesthetic experience without incurring the limitations of unquestioning commitment to a single view. [p. 4]

Just as one can regard light as a particle or a wave, or consider mathematical values within a range according to the principles of "fuzziness" being developed to advance artificial intelligence, one can interpret Joyce within a range of provisional readings; indeed, Gillespie argues, the reader is encouraged to do so by the works themselves.

In the course of the study, Gillespie traces the elements of continuity and change as Joyce developed as a writer. Focusing upon the author's reading and his developing use of free indirect discourse and polyphony, we are shown how the writings transform from being derivative of a nineteeth-century tradition to the modernism and postmodernism of the later Joyce. Regarded through the lens of an eclectic critical methodology, Gillespie tracks the movement—in Barthes's terms—from a predominantly readerly heritage (the early versions of some of the *Dubliners*) to the revolutionary writerly text (*Ulysses* and *Finnegans Wake*), and examines the growing insistence that the reader cope with the ambiguities of the text, unifying the disunities by employing both/and thinking (to put it in Burke's language).

Particularly interesting are the treatments of *Stephen Hero* and *Exiles*; rather than regarding them as failures, Gillespie considers them as evidence of lessons that Joyce had to learn. (Remember Stephen on Shakespeare: "A man of genius makes no mistakes. His errors are volitional and are the portals of discovery."[5]) By comparing the extant portions of the first draft of *Portrait* to the published version, the transformation from the primarily readerly to the frequently writerly text becomes evident. *Stephen Hero* cannot be ignored as it "captures a moment of Joyce's aesthetic transition. It maintains a commitment to the production of *lisible* works, but it also evinces a desire to begin the implementation of *scriptible* fiction" that dominates the remainder of the canon and encourages (nay, requires) the reader's participation in the creation of the text (p. 48). Likewise, *Exiles* represents an important turning point in the author's development—without it, *Ulysses* might have looked radically different. In the course of his drama, Joyce attempted to "incorporate fully developed personalities into a dialogic framework [which] provided him with the experience necessary to resolve the question of unifying disunities when he came to write *Ulysses*" (p. 120).

With the inclusion of the reader as participatory creator of the text another benefit accrues: *Finnegans Wake* cannot be considered a literary freak, as it is still sometimes regarded. In fact, Gillespie maintains that Joyce's final work does not introduce advances in style or alterations in the reader's paradigm: "Despite its reputation for linguistic formidability, in many ways *Finnegans Wake* offers the most straightforward and literal rendition of the creative inclinations in all Joyce's works. It simplifies language, in the purest sense of such an action, by stripping away the devices traditionally employed . . . to achieve misleading elisions and putative closures" (p. 200). By the nature of its punning, its multiple "layers of discourse" (whether they be historical, literary, or religious), and its willful confusion of syntax, a single interpretation becomes impossible, unless the reader ignores much and insists on retaining an either/or perspective, thus diminishing Joyce's parallactic work.

At the center of this impressive study, I find, however, one important critical issue blunted. Gillespie relies heavily on reader-response theory, which leads him to his interesting evaluation of Joyce's canon and his readers and to observations which have important implications for discussions of modernism and postmodernism. But he proscribes the notion of an infinite number of valid readings of Joyce: "I do not, of course, mean to suggest that an infinite number of texts can legitimately be derived from Joyce's fiction. Whatever pattern of coherence the reader creates *must* develop within the paradigm of Joyce's work and *must* reconcile competing and potentially conflicting impressions" (p. 92, my emphasis). If Gillespie is speaking of those readings that have critical legitimacy (however that may be defined), such lines can be drawn. But I find myself uncomfortable with the idea of allowing a range of interpretations while proscribing others. Paradigms of interpretation are, of course, culturally determined—but how can any reading be declared invalid? If it is hysteric (accepting the text "for ready money," as Barthes describes one of the neurotic reading stances in *The Pleasure of the Text*) or cabalistic, who would deny such a response to a work? While it may not be a critical reading, how can one declare invalid a prophetic reading of *Finnegans Wake* or deny its potential for bibliomancy, while endorsing selected "legitimate" responses?[6]

On balance, however, *Reading the Book of Himself* provides a skillful and valuable interpretation of Joyce's works, examining his developing style and the role of the reader with sound reasoning and lucid prose. Gillespie's consideration of the influence of Joyce's reading alone, from Flaubert and Dickens to Grant Allen and Charles Paul de Kock, makes the study worthy of attention. The book also goes a long way towards explaining why Joyceans exist. The epigraph to Don Gifford's annotations could well have served for this study: "I've put in so many enigmas and puzzles that it will keep the professors busy for centuries arguing over what I meant, and that's the only way of insuring one's immortality."[7] Not only the web of facts that require annotation serve as Joyce's perpetual memorial—as Gillespie shows, the enigmas are resolved provisionally again and again; the texts created by writer and reader evolve in perpetuity.

As these three critical works help to demonstrate, the health of

Dear Dialogic Dublin 247

Joyce studies is quite robust. With such infusions (or "in such transfusion" as the *Wake* might have ambiguously transformed it) of new perspectives and insightful uses of literary criticism, James Joyce's dream of immortality will be achieved and his readers will continue to explore the varied delights of his work: the laughter, the voices of popular literature and culture, and the participation of the reader in the creation of the text. If these qualities do not appeal, fear not—as Bakhtin suggests: "There is neither a first nor a last word and there are no limits to the dialogic context. . . . Nothing is absolutely dead: every meaning will have its homecoming festival," and yours may be celebrated soon.[8]

Notes

1. The reason is political, according to Katerina Clark and Michael Holquist's study *Mikhail Bakhtin* (Cambridge: Harvard Univ. Press, 1984), and aesthetic according to Kershner. See Kershner, p. 17.

2. Other studies which consider the relationship of Bakhtin and Joyce include: David Lodge, *After Bakhtin: Essays on Fiction and Criticism* (New York: Routledge, 1990); Patrick Parrinder, *James Joyce* (New York: Cambridge Univ. Press, 1984); and Rosalba Spinalbelli, "Molly 'Live,'" in Rosa Maria Bosinelli, et al., eds., *Myriadminded Man: Jottings on Joyce* (Bologna: Cooperativa Lib. Univ. Ed. Bologna, 1986), pp. 173–84.

3. James Joyce, *A Portrait of the Artist as a Young Man*, ed. Chester G. Anderson (New York: Penguin, 1964), p. 63.

4. Don Gifford, Ulysses *Annotated: Notes for James Joyce's* Ulysses, with Robert J. Seidman (Berkeley: Univ. of California Press, 1988), pp. 200–201 (episode 9, lines 113–14).

5. James Joyce, *Ulysses,* Hans W. Gabler, et al., eds. (New York: Random House, 1986), 9.228–29.

6. Joyceans relate tales, perhaps apocryphal, of readers who claim that *Finnegans Wake* prophesied the assassinations of John and Robert Kennedy and predicted the career of basketball star Rick Barry of the Golden State Warriors, who holds the record for the highest career free-throw percentage.

7. Richard Ellmann, *James Joyce,* new and rev. ed. (New York: Oxford Univ. Press, 1982), p. 521.

8. Mikhail Bakhtin, *Speech Genres and Other Late Essays,* ed. Michael Holquist, trans. Vern McGee (Austin: Univ. of Texas Press, 1986), p. 170. Quoted in Kershner, p. 21.

Thoreau as Reviser/ Revising Thoreau

Steven Fink

Stephen Adams and Donald Ross, Jr. *Revising Mythologies: The Composition of Thoreau's Major Works*. Charlottesville: University Press of Virginia, 1988. xii, 271 pp.

Henry Thoreau was always of two minds about revising what he wrote: on the one hand, he was drawn to the romantic emphasis on spontaneity and inspiration, and so eschewed revision and celebrated the journal as the model form of expression; on the other hand, he wanted his writing to be condensed, pithy, and multi-layered, and this required the careful reworking and crafting of his prose. He was, in fact, by nature and habit an inveterate compiler and reviser; he characteristically composed for publication by constructing elaborate mosaics of discrete journal entries. These he then painstakingly revised, often through multiple drafts. It is Thoreau the reviser who interests Stephen Adams and Donald Ross, Jr. They concede that "at the start of his writing career, Thoreau apparently was reluctant to revise," but they argue that both his practice and his written comments on his art demonstrate that "Thoreau's attitude toward revising changed" (p. 3). This, I think, misrepresents Thoreau's enduring and deep-seated ambivalence about revision. While they cite letters and Journal entries from the 1850s in which Thoreau declares the importance of re-seeing, winnowing, and reworking his thoughts, one could as easily point out Thoreau's demonstrable commitment to his Journal *qua* Journal after 1850 and string together a series of Thoreau Journal entries on the virtues of spontaneous and unrevised composition. (See, for example, *PJ* 1:35 [1838], 253 [1841]; *J* 3:239 [1852]; *J* 4:223 [1852]; *J* 10:115

[1857].)[1] Nevertheless, Adams and Ross are certainly right in claiming that Thoreau's major works (especially *A Week on the Concord and Merrimack Rivers* and *Walden*) "evolved over long periods during which he gradually discovered or created significance and poetry in incidents from his past" (p. 3), and their project is a well-justified close examination of the nature of Thoreau's revisions of works from the beginning to the end of his career.

Detailed studies already exist of the composition of both *A Week* (Linck Johnson's *Thoreau's Complex Weave*) and *Walden* (J. Lyndon Shanley's *The Making of* Walden), as well as of some of his shorter compositions, and Ross and Adams do not attempt either to refute or reiterate these efforts. The contribution their study makes is to examine these works in the larger context of Thoreau's own evolution as a writer. Both the chronology of composition and the long gestation period of his major works, for example, are graphically illustrated by the chapter divisions. After an introduction and a too-cursory survey of "Early Thoreau," the authors devote chapters to "The Early Development of *A Week*" and "Early Stages of *Walden*"; these are followed by a chapter on "Ktaadn" before picking up "The Later *Week*." Then chapters covering "An Excursion to Canada," *Cape Cod,* and "Walking" are included before we turn to "The Endings of *Walden*"; these are followed by a chapter on the later segments of *The Maine Woods* and then (violating chronology somewhat) by a chapter that includes "Resistance to Civil Government" along with Thoreau's reform essays of 1854–60. The book concludes with a brief survey of "The Late Natural History Essays" and a useful appendix charting the chronologies of Thoreau's works. While there is some awkwardness and, in my judgment, some imbalance in their arrangement, this study has the virtue of demonstrating quite powerfully what Johnson's and Shanley's studies of individual texts could not—the complex interrelations of multiple works whose compositions overlapped. Most striking, perhaps, is the juxtaposition of Thoreau's more or less simultaneous work on *A Week,* "Ktaadn," and *Walden* in 1847–48. In relatively brief chapters, Adams and Ross characterize and in some cases diagram the revisions of the entire work being discussed, but their analysis is selective, isolating a representative or particularly revealing passage for close examination. Both in charting Thoreau's revisions and in local insights on individual texts, *Revising Mythologies* is a useful complement to existing Thoreau scholarship.

Adams and Ross's presentation of Thoreau's revisions is given shape and direction by two distinct but related arguments about Thoreau's development as a writer. The first thesis, implied by their title, is that Thoreau's revisions reveal a gradual change in his attitude toward and use of mythology: beginning, they argue, with largely conventional neoclassical views which led to the essentially decorative use of mythological allusions in his work, Thoreau gradually came to a more radical and romantic understanding of mythology, in which "conscious myth-making" could reunite man and nature and in which myth "finally assumed the status of a special source of truth and aesthetic power" (p. 6). Here myth is not merely decorative but determines and informs the very structure of a work. In particular, they argue, Thoreau began to represent himself as a mythic hero in narratives brought into conformity with the myth structure of the romantic quest. Thoreau's use of mythology and Thoreau as myth-maker are not new subjects in Thoreau scholarship; Adams and Ross's particular contributions are their argument about his gradual evolution from neoclassical scholar to romantic myth-maker and their demonstration that "his views about mythology are often quite different even among the drafts of *Walden* and, especially, *A Week*" (p. 6). In general, this argument is convincing, and Adams and Ross do a genuine service in reminding us of Thoreau's early ties to neoclassical conventions and aesthetics; in the interest of advancing their thesis, however, they are far too dismissive of Thoreau's early writings, summarily labeling them as mired in eighteenth-century conventions without acknowledging the extent to which these works do, indeed, express many of the same romantic ideas and employ many of the same romantic and mythic elements that they celebrate in the later works. "The Service," "Natural History of Massachusetts," "A Walk to Wachusett," and "A Winter Walk" can all be seen as engaged in "conscious myth-making" on a more profound and more fundamentally romantic level than mere neoclassical allusiveness.

The second, related thesis of this book is both more radical and more problematic. The authors argue that, in the course of Thoreau's gradually romanticized understanding and use of mythology, he underwent a more dramatic "'conversion' to romanticism": this was a "single event, with a single date, after which time his way of talking about the world changed"—"a period during 1851 and 1852 when he began to use the formal terms regarding the imagination and poetry that had become commonplace in England and among his New England friends such as Emerson" (p. 6). Like any novel thesis that challenges the received wisdom on a given subject, this one too has the value of forcing the reader to reexamine and defend his or her original assumptions; and, indeed, Adams and Ross succeed in sensitizing us to the neoclassical elements in Thoreau's early writings and in his explicit statements about art. Ultimately, however, their argument for Thoreau's "conversion" is not convincing. Rather than supporting and enhancing their primary thesis about Thoreau's evolving understanding of myth (as they clearly intend it to), their insistence on Thoreau's "conversion" interferes with the presentation, and undermines the credibility, of that otherwise useful and instructive argument.

To borrow terms from nineteenth-century theories of evolution, Adams and Ross's first thesis, about Thoreau's changing view of mythology, is based on an essentially "uniformitarian" rather than a "catastrophic" model of Thoreau's evolution as a writer. That is, Thoreau's discovery and use of romantic mythmaking was gradual and is more or less predictably traceable through successive revisions of a prolonged composition like *A Week*. Their second thesis, however, is essentially catastrophic—they attempt to identify Thoreau's "conversion" to romanticism as a specific event with a specific date, resulting in dramatic changes in his writing. Thus, while both arguments address Thoreau's development as a romantic writer, they seem to be at odds with each other when Adams and Ross try to demonstrate that development. Thoreau's "conversion" supposedly took place in

1851-52—after the publication of "Ktaadn" (1848) and *A Week* (1849), in other words. Yet the authors also argue that Thoreau's experience on Katahdin brought him "closer to a romantic travel writing which is shaped by a romance quest and which explores the epistemological and literary uses of mythology" (p. 8); and that this same romance quest model informs the subsequent revisions of *A Week*, even while he was constrained by the essentially neoclassical language and forms of the earlier drafts. Thus, the gradualist argument represents 1834-46 as Thoreau's neoclassical phase. He was influenced, of course, by the language and themes of the romantic writers around him, they explain, but he "does not apply them with the full commitment he would later on" (p. 7). The years 1846-51, then, apparently represent an intermediate stage, when romantic myth begins to shape his narratives. This gradualist argument can account for the revisions of his major works during this period, but it seems to undercut the force of the claims that it was not until 1851, with his "conversion," that Thoreau became "emotionally committed to the ideas, terminology, and literary figures of the romantic movement" (p. 9). The results of this "conversion," they argue, are the triumphant later versions of *Walden*, written between 1852 and 1854, but it is difficult to see why these represent a significantly different vision or commitment to romanticism than he had achieved earlier. Adams and Ross then seem rather hard-pressed to account for the un-romantic tenor of the travel pieces written at just this time: "An Excursion to Canada" (1850-52), *Cape Cod* (1850-55), "Chesuncook" (1853-56), and "The Allegash and East Branch" (1858). They note that these works did not undergo the prolonged revising process of *A Week* or *Walden*, and they argue, correctly I think, that Thoreau's interest in writing for a popular magazine market imposed several significant constraints on these works, discouraging radical experiments and encouraging conformity to conventional scientific and travel writing. But while this tension between his romanticism and his professionalism might be (and to some extent is) instructively explored in terms of Thoreau's revising practices and his evolution as a romantic myth-maker, it is difficult to understand why Thoreau would turn to conventional pieces immediately during and after his "conversion" experience. Thoreau's later essays persuade Adams and Ross that "Thoreau moved away from his heightened romanticism of the mid 1850s not only because he was writing for a popular market and was himself growing more secular and scientific but also because he was increasingly involved in social concerns, as the history of his political writing reveals" (p. 12). Thus, Thoreau's "conversion" was of limited duration and was manifested principally in the late revisions of *Walden*.

In spite of the apparently limited duration and influence of this "conversion," Adams and Ross give it the central place in their account of Thoreau's career: it is the event toward which his earlier career leads and away from which his later career declines. Thus, while the 1851–52 "conversion" is not fully discussed and defended until we reach that point chronologically, in chapter 9, the first eight chapters constantly foreshadow that event. Thoreau's earlier works are not fully romantic, they argue, in the way those are that are informed by his "conversion." Their insistence on the centrality of this "conversion" is particularly frustrating because the evidence for it is so insubstantial. They succeed best in showing that during 1851–52 Thoreau began using some key terms of British romanticism with greater frequency and confidence than he had earlier—probably as a result of his rereading Wordsworth at this time, and perhaps Emerson as well; but so many of the themes and characteristics Adams and Ross identify as fundamentally romantic had already been explored by Thoreau by this time that the evidence for a "conversion" experience relies far too heavily on the evanescent claim that these things now meant more to him than they had: "It was as if," they explain, "a conventional Christian, brought up in a Christian household and familiar with its doctrines and vocabulary, underwent the transforming experience of being 'born again'—this time making the concerns and especially the language genuinely his own" (p. 156).

"Thoreau announces the first step of his conversion," they assert, "in the Journal entry for 21 May 1851 (*J* 2:207) with a declaration of religious faith, discovered or confirmed quite recently: 'Who shall say that there is no God, if there is a *just* man. It is only within a year that it has occurred to me that there is such a being actually existing on the globe'" (p. 159). Adams and Ross suggest that Thoreau "seems quite sincere" in proclaiming this faith as "something new" and then strain to make the connection to his "conversion" to romanticism by arguing that "Transcendentalism is, among other things, a religious movement, and Thoreau's newfound faith is an important starting point toward his fully joining that movement" (p. 159). But Thoreau asserted and reasserted his faith throughout his writings. Early essays including "The Service," "Natural History of Massachusetts," "A Winter Walk," and "Paradise (to be) Regained" might all be regarded as *fundamentally* declarations of his faith in the divinity of man and of creation. Epiphany *is* the way of knowing for Thoreau, and this 1851 Journal entry is but one of many exclamations of a faith revealed or discovered anew. I think, for example, of his 1840 Journal entry, "I am not taken up, like Moses, to learn the law, but lifted up in my seat here, in the warm sun and the genial light" (*PJ* 1:147); or his Journal entry ten days after moving to Walden Pond in 1845 (and later incorporated into *Walden*), "Sometimes when I compare myself with other men methinks I am favored by the Gods. They seem to whisper joy to me beyond my deserts and that I do have a solid warrant and surety at their hands" (*PJ* 2:159); or of the several epiphanic moments recounted in *A Week*, including his ecstatic moment of intuition on Monday night, of which he wrote, "I see, smell, taste, hear, feel, that everlasting Something to which we are all allied, at once our maker, our abode, our destiny, our very Selves,"[2] and his description in Wednesday's essay on Friendship of "passages of affection in our intercourse with mortal men and women, such as no prophecy has taught us to expect, which transcend our earthly life, and anticipate heaven for us" (*Week*, 268), as well as his well-known vision from the summit of Saddleback Mountain. Given such passages, it seems arbitrary and capricious to argue that just now, in 1851, Thoreau really *commits* himself to the Transcendentalist's faith.

Adams and Ross note that within weeks of this 1851 Journal entry, Thoreau explicitly calls himself a Transcendentalist: "I begin to be *transcendental* and show where my heart is" (*J* 2:228).

They suggest, "As far as we can tell, this is the first time he applies the label to himself unambiguously" (159; cf. 22, 33). They point out that the context of this entry, in which Thoreau "uses *transcendental* (with its variants) three times" (in fact, five times), is a discussion which sets the Transcendental "Instinct" against "common sense." The authors claim that "It is unlikely that a person who had long and confidently held such beliefs about epistemology and its relation between the individual and his world would rehearse them in his private writings. We conclude that they were newly formulated and that Thoreau was trying them out" (p. 159). These conclusions are not entirely justified, however. Certainly, as Adams and Ross point out, there are at least three instances during this period when Thoreau labels himself explicitly as a Transcendentalist in what seems to be an unguarded and unambiguous way not characteristic of his earlier writings (though these are still rare occurrences). This does not, however, imply that he was now embracing a movement from which he had previously held himself aloof. Thoreau's loyalty to Emerson and the *Dial* (1840–44) would seem to be sufficient evidence that he identified himself with that movement, however loosely defined. Moreover, there are early instances of Thoreau's more explicit identification with Transcendentalism. Adams and Ross cite an 1840 letter to his sister in which he refers to himself as John's "'transcendental brother,'" but they argue that "the quotation marks here suggest to us that Thoreau acknowledges his reputation as a Transcendentalist but refuses to embrace the label for himself without irony" (p. 22n). But considering the pejorative sense with which the label "Transcendentalist" was used throughout the 1830s and 1840s, it is hard to imagine Thoreau (or Emerson, or any other Transcendentalist) ever applying it to himself *without* a degree of irony. All the instances cited from the 1850s seem as ironic and self-conscious in tone as the 1840 letter, though they lack the quotation marks. Thoreau also clearly, if indirectly, identified himself as a Transcendentalist in his 1843 review-essay, "Paradise (to be) Regained." Thoreau begins this review of J. A. Etzler's Fourierist utopian tract by observing, "It would seem . . . that there is a transcendentalism in mechanics as well as in ethics. . . . One [the latter] says he will reform himself. . . . The other will reform nature and circumstances."[3] The Transcendentalist in mechanics is Etzler; initially, Thoreau avoids explicitly identifying the Transcendentalist in ethics, but by the end of the review, when he forcefully argues for individual moral reform powered by love and faith, he has clearly and unambiguously taken a public stand as just such a Transcendentalist.

It is in cases such as this that Adams and Ross's cursory treatment of early Thoreau comes back to haunt them. They devote only one slim paragraph to "Paradise (to be) Regained" in which they not only fail to acknowledge his use of the label "Transcendentalist" but also manage to misread the essay rather badly. They acknowledge Thoreau's emphasis on the reforming power of love but argue that "Thoreau's placing individual regeneration ahead of social reform here is (as his title indicates) in the future. His Miltonic title speaks of paradise not in the present (where he locates it in *Week* and *Walden*) but sometime [sic] to be" (p. 30). On the contrary it is Etzler, not Thoreau, who defers paradise, and Thoreau's title is intended to make precisely that point, which is the very basis of Thoreau's critique. "The true reformer," Thoreau explains, "does not want time, nor money, nor co-operation, nor advice. What is time but the stuff delay is made of?" And he adds, "Faith, indeed, is all the reform that is needed; it is itself a reform" (*RP* 41, 43).

Further, Adams and Ross's conclusion that Thoreau would not rehearse in his private journal the debate between "instinct" and "common sense" unless his beliefs were "newly formulated" seems naive in its assumptions about the nature of Thoreau's journalizing. Certainly it is contradicted by Thoreau's earlier writings on "instinct" and "common sense." Thoreau "rehearsed" and reworked ideas over and over in his Journal; it was not merely a private diary but the work-book and storehouse of a professional writer who, as Adams and Ross well know, could revise almost compulsively. And the celebration of intuition or instinct over the understanding or "common sense" was not a new belief for Thoreau. It informs the distinction between "facts" and "truths" in "Natural History of Massachusetts" (1842) as well as the distinction between "common sense" and "uncommon sense" in the "Friday" chapter of *A Week;* and it is at the heart of each of Thoreau's moments of epiphanic illumination cited earlier. In reformulating old ideas, Thoreau may be said to modify or refine his thinking, but the evidence simply does not suggest any newly formulated beliefs or a "conversion" experience here.

Adams and Ross identify the "next stage" of Thoreau's "conversion" as prompted by his rereading of Wordsworth in the summer of 1851, resulting in his use of a new romantic vocabulary, centering particularly on the use of "imagination" and "sympathy." They are generally more persuasive here about Thoreau's use of "imagination" than they are about his use of "sympathy" (which Thoreau seems to use in its fully romantic sense, as Adams and Ross define it, throughout "Natural History of Massachusetts" and "A Winter Walk," for example). Though they again seem to undervalue the early writing, the attention to Thoreau's vocabulary is nevertheless instructive; the greater weakness in the argument is in the effort to see this revision in Thoreau's lexicon as evidence of a "conversion" experience rather than as part of a progressive intellectual development. A particularly strained argument suggests that Thoreau's discovery of romantic "imagination" and "sympathy" was connected to a new "Faustian drive," renewed "aspirations," and a vigor associated with his "conversion" (p. 163). The evidence seems to be a Journal passage for 16 July 1851, "soon after his conversion begins," in which Thoreau admonishes himself, "Let me forever go in search of myself." The authors suggest, in turn, that the "restlessness" expressed here "is important for anticipating the 'different drummer' paragraph in *Walden*," drawn from a Journal entry for 19 July 1851. The conclusion is that "the immediate result of Thoreau's changed way of thinking and talking about the key ideas of romanticism was a searching reassessment of his personal goals" (p. 163). There is, first of all, no evidence linking Thoreau's examination of the vocabulary of romanticism to his "restlessness" or "reassessment." Secondly, the restlessness, self-examination, and ambition noted here are recurring characteristics found throughout the Journal; among other passages, one can certainly point to the first few months of 1842 (after John's death) and the summer of 1845 (with his move to Walden) as periods when his Journal was filled with similarly searching reassessments of his goals. Ironically, the "different drummer" passage cited here as evidence of his "conversion" experience is in fact an instructive example of Thoreau's habit of reworking old ideas and images in his Journal: this 1851 entry is but the latest incarnation of an image first appropriated for "The Service" (*RP* 11) and subsequently revised for inclusion in *A Week* (p. 175).

Greater attention to the ways in which Thoreau's early writings do anticipate his later major works, in spite of the constraints of a lingering neoclassical vocabulary and aesthetics, would have tempered but strengthened this book. The "conversion" thesis seems misguided, but the legitimate and insightful observations Adams and Ross make along the way could have contributed to a more compelling study of Thoreau's revisions, of his use of mythology, and of his development as a romantic writer. If one can read *that* book between the lines here, *Revising Mythologies* will still be a quite useful book to Thoreau scholars. The carefully tabulated data on Thoreau's revisions will be particularly useful, and the insistence on Thoreau's neoclassical roots is a salutary corrective. Ironically, among the freshest and most persuasive chapters of the book are those on "An Excursion to Canada" and *Cape Cod,* works which did not undergo the prolonged revisions of *A Week* or *Walden* and which were far less experimental and "romantic" because of the constraints of the periodical marketplace. Adams and Ross are sensitive to these constraints and perceptive about Thoreau's adaptations to them, while revealing the underlying mythic dimensions of these travel pieces. In the chapters that deal with more extensively revised works, Adams and Ross largely succeed in suggesting the importance of scholarship "which makes the facts about composition and revision a part of the proper study of texts and which takes relevant biographical and textual evidence fully into account . . . rather than focusing all of our interpretive energies on a fixed, authorized, and determined product" (p. 5). Such a project seems particularly appropriate for a writer with writing habits like Thoreau's, and while I am not persuaded by many of the arguments and conclusions of this book, the scholarship on Thoreau's texts will undoubtedly make a significant place for *Revising Mythologies* in Thoreau studies.

Notes

1. Throughout this review, *PJ* will be used as the abbreviation for Henry Thoreau, *The Journal,* ed. John C. Broderick, et al., 3 vols. to date (Princeton: Princeton Univ. Press, 1981–   ); *J* will be used as the abbreviation for Henry Thoreau, *The Journal of Henry D. Thoreau,* ed. Bradford Torrey and Francis H. Allen, 14 vols. (Boston: Houghton Mifflin, 1906).

2. Thoreau, *A Week on the Concord and Merrimack Rivers,* ed. Carl Hovde, et al. (Princeton: Princeton Univ. Press, 1980). Subsequent references will be cited parenthetically in the text, abbreviated as *Week.*

3. Thoreau, *Reform Papers,* ed. Wendell Glick (Princeton: Princeton Univ. Press, 1973). Subsequent references will be cited parenthetically in the text, abbreviated as *RP.*

Marxism and Its Uses as Criticism

Frederick C. Stern

Edward J. Ahearn. *Marxism and Modern Fiction.* New Haven: Yale University Press, 1989. xv, 231 pp.

Criticism has been seriously influenced, in the last fifteen or twenty years, by Marxism. I date the most significant moment of onset in this regard, in the United States at least, to the publication in 1971—now twenty years ago—of Fredric Jameson's *Marxism and Form: Twentieth-Century Dialectical Theories of Literature* by Princeton University Press. Jameson offered a Marxist approach to literature which he distinguished sharply, effectively, from what he called a "criticism . . . of a relatively untheoretical, essentially didactic nature, destined more for use in the night school than in the graduate seminar, if I may put it that way" (p. ix). Jameson's volume appeared at about the same moment and, indeed, was part of the attack on such previously established critical modes in the United States as—to use mere rubrics—the "New Criticism," "Neo-Aristotelianism," and various "socially conscious" forms.

The attacks came mostly from European sources, of course. Many names now known by every serious critic came to our attention for the first time then, given the previously rather provincial nature of American criticism, and were to help give U.S. criticism the "theoretical" cast, in the hands of Marxist as well as non-Marxist critics, which, as Jameson's perhaps a little cavalier dismissal of earlier Marxist critical ideas suggested, was needed. I think of the volume *The Structuralist Controversy: The Languages of Criticism and the Sciences of Man* (Richard Macksey and Eugenio Donato, eds., Baltimore: Johns Hopkins University Press, 1970), as the opening salvo, as it were, of this attack on accepted American critical approaches. This volume, which printed the proceedings of a conference on structuralism held at Hopkins in 1966, gave a broad segment of the American critical community an opportunity to read the work of such now-fabled figures as Derrida, Barthes, Todorov, and Lacan, among others. It also provided an opportunity for acquaintance with such an avowed, Lukacian Marxist as Lucien Goldmann, whose *The Hidden God* had been known mostly to critics of the eighteenth century, and had not been widely disseminated among the general critical community.

I mention this aspect of the recent history of criticism because it seems to me that Professor Ahearn's book must be seen as one entry in a growing and significant list of works by American critics concerning Marxism, a list that is now about twenty years old. That is, Marxist literary criticism, which at one point fell afoul of the Cold War and McCarthyism—as well as of its own, to use Jameson's term, "night-school" limitations—is now generally accepted as a perfectly respectable, significant way to approach literary matters. A number of works have appeared in recent years which avow Marxism as a useful, challenging, theoretically sustainable way of dealing with literature. I cite anthologies only as examples. Some appeared shortly after Jameson's book—e.g., Berel Lang and Forrest Williams, eds., *Marxism and Art: Writings in Aesthetics and Criticism* (New York: David McKay, 1972); and many more have been published recently—e.g., Cary Nelson and Lawrence Grossberg, eds., *Marxism and the Interpretation of Culture* (Urbana: University of Illinois Press, 1988).

Ahearn's volume, it seems to me, is an ambitious and significant entry in the list of works of Marxist literary criticism. Its style is lucid and relatively free of the cant which mars so much recent critical writing. I learned much from it and found it usefully stimulating, but I also think the work raises serious difficulties. Of necessity, in this review I must focus on the difficulties, while positing, at once and at the outset, that in many ways Ahearn's work is a fine example of at least some of the insights a knowledge of, and commitment to, Marx's thought can provide in literary studies.

Ahearn begins his book with a brief chapter entitled "The Anatomy of Civil Society," in which he attempts to set forth some central constructs by which Marx deals with culture and cultural production—a brave effort, in thirty pages. He continues with four chapters, each of which discusses one or more novels from the point of view of the social picture drawn in chapter 1. Chapter 2 deals with *Pride and Prejudice* and *Madame Bovary,* chapter 3 with *Ulysses* and *The Golden Bowl,* chapter 4 with *Le Père Goriot* and *Absalom, Absalom!* and chapter 5 with *Moby-Dick.* The very conjunctions indicated by these pairs shows the boldness of Ahearn's enterprise and the originality of his attempt. A final chapter, entitled "Conclusion: Educating the Educator," attempts to draw some lessons concerning the utility of Marxism for the project of studying and teaching literature. The major point Ahearn has attempted to make is here stated clearly and concisely. Quoting Jameson's citation of Walter Benjamin's "assertion that the documents of culture are always the documents of barbarism," Ahearn writes:

> Jameson's use of Benjamin's statement, as a warning against the tendency of "a certain radicalism" to reappropriate the classics as humanistic or progressive, might be thought to apply to the present study, which in effect appropriates Marx to enhance the appreciation of a number of classics. That would be to misread my intention and practice, since I agree with Benjamin.... I value the works treated here for achieving a greater or lesser transcendence of class limitation, a complex and sometimes contradictory degree of "world-historical consciousness." Rather than being humanistic or progressive, for me they are critical, often virulently so. [p. 199]

I take it that these lines indicate the central intentions of Ahearn's work. He proposes to demonstrate that the works he discusses criticize, consciously or not, aspects of "civil society" in ways which parallel or echo Marx's critiques, that they are critical of the societies in which they are set—e.g., capitalist society since 1813 (the publication date of *Pride and Prejudice*). He makes his case well, on the whole. He argues effectively that one can read, as "critiques" of capitalism, the novels he uses. He demonstrates over and again that a reading of even so seemingly "apolitical" a work as *Pride and Prejudice,* when undertaken with a consciousness of Marx's description of such matters as alienation, the division of labor, primitive accumulation and other categories, leads to an understanding of the society of the novel's present. That understanding is profoundly critical, and in turn buttresses Marx's description. Repeatedly, Ahearn emphasizes that the works he is examining can be read, as it were, as demonstrations of Marxist ideas about the nature of the world and society. Some examples may clarify the point here:

In a passage near the end of the *Ulysses—Golden Bowl* chapter: "I hope to have shown that the range of what is thus depicted *expands the contexts furnished by Marx* and Joyce" (p. 117).

In a passage early in the *Le Père Goriot—Absalom, Absalom!* chapter: "Here we encounter a New World realization of what Vautrin explains to Rastignac as a general principle, *something like Marx's* dissection of the concept of 'primitive accumulation'" (p. 125).

Specifically in relation to *Goriot:* "In Balzac's book, Rastignac (unlike the other boarders, whose indifference to Goriot's plight *parallels Marx's* argument about the atomization of nineteenth-century society)" (p. 155).

In the *Moby-Dick* chapter: "The universal extension of the category of ownership, so devious a force in fiction by Austen, Flaubert, and James, is justified immediately by Ishmael's first examples of Fast-Fish: 'the sinews and souls of Russian serfs and Republican slaves.' The *Marxlike equation* neatly demystifies the passages on the czar's imperial brain and democratic equality that we have just discussed" (p. 196). (Italics in these citations are mine.)

These examples, typical of a great many more in this volume, are the meat of this book, if we take its title and first chapter seriously. They show that ideas about society that the seminal nineteenth-century mind of Karl Marx conceived can be *construed to be* present in the minds of writers who have lived in the world Marx analyzed. The demonstration is that what Marx saw in, say, 1848 (I take the date of the *Manifesto* only as sign for the entire body of Marx's thought) as characteristic of the world he analysed, can also be seen, at least partially, to be reflected in the works of writers who lived in it. Furthermore, in examining these works through the lens of Marx's description of "civil society" as redacted by Ahearn, we can find "Marxlike" features, or features which are "something like" Marx's view or something which "parallels" Marx.

On the whole, Ahearn's demonstrations are quite successful. It is precisely *because* Ahearn succeeds so well in what he has set out to do that his book, despite its many merits, is disturbing. Finally Ahearn's position is a kind of tautology which can be stated as follows: if we read novels (or, perhaps, any fictional text) with Marx's descriptions of "civil society" in mind, we can find that, consciously or not, the descriptions the writers offer of the lives and times they have chosen as their subject echo or otherwise reflect Marx's description—and that such readings in turn validate Marx's description. To put this another way: Ahearn shows us, through clever and intelligent readings, that it is possible to "appropriate" Marx in order to validate the verisimilitude of fictional description, and, in turn—since the dialectic must apply—that such works of fiction validate Marx's description of "civil society."

It is difficult to disagree with Ahearn. Indeed, given my own life-long preoccupation with Marxism as a means of understanding society and its cultural products, I would have *assumed* this to be the case, and Ahearn states and demonstrates this proposition usefully and well. However, an equally clever reader of texts could make a similar argument for, say, Christian readings of these texts; or a myth critic, following Frye, could make such an argument for mythic readings; or, at the opposite pole from Ahearn, a critic might well argue that these texts demonstrate the viability and permanence—especially in light of recent events—of free enterprise social arrangements, of capitalist visions of the nature of "civil society" and of the human beings who people such a society.

The work of art, especially (though not only) if it has withstood the test of time and continued to arouse interest, will always reflect its society in myriad ways. Indeed, part of the attraction of the novel, especially what one might call the realistic novel, is that it renders the individual *in situ*, in his or her social setting. It becomes the task of interpretation, of the hermeneutic enterprise, to understand how the text works, to point out that the world described by the writer fits into the critic's sense of reality—and it will be the critic's sense of the nature of "civil society," the critic's reality, which will underlie the reading offered. Such a pointing adds something to our understanding of the text, though its greatest use may be to help us to verify our own view of the world, of "civil society," of the nature of human beings. It helps us to demonstrate that authors (Foucault's *caveat* not withstanding), who after all live in the world, can present to us character, incident, and setting that help verify a variety of ways of seeing the world, one of which—for Marxists the most important of which—is Marxism.

Ahearn's project adds a good deal to our understanding of the texts he discusses. His juxtapositions of such disparate works as *Ulysses* and *The Golden Bowl* or *Le Père Goriot* and *Absalom, Absalom!* are fascinating and give us a fresh angle of vision through which to see these familiar and always intriguing works. But the part of Ahearn's project implicit in his title—i.e., the relationship between Marx or Marxism and the novel—seems to me flawed, finally, because despite the ingenuity of the readings, the results are only that Balzac's novel can be seen as "something like" Marx's conception of primitive accumulation, or that *Moby-Dick* has "Marxlike" features, or that something in *Goriot* "parallels" Marx.

Why is this so? I am a little loath to offer even a tentative answer. I will do so, however, in what I hope is a suggestive fashion, in the spirit that all of us who think of ourselves as Marxists (in one or another way) need to consider together what uses we can make of our now-much embattled philosophy. The problem, I think, lies first in the use Ahearn makes of the "tool," if the term applies, of Marxist analysis. Marxism, especially as necessarily modified by later Marxist thinkers in the years since Marx wrote, is a complex, delicate, difficult scalpel with which to dissect anything, be it society, literature, or other aspects of human behavior. Any notion that it can be simply applied has surely been destroyed by the uses to which Marx has been put wherever practical politics has created societies which have put themselves forward as Marxist. Ahearn's tool, his use of Marxism, is not scalpel-like. It is more like a trowel, a tool with which one does not cut into or away, but with which one adds on and

Marxism and Its Uses as Criticism 267

binds together. The conclusions—"Marxlike," "parallels" Marx, etc.—do not do much to enhance our understanding of the uses of Marxism as a means for literary analysis, or of the world the Marxist tool analyzes, though they may assign Marxist readings to the texts in question. Our understanding of the texts Ahearn discusses *is*, however, enhanced because his own mind offers us insights into the events, characters, language and sign-systems of these texts. Ahearn's eye is informed by his knowledge of Marx, and it thus sees the literary text as a product of the society in which the writer exists. Such an eye, such an awareness, Marxist or not, is useful in helping to see the text as product of its society, as mediated through the writer, regardless of the possibility of assigning "Marxlike" features to the text.

Another aspect of the problem with Ahearn's approach derives from his brave effort to delineate Marx's vision of "civil society" in his thirty-page-long first chapter. Although this chapter is a remarkably good effort at presenting Marx's vision, it does leave a good deal open to question. In the space afforded even by a lengthy review, one example of the problem must suffice. After a discussion of Goriot's status as "once a capitalist," a "fact" that "is obscured and must be revealed" (p. 23), Ahearn continues:

> Readers used to conventional approaches might suspect me of being guilty of the error ascribed to Marx by Peter Demetz, who accuses him of naively treating the characters in Eugene Sue's *Mysteries of Paris* as if they were real people. I do not take the creations of my writers to be real in this limited sense, but I do take these fictions to be every bit as much reproductions, representations, workings up, appropriations of human reality as those of political economy or other social sciences. . . . Literary works by our most powerful authors are often concrete representations of world historical developments in Marx's sense of those terms. [p. 24]

But it seems to me that Ahearn's book is, indeed, subject to a charge like Demetz's. This becomes clearest if we compare Ahearn's work with that of the Marxist critic I consider preeminent in the United States today.

Ahearn seems to take his lead from Fredric Jameson, and especially the Jameson of *The Political Unconscious* (Ithaca: Cornell University Press, 1981). In that volume Jameson offers analyses of aspects of a startlingly large number of texts, with intentions not unlike Ahearn's. Though in a more complex fashion, Jameson offers us what he calls a "Marxian vision of history" (p. 103) in his first chapter—a chapter which does many other things, but which also presents a description of Marxism, somewhat like Ahearn's "The Anatomy of Civil Society." His application of that vision, however, never leads him to the conclusion that works or parts of works, or ideas expressed in works, are "Marxlike," or construable as verification of a Marxian view of the world. For Jameson,

a Marxist hermeneutic—the decipherment by historical materialism of the cultural monuments and traces of the past—must come to terms with the certainty that all the works of class history ... are all in one way or another profoundly ideological, have all had a vested interest in and a functional relationship to social formations based on violence and exploitation; and that, finally, the restoration of the meaning of the greatest cultural monuments cannot be separated from a passionate and partisan assessment of everything that is oppressive in them and that knows complicity with privilege and class domination, stained with the guilt not merely of culture in particular but of History itself as one long nightmare. [p. 299]

Jameson will not find "Marxlike" features in the works he examines. Rather, he will find in them evidence which reflects the ideology of the society in which the work is created, evidence of "History itself." One example again must suffice. Discussing Balzac's *La Rabouilleuse,* Jameson writes:

Yet this representation of a historical dialectic is at one and the same time the locus of an essentially ideological reflection, or in our previous terminology, of the mediation on a conceptual antinomy. From this angle, the problem is one of the ideological category of "violence" and can perhaps best be conveyed in the following formulation: how is it conceivable for the family to generate a force explosive enough to wrest the fortune away from its other branch without being itself blown open and destroyed in the process? When we understand that the family is here, according to the canonical logic of Balzac's conservatism, the figure of society, it will become evident that the "political unconscious"

Marxism and Its Uses as Criticism 269

of this text is thereby raising, in symbolic form, issues of social change and counterrevolution, and asking itself how the force necessary to bring about a return to the old order can be imagined as doing so without at the same time being so powerful and disruptive as to destroy that order itself in the process. [pp. 172–73]

There are no "echoes" of Marx. Jameson shows rather that the vision of the writer, *as mediating force,* and from its own logic, can be seen to explore the social arrangements of the writer's society, if we examine it from the point of view of the historical dialectic. Jameson's use of Marxism as scalpel, to follow my earlier metaphor, helps us to recognize that in a reading of this novel we can best understand its intersection of what he calls somewhat earlier "an essentially objective or sociological diagnosis with an essentially subjective or protopsychoanalytic one" (p. 171) by *our* use of the historical dialectic. Jameson avoids Demetz's charge by dealing with the novel not as "Marxlike" in any sense, but by perceiving it as a mediating force in which ideology *necessarily* finds reflection in the "intersection" between sociology, and some form of psychology. This is not so much a construing of the novel according to Marx, but an analysis of the text—a dissection of it—which reveals its ideological core.

I am not for a moment suggesting that Ahearn is unaware of Jameson's stand. Clearly, as his entire book shows, he has taken Jameson very seriously. But the result of Ahearn's seriousness and his use of Jameson is not the exploration of his works in regard to their "complicity" and their "ideology." Rather it is an effort to show "Marxlike" features in the works he discusses, and that is quite the opposite of Jameson's sense of ideology. Ahearn is a sophisticated Marxist, aware of the complexities of Marxism. His learning is extensive, as his entire book shows. However, it seems to me that in the book under review he has troweled too much and not scalpeled enough. The work, for all its sophistication, comes to conclusions which seem reductive of Marxism's power to aid our understanding of literary texts, and reductive of Ahearn's own analytical capabilities.

I shall mention two other matters—perhaps merely cavils. First, the economic analysis of James's *The Golden Bowl* does not give credit to, and does not use, F. O. Matthiessen's similar—though perhaps less extensive—analysis in his *Henry James: The Major Phase* (New York and London: Oxford University Press, 1944). Matthiessen also raises this issue in his more casual discussion of James's work in *American Renaissance* (New York and London: Oxford University Press, 1941), a volume in which he also writes a chapter entitled "Hawthorne's Politics and the Economic Structure of *The Seven Gables*" (pp. 316–37). Ahearn seems to think that economic analysis of a more-or-less Marxist cast in literary studies is entirely a recent product. Indeed, in several places he asserts that (for one example) "Marx's work is not extensively or intimately known to Americans" (p. xi).

But if so important a critic as Matthiessen has asserted economically influenced readings in the works he discusses, based on his own admittedly limited understanding of Marxism (a world view he could not fully accept, though he respected it, because of his own profound Christianity), then the lack of knowledge of Marx which Ahearn so regrets is not as great as he suggests. Marxism, though hampered by its own limitations and by attacks upon it, has been a presence of sorts in American criticism for more than half a century. One can suggest others besides Matthiessen, from the Communist-Party-dominated period in Granville Hicks's career to the anti-Communists at the *Partisan Review,* who used Marxism in one or another way. The problem was not that Marx was so little known. Rather, the problem was that the use of Marxism as a tool for literary or cultural analysis had to await a broader acquaintance with such European Marxists as Adorno, Benjamin, and Gramsci before its uses became clear, and had to await a theorist as powerful as Jameson before it could have a wider currency than it did in the Cold War era.

A significant thing about the publication of Ahearn's book, and of the anthologies I have mentioned and other recent works of Marxist criticism, is how acceptable Marxism has become—or, if one prefers, how open the academic community is at least to considering Marxist works of criticism seriously. Many works can be cited here, and this rather weakens Ahearn's comment, "It is also my experience that many good scholars and teachers of literature who have worked their way through the intricacies of

Derrida, Lacan, or Althusser have paid rather little attention to, have read rather little in, Marx" (p. xii). What is surprising to a person who has lived through the Cold War years, and experienced McCarthyism and all that it implied, is how *much* knowledge of Marx has been developed by younger scholars in recent years. To compare such knowledge to knowledge of "Derrida, Lacan, or Althusser" serves little purpose. The point is that Marx *is* known, along with these fashionable, but also highly important, thinkers.

Finally, and very briefly, I am also a little uncomfortable with Ahearn's treatment of *Moby-Dick* as extensively a homosexual novel. Ahearn writes: "Earlier, too, 'The Cassock' had shown us the sheath of the whale's 'unaccountable cone' as like an enormous homosexual version of Quequeg's jet-black idol, Yoyo" (p. 177). A little later, citing Irigaray's "vision of the oppressively male nature of the societal order," which, he says, "coincides with the figure of Ahab," Ahearn writes: "Homosexual through and through, having dented the pillow once for the form, he represents not pleasure but a bizarre collusion with the commercial order" (p. 191). These citations show the degree to which Ahearn insists that homosexuality is a major theme in Melville's novel. That idea is hardly original, but it is also not self-evident. Ahearn bases much of his economic reading of *Moby-Dick* precisely on what he sees as its "phallic and anal imagery that is part of the dominant homosexual motif of the book" (p. 170). This argument can certainly be made, but Ahearn has not sufficiently demonstrated the premise of his argument—that *Moby-Dick* is "homosexual throughout"—to base so strong a reading upon it as he offers us.

I have other concerns which I cannot and need not list here. It is sufficient to summarize as follows: Ahearn has written a useful, graceful, enlightening study of these novels, based on his reading of Marx. He has not, however, demonstrated the utility of Marxism as a tool of literary analysis any more than to show us that one can find, in the works he examines or, for that matter, in any novel, "parallels" to Marx, "echoes of" Marx, or "Marxlike" features. Ahearn's book is so good that I only wish he had taken his lead from Jameson more fully, and had worked more closely with "the political unconscious" than he does.

Samuel Beckett, Revisionist Translator

Rubin Rabinovitz

Brian Fitch. *Beckett and Babel: An Investigation into the Status of the Bilingual Work.* Toronto: University of Toronto Press, 1988. x, 242 pp.

For Samuel Beckett, the task of translating his works was a tiresome distraction from more creative endeavors. As he wrote in 1957 to a friend, the Irish poet Thomas McGreevy, "Translation of *All That Fall* into French and German, of *Fin de Partie* into German and English, of *L'Innommable* into English, of *Malone Meurt* into German, of *Echo's Bones* and other odd poems into German, and sick and tired I am of translation and what a losing battle it is always. Wish I had the courage to wash my hands of it all. I mean to leave it to others and try and get on with some work."[1] But Beckett never did give up that "losing battle." A few minor texts he left untranslated; a few he worked on in collaboration with others; but the majority, he translated on his own.

In *Beckett and Babel,* Brian Fitch has two main purposes: to study some of Beckett's texts in their original and translated forms, and to consider Beckett's methods of translation from a theoretical perspective. As will be seen, he achieves only limited success, particularly when his discussion centers on theory.

Fitch feels his subject has too often been ignored by other critics who, he says, tend to read Beckett's works only in their native languages. While many critics have in fact pointed out how Beckett's translations led to variants in specific passages, Fitch is right in claiming that little attention has been given to a detailed, systematic comparison of Beckett's works in their original and translated forms.[2] Fitch begins in just this way, with a series of side-by-side comparisons of Beckett's texts and translations, and these are among the most useful and informative sections of his book. He describes, for example, the obstacles that Beckett encountered while working on the French translation of

Murphy: puns, ambiguous passages, and rhymes were among the elements he found difficult to reproduce. Fitch concludes that because of such factors the French version of the novel lacks some of the impact of the English original. Beckett seems to have run into fewer problems when he translated *L'Innommable* into English. Although he did make some changes, they seldom led to conspicuous losses. Fitch, after reviewing portions of the French and English versions of the novel, feels that the two versions are about equal in terms of their accuracy and effectiveness.

As Fitch discusses various texts, it becomes clear that the outcome of the Beckettian translation process is seldom easy to predict. Often the reason is that Beckett, like Joyce, varied his style considerably from work to work. In places one finds devices like alliterative phrases or colloquialisms that impose barriers for the translator; elsewhere, there are fewer impediments of this type. What does seem consistent in different works is Beckett's tendency to introduce significant changes while translating. For example, Fitch found that about a third of the sentences in the English *Ping* were enough altered to vary in considerable ways from those in *Bing*, the French original. Fitch's comparison of *Still* and its translation *Immobile* led to the discovery of even more differences of this kind: some two-thirds of the sentences in *Immobile* underwent discernible shifts in meaning.

Most of the time, says Fitch, although Beckett's English texts tend to be somewhat longer than their French counterparts, they are not necessarily any richer in meaning as a result; apparently, the shift into French encouraged Beckett's penchant for brevity. But this rule has some exceptions. In the transition from *Company* to *Compagnie*, for example, seventeen sentences were dropped. In addition, descriptive details were omitted; verb tense and narrative perspective were changed; and at times the text of *Compagnie* even contradicts the original. On the other hand, *Company* often seems more ambiguous than its French counterpart: to some degree, the movement away from English seems to have clarified certain cryptic concepts and verbal complexities that existed in the original. The presence of so many modifications in the translated works leads Fitch to conclude that there is something puzzling about Beckett's method, a paradoxical element related to his unique situation as an author who alternated between two languages.³ At this point Fitch's discussion moves into a theoretical arena, as he tries to provide a clearer understanding of Beckett's unusual approach to translation.

Fitch has read widely in the area of translation theory, and some of the critical material he reviews is helpful. But again and again, after giving a lengthy synopsis of some concept, he decides that the paradox of the Beckettian method is still not resolved and turns to another authority. Fitch surveys virtually an anthology of theories—those of Friedrich Schleiermacher, Henri Meschonnic, Tzvetan Todorov, George Steiner, Walter Benjamin, Jacques Derrida, Noam Chomsky, and Julia Kristeva, among others—without finding the sought-after concept. Indeed, Fitch ultimately concludes that none of the theories he has cited can provide an adequate explanation of Beckett's singular approach to translation.

The pivotal issue, says Fitch, is establishing "the existence of an *intrinsic* difference" between ordinary translations and Beckett's. This he considers impossible because "in order to be able to speak of an intrinsic difference in the constitution and functioning of the text, we would require an analytical tool that would allow for the rigorous comparison of two texts in different languages. Such a tool does not (yet?), to my knowledge, exist. Here we run up against one of the perennial topics of translation theory: the problem of equivalence between a translation and its original, which appears no nearer to solution than it ever did!" (pp. 226–27). This comment, in the closing pages of *Beckett and Babel*, raises the question why—if none will finally meet his purposes—Fitch summarizes so many theories. It also touches on a related question: whether there truly is no way of defining an intrinsic difference between Beckett's methods and those of other translators.

The problem Fitch poses remains insoluble only if one blurs the distinctions between two disparate activities, translation and emendation. Translators, of course, try to limit themselves to minor changes, those demanded by the prerequisites of a new language. But Beckett usually went further than this. He used the opportunity afforded by translation as a way of introducing other modifications, at the same time expanding, pruning, polishing, refining—in a word, revising. One hardly needs an army of experts to establish that Beckett's blend of revision and translation would be prohibited to other translators.

It might seem that differentiating between revision and translation is so subtle and delicate a process that it can never in practice be achieved. But this is hardly the case. There are numerous examples (some mentioned in *Beckett and Babel*) where Beckett clearly crosses the line between translation and revision. For instance, the large-scale dropping of sentences in *Ping* and *Immobile* that Fitch discusses certainly represents the kind of emendation that goes beyond the commonly accepted bounds of translation.

There are many other occasions when Beckett introduced revisions while translating, and some of those Fitch doesn't mention are worth considering. In *En attendant Godot*, Estragon refers to himself as "Catulle"; in the English translation he calls himself "Adam." In the same play, Lucky alludes to Voltaire in the French version and to Berkeley in the English translation.[4] Adam is hardly the equivalent of Catullus; and if Voltaire and Berkeley were both philosophers, the first was a religious skeptic and the second an Anglican bishop. Clearly, only an author could introduce changes of this magnitude with impunity. And if no theory of translation can explain such modifications, it is because they are not really translations.

Richard Seaver, who assisted Beckett with the English translation of "La Fin," described the process in a way that underlines the special role of the author-translator. "What we ended up with was not a translation but a complete redoing of the original," Seaver recalled. "It was a completely new creation. I could not have taken the liberties that he did."[5] It seems reasonable then, that a study of Beckett's translations should consider the effects of such "liberties"; only in this way can any gray area between emendation and translation be defined. But Fitch, persuaded he has stumbled onto a problem that has confounded the experts, never discusses this question.

A reluctance to test long-held assumptions recurs in Fitch's comparison of *L'Innommable* and *The Unnamable*: here he claims that the novel's central theme (again, one overlooked by the critics) is a concern with bilingualism. In putting this theory forward, Fitch abandons traditional forms of explication in favor of what he calls a "a critical commentary of the Beckettian text in both languages" (p. 141). His commentary consists of a series of passages from *L'Innommable* and *The Unnamable* among which he intersperses material of his own—passages that follow the style of the novel and utilize the speaker's first-person voice. It is with this intermixture of quotation and imitation that Fitch hopes to establish the thematic importance of bilingualism in the novel, indeed, "to reveal and bring to the fore this main concern of *L'Innommable / The Unnamble*" (p. 155).

In order to identify the sources of the different passages, Fitch gives page numbers after the material taken from Beckett and uses italics for his own interpolations. A short excerpt will illustrate his approach:

> Je ne serai pas seul les premiers temps. Je le suis bien sûr. Seul . . . Je vais avoir de la compagnie (8). *Tout en me trouvant seul ici, je ne le suis jamais tout à fait puisque mon autre persona, l'anglophone, n'est jamais loin.* I shall not be alone, in the beginning. I am of course alone. Alone . . . I shall have company (292). *There shall always be this other me who speaks another tongue to keep me company.* Un de ces jours je l'interpellerai, je dirai, je ne sais pas, je trouverai le moment venu. Il n'y a pas de jours ici, mais je me sers de la formule (9). *Et les formules ne sont-elles pas l'apanage privilégié de qui pratique une seconde langue?* One of these days I'll challenge him. I'll say, I don't know, I'll say something, I'll think of something when the time comes. There are no days here, but I use the expression (292). *For such expressions really come in handy since they sound so natural.*[6]

After a dozen pages of this "critical commentary," Fitch, satisfied that he has provided the equivalent of a well-argued polemic, is ready to rest his case:

> In the preceding pages I have, of course, attempted to show that among the various problems addressed or, if one prefers, themes treated in those remarkable texts *L'Innommable* and *The Unnamable*—

the identity of the self, the relationship between writer and language, reader and language—perhaps the most central one or at least the one that is most specifically Beckettian has failed to be identified by the critics. I am speaking of the situation of the bilingual writer. This work can be seen first and foremost about bilingualism and more particularly about the manner in which bilingualism is lived by him who writes. [p. 154]

Never mind that author and persona are confused in Fitch's description of the novel's concern with "the manner in which bilingualism is lived by him who writes." Never mind that bilingualism seems trivial compared to the issues traditionally considered predominant in *The Unnamable:* the pain of existence, the loneliness of isolation, the difficulty of artistic creation, the poverty of linguistic expression, the ultimate incomprehensibility of the self and of the world. Never mind that positing a favored interpretation to the exclusion of others undermines Beckett's many-layered metaphorical structure. The overriding question for Fitch is why, if he hopes to prove that *The Unnamable* is "first and foremost about bilingualism," he can never find any factual evidence to substantiate his claim.

In the twelve pages where Fitch intersperses passages from *The Unnamable* with his own responses, the only allusions to bilingualism come in his material. Indeed, the novel seems notably devoid of references to bilingualism. The words *bilingual* and *bilingualism* never appear in it; nor do *translator, translation, linguistic, monolingual, dialect, argot, idiom, parlance, vernacular, colloquialism,* or *vocabulary.* Of the infrequent appearances of the words *language, tongue,* and *interpret,* none are in contexts that touch on the subject of bilingualism.[7] The word *English* is never used in the novel. And if the word *French* does occur once, in a reference to "the French breakfast," its equivalent does not appear in *L'Innommable,* where the corresponding passage reads "le petit déjeuner."[8]

Justifying his own approach, Fitch asserts that "a bilingual work should call for a bilingual critical commentary" (p. 155). Here he not only forgets that Beckett never published *L'Innommable* and *The Unnamable* in a bilingual edition; he snubs monolingual readers in need of commentary on Beckett's translations while employing a logic that might equally insist on studies of *Hamlet* being written in pentameter. There are other instances when Fitch's assertions seem extravagant. Arguing that the Tower of Babel "furnishes the only adequate symbol" for Beckett's bilingual dilemma, Fitch claims that "it is as though Beckett's whole life's work, the process of its realization and indeed of its very conception, were a direct assault on the mythical tower itself . . . " (p. 180). A similar lack of moderation leads to an unwitting slight when Fitch insists that Beckett's translated works "are completely cut adrift from any reality other than that which they manifest by their mere presence as language" (p. 191).

If overstatement is one of Fitch's failings, minimizing challenges to his thesis is another. Eager to depict a figure bedeviled by the problem of bilingualism, he ignores Beckett the polyglot who read Greek, Latin, Italian, Spanish, and German authors in the original.[9] Fitch similarly skirts a related issue: that if Beckett mainly produced French and English versions of his works, he also translated some of them into German.

The subtitle of *Beckett and Babel* promises "an investigation into the status of the bilingual work," but Fitch, ignoring the plays and poems entirely, deals only with four of the shorter fictions and with excerpts from two novels. Although he devotes half of one chapter and three-quarters of another to *L'Innommable,* he says nothing about *Molloy* and *Malone meurt*, the first two novels in Beckett's trilogy.[10] *Molloy* is of particular interest because the South African writer Patrick Bowles assisted Beckett with its translation; hence a comparison of *Molloy* and the novels Beckett translated by himself would be illuminating. But Fitch chooses not to discuss the works Beckett translated in collaboration with others. Nor does he ever compare Beckett's self-translations with his translations of other writers; the list of these includes such names as Guillaume Apollinaire, André Breton, Paul Éluard, and Robert Pinget.

Providing detailed comparisons of Beckett's French and English texts is painstaking work that yields few ground-breaking discoveries. So long as Fitch is content to focus on this topic, his careful observations lead to valuable, if undramatic, insights.

But when he turns to more abstract issues, he finds himself scrambling for evidence. On occasion Fitch proceeds without the requisite evidence, as in assigning a central role to bilingualism in *The Unnamable*. The result is a series of observations in which he confuses his own concerns and Beckett's. If Fitch often proves himself a skillful microscopist, he sometimes needs to ask whether the object under scrutiny might not be a reflection of his own eye.

Notes

1. Deirdre Bair, *Samuel Beckett: A Biography* (New York: Harcourt Brace Jovanovich, 1978), p. 485.

2. Thus, in his perceptive essay on Beckett's methods of translation, Raymond Federman calls for a "solid, thorough, definitive study of Beckett's bilingualism and his activity as a self-translator." See Raymond Federman, "The Writer as Self-Translator," in Alan Warren Friedman, Charles Rossman, and Dina Sherzer, eds., *Beckett Translating / Translating Beckett* (University Park: Pennsylvania State Univ. Press, 1987), p. 9.

3. Melvin J. Friedman, on the other hand, argues persuasively that Beckett's bilingual approach is not unique. In an essay published thirty years ago but still very much worth reading, Friedman points out that like Valery Larbaud, Beckett is part of a group "of modern authors who have made polyglot tendencies an essential aspect of their craft." Other members of this multilingual group are Rilke, Eliot, Pound, Joyce, and Nabokov. Friedman mentions, for example, that Nabokov collaborated with his son on the translation of *Invitation to a Beheading*. See Melvin J. Friedman, "The Creative Writer as Polyglot: Valery Larbaud and Samuel Beckett," *Transactions of the Wisconsin Academy of Sciences, Arts, and Letters,* 49 (1960), 229–36, esp. 229, 234.

4. Actually the situation is even more complicated than this. The name Voltaire was changed to Samuel Johnson in the first British edition of *Waiting for Godot* (published by Faber); Berkeley was introduced in the first American edition (published by Grove). See Colin Duckworth, "Introduction," *En attendant Godot* (London: Harrap, 1966), p. cviii.

5. Quoted by Bair, *Samuel Beckett,* p. 438.

6. *Beckett and Babel,* p. 142. The ellipses in the passage are Fitch's; they mark places where he has omitted material from Beckett's text. Page references after the French excerpts are to Samuel Beckett, *L'Innommable* (Paris: Éditions de Minuit, 1953); those after the English excerpts are to Samuel Beckett, *Three Novels* (New York: Grove Press, 1965).

7. For the six occurrences of the word *language* in the novel, see Samuel

Beckett, *The Unnamable* (New York: Grove Press, 1958), p. 51, line 3; p. 52, lines 29 and 30; p. 57, line 20; p. 63, line 21; and p. 66, line 1. In these passages the speaker of the novel does not refer to a foreign language; his concern is with understanding the utterances of the inner voices he hears. The same is true of the references to the word *tongue* (p. 68, line 28; and p. 70, line 10) and the word *interpret* (p. 31, line 30; and p. 56, line 31). I am relying here and in subsequent discussions about the presence or absence of words in *The Unnamable* on my concordance to Beckett's trilogy. See Michèle Barale and Rubin Rabinovitz, *A KWIC Concordance to Samuel Beckett's Trilogy: Molloy, Malone Dies and The Unnamable* (New York: Garland Publishing Company, 1988).

8. Samuel Beckett, *The Unnamable* (New York: Grove Press, 1958), p. 91, line 4; *L'Innommable* (Paris, Éditions de Minuit, 1953), p. 134, line 5.

9. Here again one can point to the importance of Melvin J. Friedman's idea that Beckett belongs to a tradition of polyglot authors.

10. The best discussion of the translation of these works is still in Ruby Cohn's essay, "Samuel Beckett, Self-translator," *PMLA,* 76 (December 1961), 613–21. Cohn, of course, discusses the translations of all three novels of the trilogy; she also anticipates much of what Fitch has to say about *Murphy.*

Unspeakable Plots and Unamazing Puzzles

Virginia A. Smith

Marianne Hirsch. *The Mother/Daughter Plot: Narrative, Psychoanalysis, Feminism.* Bloomington: Indiana University Press, 1989. xii, 244 pp.

Mickey Pearlman, ed. *Mother Puzzles: Daughters and Mothers in Contemporary American Literature.* Westport, Conn.: Greenwood Press, 1989. x, 203 pp.

The feminist consciousness of the 1960s has been aptly characterized as anti-natal and matraphobic—hostile to the biological and cultural actualities of women giving birth and disdainful of mother-centered identities. The effect that the 1976 publication of Adrienne Rich's *Of Woman Born: Motherhood as Experience and Institution* had on the dialogue about second-wave feminism and motherhood cannot be overstated. Rich separated the troubling history of the institution that has "ghettoized and degraded female potentialities" from the positive and potential ways women might choose and experience motherhood.[1] This contribution to feminist discourse was constructive and provocative. In articulating for millions of women their inchoate ambivalence and rage about their experiences as mothers and daughters, Rich also mapped new terrain for public and private feminist agendas for motherhood. Rich did more than realign feminism with motherhood—a natural enough union for many first-wave feminists such as Elizabeth Cady Stanton and Harriet Beecher Stowe. She also channelled both popular and academic American feminist scholarship in what has proven to be one of its most productive and profitable directions.

I wonder, though, if in postulating the cathexis between mother and daughter as "the great unwritten story," Rich herself could have anticipated the abundant diversity of theoretical-critical and creative stories feminist scholars have recently written about mothers and daughters. In a number of monographs published over the last decade, feminist critics have "unpacked" mother-daughter texts and subtexts; editors of feminist essay collections exclude at their peril mythic, psychoanalytic or social theories about the maternal and the mother/daughter dyad; and contemporary women fiction writers have sung in dissonance and harmony the previously silent story of mothers and daughters.

While the texts reviewed here are embedded in this matrix, as books dedicated solely and explicitly to the mother-daughter theme in literature they have only a single bona fide antecedent: the collection *The Lost Tradition: Mothers and Daughters in Literature,* edited by Cathy N. Davidson and E. M. Broner (1980). The strength of this text emerges in part from its strong historical and multicultural structure. Individual topics range from ancient Near Eastern and Greek to contemporary English-Canadian and southwestern Native American literature. The collection concludes with an impressive, cross-cultural primary bibliography on mothers and daughters in literature. It also bears the mark of what a decade earlier had yet to become commonplace in feminist scholarship: theoretical work on women's autobiography and several collaborative essays, including the work of a mother and her two daughters. The foreword to *The Lost Tradition* cites the exclusion of the mother-daughter plot in fiction even as it invites revisionary literature and scholarship on mothers and daughters: "We have already heard the story of fathers and sons, of mothers and sons, even of fathers and daughters. But who has sung the song of mothers and daughters?"[2] *Mother Puzzles* and *The Mother/Daughter Plot* answer with differing degrees of originality and sophistication Davidson and Broner's call nearly a decade earlier for continuing projects that would unearth and preserve, as well as create, mother-daughter tales as sustaining cultural myths.

Hirsch's delineation of purpose in the introduction suggests the ambitiousness of *The Mother/Daughter Plot:*

Unspeakable Plots and Unamazing Puzzles 285

This book takes as its point of departure the intersection of familial structures of plotting, attempting to place at the center of inquiry mothers and daughters, the female figures neglected by psychoanalytic theories and submerged in traditional plot structures. It concentrates on novels by nineteenth- and twentieth-century women writers from the Western European and North American traditions, reading them with psychoanalytic theories of subject-formation in the context of the narrative conventions of realism, modernism, and post-modernism. Thus its aim is to reframe the familial structures basic to traditional narrative, and the narrative structures basic to traditional conceptions of family, from the perspective of the feminine and, more controversially, the maternal. [p. 3]

The focus on mothers and daughters in the Pearlman collection is more specific and less theoretical. The nineteen contributions to *Mother Puzzles,* including Pearlman's introduction and a selected bibliography of nonfiction, include essays on the figures of mothers and daughters in contemporary American poetry, science fiction, domestic realism, short fiction, and postmodern fable written by women. Readers alienated by Hirsch's relentless theorizing may find Pearlman's theoretically truncated introduction a relief. Rather than aiming for the matriarchal moral high ground Hirsch sometimes imagines she occupies, Pearlman poses the darker question of why "the mother as currently depicted in American literature by women has moved from sainted marginality (as icon) to vicious caricature (as destroyer), to the puzzling figure that emerges here" (p. 2). To one's disappointment, though, and to the detriment of the rather pedestrian book as a whole, Pearlman's introduction fails to sustain a unifying direction for her project.

But *The Mother/Daughter Plot* is as formally tight as it is ideologically elaborate. Borrowing Luce Irigaray's notion that "with some additions and subtractions, our imaginary still functions according to the patterns established through Greek mythologies and tragedies," Hirsch establishes in the prelude what becomes the abiding center of her text: an illustration of the connection between the plots of literature and culture. Revising both the Freudian family romance and traditional humanist readings of Greek mythology, Hirsch's fundamental argument is that the symbolic matricide of Clytemnestra marks the "founding moment of civilization under paternal law" (p. 28). Hirsch sees the transformation of the Furies into a new Athenian order not as the symbolic moment in which Western humanism rejected passion for reason but as a metaphor for the erasure of the maternal in which "the mother is supplanted and the father comes to control the laws of justice and discourse" (p. 37). Maternal plots are thus subverted and rendered "unspeakable." In exploring the "slow emergence of maternal speech from silence," Hirsch takes her reader from Jane Austen and the Brontës to Toni Morrison and Alice Walker, from a feminist psychoanalytic critique of *The Oresteia* and the Sophoclean Trilogy to a meditation on the future of "maternal narratives in feminist fiction" (p. 198).

Hirsch's text resonates structurally with two precursors. The confident movement from Greek myth and drama to contemporary African-American women's novels, or from Anglo-American realism to Anglo-American and French postmodernism, recalls the historical and global format of *The Lost Tradition*. While the cross-cultural continuities established in that collection were admirable editorial feats, such freewheeling range in a monograph is dazzling. Preceded by an introduction and prelude, the tripartite body of Hirsch's work is a fusion of historical and thematic progression: Realism and Maternal Silence, Modernism and the Maternal, and Postmodernist Plots/Maternal Subjects. It is nearly impossible to scan the chapter divisions and names in *The Mother/Daughter Plot* without also reading it as a kind of palimpsest to Elaine Showalter's *A Literature of Their Own: British Women Novelists from Brontë to Lessing* (1977). While both authors see the development within a female narrative tradition from a female or feminine plot to a feminist discourse or aesthetic, each locates the latter at various historical moments. Showalter illustrates convincingly the presence of a British feminist novel during the "new woman" cultural upheaval at the turn of the century. Hirsch develops her theory of a feminist family romance using the contemporary discourse of Adrienne Rich, Nancy Choderow, and Luce Irigaray, and the novels of Margaret Atwood and Marguerite Duras.

Showalter and Hirsch's conclusions about salutary future directions for women's narratives mark what is probably the single most significant change in feminist theory from the seventies to the eighties and nineties: the shift into a rhetoric of difference, sometimes even of essentialism. Showalter urged a female tradition rooted in narrating female experience, though she resisted "yoking women writers to feminist revolution and denying them the freedom to explore new subjects."[3] But Hirsch's discourse is consciously visionary and political. What might seem a fatuous politically correct conclusion in other texts becomes, in Hirsch's, a well-earned illustration of her intended aim: to demonstrate the feminine, maternal reframing of narrative and family structures. Jean Wyatt has recently theorized about possibilities for social change in female lives and in families via discursive practices and the processes of reading and imagining.[4] Hirsch imagines a similar interchange in which new maternal theories and fictions, and redefinitions and revaluations of maternal practices, engender one another. Hirsch's lengthy wish-list includes theories and fictions that

> will have to be supple enough to respect and reflect the vast differences among mothers who mother in vastly different social and cultural conditions . . . will have to respond to the practical needs of women's, men's and children's lives . . . [and] will have to oppose, as rigorously as possible, mystifications of maternity and femininity, by creating ways to theorize adult, maternal as well as paternal, experience and by transcending the limited perspective of the developing child. [p. 199]

Hirsch here charts a territory where the borders between psychoanalytic, narrative, and feminist theory, between lived experience and scholarly meditation not only overlap but also reform. For some readers, this unabashed fusion of social criticism, literary theory, and personal politics will be distasteful. It will appear aberrational, however, only to an academic who has spent the last decade in deep freeze and has awakened innocent of the cultural studies phenomenon. In their insistence on literature as a dynamic sociohistorical formation rather than an immutable object hovering above history, practitioners of cultural studies, Hirsch among them, have provided the most comprehensive critique of the failures of New Criticism. Hirsh's very subtitle—*Narrative, Psychoanalysis, Feminism*—signals her participation in a discourse which covers the broad terrain of cultural interpretation defined by the conjunction of interdisciplinary studies and methods.

Hirsch's use of self-description in the introduction of *The Mother/Daughter Plot* figures as one of the text's earliest markings of her method as well as one of its stumbling blocks. The adoption by feminists and cultural critics of this radically subjective epistemology originated as a challenge to the unspoken norm of white or male or heterosexual readings by subverting the notion of a universal viewpoint. By calling sustained attention to a socially constructed reading, interpreting "I," this rhetorical stance implies that knowledge is not monolothic but is shaped by the knower. Hence in "The Location of the Critic," the last of three subsections in the introduction, Hirsch develops her own "formation and 'location' as a feminist critic within the context of the rapidly expanding field of psychoanalytic feminist theory . . . [to] help articulate some of the assumptions that underlie the analyses to follow" (p. 17). However, like many current feminists, Hirsch speaks her differences not only to decenter the unspoken centrality of white male perspectives but also to expose the new critical hegemony of white, middle-class, academic feminists who have unwittingly rendered marginal the voices of other women. Most readers will either celebrate or tolerate the litany of "location" that names the critic as

a woman, a teacher, a daughter, a mother, a feminist (should I add a heterosexual, a Jew, an immigrant, middle class, an only child, a mother of sons?), within the institutions of patriarchy, of motherhood, of literary studies, of feminist studies, of the university in the United States (should I add of marriage, of divorce, of the Ivy League, of Comparative Literature and French Studies, of the development of Women's Studies?). [p. 17]

But the pages delineating this "location and formation" test the patience of even the most sympathetic reader as well as the serviceable limits of an autobiographical criticism. After reading ten pages detailing the author's feminist evolution in these roles and revelatory experiences in these institutions, I felt as if I had been backed into a corner at a cocktail party by a well-meaning boor. Jane Gallop, the academy's most visible feminist psychoanalytic theorist, succeeds in crossing and recrossing the borders between self- and textual revelation with her irreverent posturings. But Hirsh's seriousness, and her hold on a narrowly theoretical lexicon, sabotage her intent. After finishing her introduction, one may well understand the dynamic between self and text, experience and theory, knower and known; but one may feel as though one has been coerced into it.

If Hirsch is truly searching for a feminist alternative to traditional scholarly writing (as she insists that she is) she would have done well to model her style more consistently on "Adrienne Rich's unusual combination of autobiography, incisive analysis, scholarly research and poetic expression" (p. 17) than on the ugly constructions of many (male) poststructuralist theorists. There are moments when Hirsch's discussion of "unspeakable maternal plots" gets lost in unreadable prose. At the conclusion of her introduction to Part 2, "Modernism and the Maternal," Hirsch inserts this commentary into her discussion of the Demeter myth as a modernist paradigm: "Narratibility itself, the Homeric hymn suggests, demands some form of breech [sic], some space of anxiety and desire into which to inscribe itself. The perpetuation of infantile plenitude cannot offer a model for plot" (p. 102). Or this, in which Hirsch gets us (and perhaps herself) lost in the labyrinth of French feminist theory: ". . . in Kristeva, Cixous, and Irigaray, the very process of metaphorization, which would make the maternal into the unrepresentable capable of shattering the scene of representation, actually leaves the maternal firmly rooted in the very structures of representation these writers wish to escape" (p. 173). Finally, there is the occasional sentence in this text that simply does not make sentence sense, such as the following: "If maternal discourse can emerge in a particular feminist tradition it may not be surprising that it should be in one that is itself marginal and therefore perhaps more ready to bond with women—mothers and daughters—letting go of male, paternal, fraternal, or filial approval" (p. 177). Is "discourse" or "tradition" the antecedent for the second "it"? Never mind—both are quite friendly if, as literary constructions, they can "bond with women."

I rush to mention that Hirsch adds a lucidity to the field of literature and psychoanalysis that has been absent in much postmodern literary theory since the humanities mysteriously became the human sciences over a decade ago. For the most part, Hirsch avoids the needless opacity and "inspeak" characteristic of the *de rigueur* attitude that would have all professors of English conversant in Western philosophy from Plato to Derrida. Like a good teacher, Hirsch unobtrusively walks her reader through her argument, explaining here her own rethinking of Juliet Mitchell's feminist revisions of Freud, there Freud's codification of family romance and its impact on narrative, or elsewhere distinctions between classical Western and African-American cultural and literary paradigms. She is most effective during transitions like the following, when she moves from one chapter or chapter-section to another, summarizing for her reader the conclusions that have accrued and drawing them onward with a series of provocative questions and fresh connections:

This chapter has argued that feminist discourse has suffered from its "inner splitting" and "radical surgery," from the absence of the mother as subject in favor either of a celebration of women as sisters and friends, or of the maternal as function and metaphor. If maternal voices are not to be found in feminist theoretical writing, is it possible to turn to feminist fiction for an articulation of maternal subjectivity? Do mothers write their own experience as mothers? What shapes and plots accommodate these experiences, and what is the relationship of maternal narratives to the cultural projections this book has traced? To what extent do women writers who are mothers co-conspire in their own silence, hesitant to reveal their stories to their children? [p. 176]

Pearlman's introduction to *Mother Puzzles* would have been much improved by the presence of similar rhetorical strategies and theoretical coherence. Instead, it becomes the most puzzling of the "mother puzzles" in the collection. She strews commentary about mothers, daughters, and contemporary women's fiction around in a discursive style that substitutes non sequiturs and scattered context for suggestion and synthesis. In one of the few instances in which she attempts a directive generalization about the essays, she fails to develop or provide a context for this assertion: "The editor would suggest that one of the revelations in this volume is that most of the novels are profoundly stories of a daughter's experience, that many daughters are, as Gottschalk says, trapped in 'memories of . . . mother and grandmother . . . nagging, unstoppable voices from heaven'" (p. 7). Hirsch agrees. Aware that "feminist theory situates itself in the position of daughter and at a distance from the maternal," Hirsch (sometimes painstakingly) thinks through the implications of this premise (p. 25). But Pearlman flies from her suggestion only to light on a slimly related comment by essayist Abby Werlock, thus concluding the two-sentence paragraph about "the revelations of this volume."

Perhaps the less-than-exemplary *Mother Puzzles* provides a lesson in pacing one's publications. Pearlman has elsewhere done a fine job as a collection-editor balancing the shape, context, and scope of her project, its shared and divergent directions, with a commentary on individual essays and authors. In her introduction to *American Women Writing Fiction: Memory, Identity, Family, Space* (1989), Pearlman cogently questions what becomes of the (male) American mythology of open space and quest in a diversely regional contemporary American literature written by women. But *Mother Puzzles* not only seems to suffer in quality as a result of appearing in the same year as *American Women Writing Fiction;* it also seems to duplicate that work. While it is possible that Pearlman had in mind two separate projects to collect and edit, she herself does not always seem aware of the individual identities of each. In the introduction to *Mother Puzzles*, she fails to distinguish between writers whom she mentions referentially and those who are the subjects of essays in that collection. Pearlman begins a relatively lengthy discussion on mothers in Louise Erdrich's *The Beet Queen*. Yet no essay on Erdrich appears in that collection—although one is included in *American Women Writing Fiction*—thereby leaving the context and purpose of that commentary nebulous. (References to Joan Didion, Joyce Carol Oates, and Josephine Humphries, authors also not included in *Mother Puzzles*, cause the same confusion.) Essays on Gail Godwin, Susan Fromberg Schaeffer, and Mary Gordon appear in both collections. While the pieces on Schaeffer and on Godwin in

American Women Writing Fiction are far superior to those in *Mother Puzzles*, articles discussing the use of doubling in Mary Gordon's *Men and Angels* appear in both collections under the individual authorship of John W. Mahon and Ellen Macleod Mahon. (Of course the deconstructive potential of this *mis en abyme* is mind-boggling: two essays about doubling in the same novel are individually authored by a husband and wife or brother and sister and appear in two separate volumes published in the same year by the same editor.) A stated awareness on Pearlman's part of the ways in which her texts overlapped and echoed one another might have transformed these collections from siamese twins struggling for separation into healthy and autonomous sisters.

The scope of *Mother Puzzles,* though, is arguably more ambitious than that of *American Women Writing Fiction*. In both texts the operative buzzword is "inclusiveness." In decentering male American mythologies of space, identity, and gender in *American Women,* Pearlman's contributors examine a diversity of writers for whom regional identity becomes bound up with race and ethnicity. This range is more extensive in *Mother Puzzles*. In three individual essays—"Breaking the Silence: Marilyn French's *Her Mother's Daughter,*" "Tasting Stars: The Tales of Rabbi Nachman in Anne Roiphe's *Lovingkindness,*" and "Jewish Mothers' Stories: Rosellen Brown's *The Autobiography of My Mother*"—the maligned Jewish mother becomes transformed through the redeeming perspectives of daughters who are also Jewish mothers. On the other hand, as the sole representation of a text about mothers and daughters of color, an essay appears on what has by now become the most celebrated of African-American women's novels, Toni Morrison's *Beloved*. The article on Mary Gordon' *Men and Angels* lends an Irish Catholic voice to the collection (although that is Gordon's least explicitly Catholic novel).

Given Pearlman's eye for inclusiveness in *Mother Puzzles,* her exclusion of contemporary Native American and Asian-American literature seems less than judicious. Louise Erdrich's *Tracks* contains a powerful subtext about the mythical Chippewa named Fleur and her daughter. Although much has been written about the significance of women's speech and silence and mother-daughter relations in Maxine Hong Kingston's *The*

Woman Warrior, Amy Tan's more recent *The Joy Luck Club* remains unexplored. In Tan's novel the relations between immigrant mothers and their modern daughters, involving mother absence as well as maternal lineage, provide the novel with its most central and compelling tensions.

Pearlman leads through strength in placing as the first essay in the collection Roberta White's "Anna's Quotidian Love: Sue Miller's *The Good Mother.*" Miller's first and bestselling novel, further catapulted into the limelight by Hollywood's screen version, is a text which defies a simple reading. For many feminists, this tale about a mother who loses her young daughter in a custody trial as a result of her allegedly aberrant sexuality reads as a female author's conscious or unconscious complicity in women-punishing plots. Disappointingly, White fails to take on that argument. Her only nod to explicitly feminist issues in the text is her rather trivializing comment that "to the dismay of some feminist readers, Anna will never be aggressive and never achieve much in the world" (p. 18).

But White's implicitly conservative cultural feminism, aligning women with private spheres and emotional values, informs her provocative thesis: that Anna's single-minded love of her daughter, her life devoted to non-custodial visitation, "affirms the value of private over public values, of love over law" (p. 22). Maternal and womanly love as an alternative to the iron law and emotional aridity of the world of the fathers might have appeared subversive to nineteenth-century readers of *The Scarlet Letter.* But novels such as Lisa Alther's *Kinflicks* and Lee Smith's *Fair and Tender Ladies* offer what one might expect from a contemporary woman author: less punishing versions of women who suffer the loss of a child as a result of their illicit love affairs and who resist martyrdom. However, White makes clear that she is dealing with what Miller wrote and not what we might wish her to have written. While her vision of Anna as a tragic (albeit surviving) heroine is a powerful one, White is at her best in illuminating the hidden recesses of the "rich poetry of domestic life" she believes *The Good Mother* shares with Woolf's *Mrs. Dalloway* and *To the Lighthouse.*

Helen Pike Bauer's "'A child of anxious, not proud love': Mother and Daughter in Tillie Olsen's 'I Stand Here Ironing'" is one of several disappointing if not pointless essays in *Mother Puzzles*. Given the feminist revival of interest in Olsen, to say nothing of the technical originality of much of her prose, one expects far more from this essay than what is delivered: a preachy paraphrase of the short story that diminishes rather than enriches the significant rhythms, gaps, fits and starts of its interior monologue. Bauer's essay fittingly begins with the words "I stand here ironing," which also open Olsen's short story. Bauer moves on to assert that "these are words that would never introduce a male narrator, and the facts of her woman's life, its emotional as well as its economic exigencies and constraints, provide the context for this unnamed mother's meditation on her daughter" (p. 35). What seems likely to follow, given Bauer's immediate attention to gender difference and voice, is a framing of the short story in these terms. Instead, she robs the story of the genius of its measured unfolding by telling us, as in this example, what we obviously know from reading it: "The narrator has struggled through intensely difficult times. Without money, education, skills, deserted at nineteen with an eight-month-old child, she worked to support the two of them" (p. 37).

Other failures to deliver analyses equal to the complexity of the original work surface in this collection. The essays on Gail Godwin and Susan Fromberg Schaeffer come most readily to mind. When Kim Lacy Rogers states in "A Mother's Story in a Daughter's Life: Gail Godwin's *A Southern Family*," that "these intense, unresolved, and unhappy primal female relationships resemble other lost causes of the southern past," she places her treatment of the mother-daughter theme within the regional romance tradition of the southern gothic (p. 60). Significantly, Rogers's conclusion resonates with Hirsch's desire for female plots that are mature and maternal, that move beyond the daughter's arrested childhood perspective: "We can expect that [Godwin] will move beyond this kind of family romance—which is essentially a daughter's story—and on to a woman's story, free of a mother's powerful charm and feminine delusions" (p. 66).

However, Rogers's article echoes the essay on Olsen and anticipates the piece on Schaeffer in its maddening overreliance on plot recapitulation. Her claim early in the essay to examine "a mother's story in a daughter's life" goes nowhere. Inasmuch as the polyphonic *A Southern Family* is a postmodern novel about the failures of written discourse, Rogers is on the right track. But in her pursuit of the mother's story in a daughter's life, she would have done well to frame her inquiry briefly within the context of Godwin's oeuvre as a whole. The real center of most of Godwin's mother-daughter subtexts, from *The Odd Woman* and *Violet Clay* to *The Finishing School* and *A Southern Family,* is enfolded within the self-reflexive tension between narrative and self-creation, between the daughter's desire to discover the mother's silenced story and her struggle to revise or to write beyond the ending of the destructive or formulaic romantic plot. Under the guise of unmasking the family myths and illusions operating in the novel, Rogers lapses into a laborious stretch of character analysis and narrative retelling only dimly illustrative of her thesis.

The essay on Susan Fromberg Schaeffer is similarly sophomoric. Although eager to join the swelling ranks of Fromberg Schaeffer devotees, I remain unconverted after reading Katherine K. Gottschalk's piece, "Paralyzed in the Present: Susan Fromberg Schaeffer's Mothers, or Daughters." While Gottschalk maintains that "Schaeffer's first novel, *Falling* (1973), begins an investigation of alienated women writers that will continue in *Mainland* (1985) and in *The Injured Party* (1986)," she fails to cultivate a fertile field of inquiry: the link between writing and sexual difference (p. 142). After detailing these fictional women writers' alienation from other women as well as from their husbands and children, Gottschalk avoids either drawing conclusions or posing questions. Hovering outside the margins of her argument is the question concerning received notions about gender, artistic alienation, and womanly or motherly love. That is: if male modernists from Joyce to Eliot treated the alienated preciousness of the artist with ambiguous acceptance, and contemporary women artists from Judy Chicago to Ursula K. LeGuin debate whether women artists must or should choose between creation and procreation, what are the implications of *künstlerromane* in which the writers are mothers and are socially and emotionally alienated? But the faults of Gottschalk's article are more basic than her lack of curiosity about or familiarity with the theoretical issues she raises. With few exceptions, she even dispenses with any organizing or summarizing transitions, regurgitating plot after plot and providing minimal direction for her argument.

I don't intend to sound a death knell for this book. There are a few treasures worth uncovering here, and Deborah Denenholtz Morse's "The Difficult Journey Home: Mona Simpson's *Anywhere but Here*" is one of them. Morse provides an insightful discussion of a rich and disturbing novel about the love, power, homoeroticism and ambivalence in a mother-daughter relationship. In their unraveling of what is at stake here, both Simpson and Morse refuse to make nice. In the novel a mother peddles her daughter to Hollywood, then abandons her; Morse discusses a graphic scene in which the abused and neglected Anna in turn molests a young female friend. Morse's reading of the comically grotesque journey west as a woman's quest for maternal origins avoids some of the more fashionably prescriptive language about mother-daughter union. (Not a single mention here of the pre-oedipal!)

But what remains troubling about Pearlman's *Mother Puzzles* is both what it is and what it might have been. Several of the essays that go beyond plot summary appear crudely tailored for this collection or fall short of complete realization. An essay on *Beloved* certainly belongs in this book about puzzling mother-daughter plots. However, in "To Embrace Dead Strangers: Toni Morrison's *Beloved*," Karen E. Fields surprisingly focuses on agape and erotic love between men and women. She almost totally avoids what is at the mythic heart of this novel: the nearly unspeakable, undecipherable desire for what Morrison calls "the join," a literal and mythic reunion between African-American mothers and daughters that had been unnaturally disrupted and denied by slavery. Pearlman unfortunately ignores or fails to apprehend what remains the most puzzling unifying element in at least half of the essays in *Mother Puzzles:* an ambivalence about female, maternal discourse; about women writing; about the difficulty of providing daughters with mothers' stories; and about men's and mothers' stories that daughters feel both compelled and afraid to revise.

Although Pearlman's collection does nothing to develop the direction of feminist theory, it would serve as a modestly useful reference book for an undergraduate course on contemporary literature or for an introductory women's studies course on mothers and daughters. In targeting an audience for Hirsch's book, I am reminded of Joyce's desire for everyone to read *Finnegans Wake*. No doubt miners and mill workers everywhere would have been uplifted by his cyclical tale of the power of love, dreams, and the mythic riverrun if they could have made their way through the first sentence, or any of the other sentences, in that text. Similarly, Hirsch seems either oblivious to or untroubled by the gap between her grass-roots political agenda and the fundamental inaccessibility of her book to even general academic readers. Nonetheless, *The Mother/Daughter Plot* is original in its conception and impressive in its breadth and depth. To the degree that this book both illuminates and creates the intellectual and social context in which current feminist literary theory and politics mirror one another, it is one of the best of its kind to be published in over a decade.

Notes

1. Adrienne Rich, *Of Woman Born: Motherhood as Experience and Institution* (New York: Bantam Books, 1976), p. xv.

2. E. M. Broner and Cathy N. Davidson, eds., *The Lost Tradition: Mothers and Daughters in Literature* (New York: Fredrick Ungar, 1980), p. xi.

3. Elaine Showalter, *A Literature of Their Own: British Women Novelists from Brönte to Lessing* (Princeton: Princeton Univ. Press, 1977), p. 318.

4. Jean Wyatt, *Reconstructing Desire: The Role of the Unconscious in Women's Reading and Writing* (Chapel Hill: Univ. of North Carolina Press, 1990).

Correspondence

To the Editors:

On page 264 of "Author, Intention, Text: The California Mark Twain" (*Review* 11 [1989]: 255–88), Guy Cardwell asserts that our Mark Twain Library edition of *Huckleberry Finn* "contains more than two hundred pages of apparatus." He later repeats this claim, saying that the book "contains a foreword (4 pages), maps (6), explanatory notes (151), glossary (7), references (35), and a note on the text (4). Total, 207 pages" (p. 286).

The *correct* number of pages for these several parts of the book are: foreword (4), maps (5), explanatory notes (52), glossary (8), references (16), and note on the text (5). Total, 90 pages, not 207 pages. The text of the novel itself comprises 372 pages—not 362, as Cardwell has it.

Perhaps your readers can decide for themselves whether or not Cardwell's misstatement of these facts (tripling the pages of notes, more than doubling the total for apparatus) has unduly influenced his conclusion that readers are therefore "over-informed" by that apparatus.

> Robert H. Hirst
> *General Editor, Mark Twain Project*

MR. CARDWELL REPLIES:

In a letter to me of 13 January 1990, Robert Hirst called my attention to arithmetical errors which led me to refer in my review to 207 pages of editorial matter in the Library edition of *Huckleberry Finn,* whereas his count of pages totaled only 89. He also remarked that my page count would be used "again and again by those who would prefer admittedly scarce resources redeployed in their direction." On 18 January 1990, I answered, acknowledging two (incredible) errors and expressing my deep regrets. I am glad to reconfirm here the correctness of Mr. Hirst's page count and to express regrets for my blunder.

I would add, however, that my query as to whether the general reader (for whom the Library editions are intended) may be over-informed by the apparatus for *Huckleberry Finn* was formulated in advance of adding up the pages. Munificence in editorial apparatus may be defended or queried. Policies in matters like this are not constant. For example, John Gerber, then chief general editor of the Iowa project for editing Mark Twain's published works, assured Edmund Wilson some years ago that cheap editions made from established scholarly texts would restrict themselves to short introductions and explanatory notes.

Contributors

NINA BAYM is Jubilee Professor of Liberal Arts and Sciences at the University of Illinois at Urbana–Champaign.

THOMAS L. BURKDALL is Instructor in English at Loyola Marymount University.

KEEN BUTTERWORTH is Associate Professor of English at the University of South Carolina.

ROBERT CASILLO is Professor of English at the University of Miami.

MICHAEL D. CHERNISS is Professor of English at the University of Kansas.

STEVEN FINK is Associate Professor of English at The Ohio State University.

DONALD W. FOSTER is Associate Professor of English at Vassar College.

THOMAS GARDNER is Associate Professor of English at Virginia Polytechnic Institute and State University.

JOHN GOODE is Professor of English at Keele University.

J.A. LEO LEMAY is H.F. du Pont Winterthur Professor of English at the University of Delaware.

RICHARD A. MCCABE is Lecturer in English at Trinity College, Dublin.

JULIET MCMASTER is University Professor of English at the University of Alberta.

JAMES NAGEL is J.O. Eidson Distinguished Professor of American Literature at the University of Georgia.

MARJORIE PERLOFF is Sadie Dernham Patek Professor of Humanities at Stanford University.

JOHN PFORDRESHER is Professor of English at Georgetown University.

RUBIN RABINOVITZ is Professor of English at the University of Colorado at Boulder.

J.E. RIVERS is Professor of English at the University of Colorado at Boulder.

VIRGINIA A. SMITH is Lecturer in English at The Pennsylvania State University.

FREDERICK C. STERN is Professor of English at the University of Illinois at Chicago.

STANLEY WEINTRAUB is Evan Pugh Professor of Arts and Humanities at The Pennsylvania State University.

ALEXANDER WELSH is Professor of English at the University of California at Los Angeles.